Plaschke

Plaschke

GOOD SPORTS, SPOILSPORTS, FOUL BALLS AND ODDBALLS

■

BILL PLASCHKE

Los Angeles Times
BOOKS

To my parents, Grover and Mary Plaschke,

for 50 years of showing me how.

To the love of my life, Lisa Ann Jacobs,

for 20 years and counting.

To Tessa, Willie and Mary Clare . . .

one, two, three . . . grrreattt dayyy!!!

Los Angeles Times
BOOKS

Editor: Kristen Walbolt

Designer: Mike Diehl

ISBN: 1-883792-65-7

Copyright: Los Angeles Times 2002

Published by the Los Angeles Times

202 West First Street, Los Angeles, CA 90012

First printing October 2002

Printed in U.S.A.

Los Angeles Times

Publisher: John P. Puerner

Editor: John S. Carroll

Book Development Manager: Carla Lazzareschi

TABLE OF CONTENTS

INTRODUCTION

Mostly, I remember the lights. They flickered in the windows of the tiny homes we passed on our Sunday night drives toward the mail slot in the door of my favorite place.

My mom clutched the wheel while I clutched my life, a manila envelope containing my youth-league story for The Voice, the weekly newspaper for our Louisville, Ky., neighborhood.

I was 13. I had scribbled the story in a tiny binder. My mom had banged it out of our rattling electric Corona. She started the Pinto, I grabbed an envelope, and off we went on a journey of promise so palpable, I can feel it in my fingers as I type this today.

It was always late. We never talked much. It was all about the lights. I spent most of the time looking out the window at those lights, tucked behind shades, nestled in curtains, a story in every shadow.

How I wanted to tell those stories! How I longed to pull up in one of those gravel driveways, knock on a door, carefully pull out one of those lights, and shine it for the rest of the neighborhood to see. Maybe it would reveal happiness; maybe it would burn pain. But always, it would reflect us. And always, I hoped, we would be enriched by the understanding of its glow.

I was certain that each block on our drive was filled with stories that could teach us and touch us. Everyone had a message. Everyone could inspire anger or laughter or tears. I wanted to be the curator of that inspiration. As I later realized, I wanted to change my neighborhood by reminding my neighborhood that it could change itself.

Admittedly, it was a lofty goal attempted with crude means.

Some of my friends wanted to fix cars or build bridges. I wanted to plug in a lamp.

I also wanted my work to be in a language I loved, and that most people understood. So from the time I first dropped that manila folder in that mail slot 31 years ago, I have been writing about sports while really trying to write about people.

There is a column here about the greatest athlete of the 20th century. There is also a column about a tap-dancing golf teacher. Don't ask which one I like best. There is a column about the New York Yankees. There is also a column about the Garfield High Bulldogs. Only one of those teams has ever made me cry.

I wish I could claim this collection of my stories to be something a tad more sophisticated or dramatic than the dreams of a 13-year-old boy. But what follows on these pages is mostly that. A slow drive through the neighborhood. A collection of those lights. Some are fancy. Some are frayed. But all of them, I humbly hope, shine real.

I would like to thank the man who taught me to write, Bill Ward, and the man who taught me to climb, Uncle Bill McLaughlin. I thank Fred Turner for taking that first chance, and Blaine Johnson for making it stick. I thank Dave Distel for understanding the lights, John Cherwa for understanding the drive, and Bill Dwyre for giving me that mail slot. I thank Rick Jaffe for my inspiration, Gene Wojciechowski for my ideas, and Kristen Walbolt for being my book editor and believer. I want to thank the subjects of each of these stories for their unbelievable patience with this old fool as he searched for the right bulb. And I want to thank Carla Lazzareschi for having the flattering, but completely hare-brained, idea to put all those stories together.

Finally, I want to thank all the folks at Section D at the Los Angeles Times. The best damn sports staff, period.

— *Bill Plaschke*

CHAPTER ONE

Slam Dunks

September 9, 1998

McGuire's 62nd Sets a Mark of Excellence

ST. LOUIS — It was the longest 341-foot home run in history, sailing from a grainy pale bat into the hearts of a nation.

Although the big man stumbled around first base, he eventually touched them all; his son, his teammates, his town, our towns.

With his 62nd home run, a brilliant white streak through a sea of murky red, Mark McGwire did a number on America.

One swing, one line drive, one dizzying trip around the diamond, a father hugs his son, a hero hugs the former hero's family, a slugger hugs his rival.

One swing, and suddenly all things seem possible.

Courage under pressure. Dignity under fire. Greatness that does not come at the expense of class. A competition in which there are no losers.

The facts can fit in one sentence.

The St. Louis Cardinals' Mark McGwire broke Roger Maris' allegedly unbreakable single-season home run record with his 62nd homer in the Cardinals' 145th game, a bases-empty shot in the fourth inning against Chicago Cub pitcher Steve Trachsel.

The moment, however, will be replayed for years.

"It was absolutely incredible," McGwire said, eyes filling with tears. "I told myself, when it happens, I think I'll be floating. And I sure as heck was floating."

After six months of going and going, he didn't know this one was gone. Imagine that.

While the ball was shooting toward the Busch Stadium left-field fence, McGwire was sprinting 12 heavy steps toward first base.

"I thought it was going to hit the wall," he said.

It surprised him when the line drive sank over the left-field fence, directly underneath an advertisement for an office supply company, his shortest home run of the season. Imagine that.

"The next thing you know, it just disappeared on me," he said.

When he realized it was gone, he leaped in apparent shock in front of first base, so quickly and awkwardly that he missed the base. In a wisely unpunished violation of the rules, first-base coach Dave McKay grabbed him and pushed him to the bag.

"McKay jumped up and said, 'Uh, Mark, you've missed one big thing — first base,'" McGwire said. "I've never done that before."

And nobody caught the ball. Imagine that.

All this talk about million-dollar souvenirs and fans holding McGwire hostage and guess what? It plopped into a tunnel underneath the seats and was picked up by a groundskeeper who dutifully handed it to his hero.

"I want to be like Mark McGwire," Tim Forneris said.

This red-haired, goateed, balloon-armed hero soon showed why, after all the bumps and turns of this crazy summer chase, maybe it is not a bad thing to want to be like Mark McGwire.

After he crossed home plate, he grabbed and lifted his 10-year-old son, Matthew, who lives with his former wife in Orange County. Then, after being mobbed by teammates, he turned and grabbed Matthew again, hugging and kissing him alone in a tender moment behind home plate.

Moments later Cub rival Sammy Sosa — stuck on 58 homers after not connecting in this two-game series — ran in from right field. McGwire hugged him, and together they exchanged Sosa's two-finger trademark celebration gesture.

Then came perhaps the most tender part of a most touching 11-minute trot.

McGwire ran down past the Cardinal dugout, through 37 years of history, and climbed into the stands to hug five children of the late Roger Maris.

"I touched your father's bat today, I touched it with my heart," he told them.

Several Maris family members wept.

Since he broke Babe Ruth's single-season record of 60 in 1961, their father has been denied the respect he deserved.

In one giant gesture, McGwire wanted to make it right.

"It's Mark McGwire's day, Mark McGwire's moment, and for him to greet our family and give us a hug . . . that's something I'll never forget," Roger Maris Jr. said.

McGwire ended his historic journey as he had started it last spring, when he was surrounded by snowbirding Cardinal fans in the small Florida town of Jupiter, peppered with questions about whether he could actually break the unbreakable.

He faced those fans again Tuesday, this time grabbing a microphone and shouting, "I dedicate this to the whole city of St. Louis."

The 49,987 in attendance — nearly 7,000 more than capacity — roared.

They did not leave, or quiet, until the postgame celebration ended nearly 90 minutes after the final pitch, after McGwire toured the field in a 1962 car, about 11:15 p.m. local time.

McGwire's homer came only two plate appearances before he and the team would be leaving town for five days.

That he hit his historic home run just in time, he said, was not coincidence.

He said baseball's best city deserved to see baseball's best record, and he was right.

"When I drove to the ballpark today, I honestly and truly wanted to hit it in this city," he said.

Now, like that sinking fourth-inning line drive, the painful weight of this city's expectations has disappeared.

Afterward, when McGwire wasn't fighting off tears, he couldn't help but laugh.

"I don't know how heavy the [Gateway] Arch is, but I just got that off my back," he said.

And gave America another landmark.

Today, somewhere, somebody will be trying to get a child to eat his vegetables.

"Don't you want to grow up big and strong like Mark McGwire?" they will say.

Today, somewhere, somebody will be scolding a child for being nasty to his parents.

"Do you think Mark McGwire treats his parents like that?"

they will say.

For the immediate future, any young baseball player taking huge swings and striking out will be issued a new reprimand.

"Who are you trying to be?" somebody will say, "Mark McGwire?"

It was not simply about a bat hitting a ball, but an athlete connecting with our consciousness.

We were reminded that our sports heroes can be gifted and polite. They can do great things, and kind things. They can not only endeavor to make themselves feel good, but us feel good.

We were reminded that sometimes, it feels like we really are all in this together.

"People say the country was brought together by this . . . so be it," McGwire said. "I'm happy to bring the country together."

Standing on the crowded field, just before handing the home run ball to a representative of the Hall of Fame, McGwire tossed it high in the air like a little boy. It felt like we were tossing it with him.

He then caught it in his palm and laughed. It felt like we all caught it together.

October 6, 2001

Moment Has All the Thrills, Lacks the Chills

SAN FRANCISCO — The ending was the journey. The moment was the man.

Barry Bonds hit his 71st homer with the passion of a welder and the magic of a shrug.

There were fireworks, family hugs, a five-minute standing ovation.

Some of which Bonds missed because he was in the dugout on a cell phone.

Talking to his father, Bobby.

Who missed his son's defining evening to host a golf tournament.

Be still, my goose bumps.

There was a fist pointed to the sky, a child thrust in the air, video images of Babe Ruth looming above it all.

Yet there were no chills.

Where were the chills?

When Mark McGwire broke Roger Maris' 37-year-old home run record in 1998, ordinary people wept. And I was not alone.

When Bonds broke McGwire's record in the first inning against the Dodgers' Chan Ho Park at Pacific Bell Park, ordinary people wondered, what was that stuff jiggling beneath his lower lip?

It was sunflower seeds, which he casually chewed as he casually rounded the bases amid 41,730 fans desperately trying to inflate the feeling.

The record does mean something, of course. It is the most glamorous record in all of sports. It is about the power of Ruth, the will of Roger Maris, the strength of Mark McGwire.

But the record also is just three years old.

And you know what they say about three year olds.

In the end, Barry Bonds' home-run spectacular was appropriately seen but not heard.

When McGwire hit his record 62nd homer, members of the Chicago Cubs congratulated him as he rounded the bases.

On Friday, the Dodgers didn't go anywhere near.

When McGwire broke the record, the game halted for more than 10 minutes not because of any planned ceremony, but because the emotion overwhelmed the moment.

He had just surpassed the unreachable. He was surrounded with dignity and majesty as he climbed, unplanned, into the stands to hug the family of the forgotten Roger Maris.

When Bonds broke the record, the game stopped for only a few minutes, and just long enough for Bonds to run behind home plate and hug his family.

He couldn't hug McGwire's family, because, well, McGwire was in St. Louis, striking out against the Houston Astros at approximately the same time.

He couldn't hug baseball Commissioner Bud Selig because, like Bonds' father, Selig was otherwise disposed, hanging out in San Diego to bid goodbye to Tony Gwynn.

That's what happens with a record so young. It carries no link to the past. It has little connection to anything but itself.

Sort of like that sign adjacent to the wall over which Bonds' 442-foot drive sailed.

It advertised webvan.com, a company which will now forever be remembered through endless video replays of the homer.

It is also a company that has gone bankrupt.

None of this has been helped by Bonds' personality, distant at best, churlish at worst.

While McGwire wasn't much more embraceable when his record season began, he eventually became understanding and even engaging. His mood also lightened when the delightful Sammy Sosa joined his chase.

This time, Bonds had no sidekick, no funny foil, no help. He had to endure the last several months being, well, Barry Bonds.

His statements were often short, his mood even shorter. Then, because the Giants were in a championship race, opponents wouldn't pitch to him, which increasingly turned what should be a dance into a grind.

Before Friday's game, he was in what some call his "Bad Barry" state.

He was asked about what it would be like to have a championship ring, something he has discussed often in recent days.

"I'll let you know after it happens," he said tersely.

Then he was asked about when he would revel in his personal achievements.

"When I'm retired and none of you guys can ever see me again," he said.

Years from now, perhaps, time will supply the emotion.

Years from now, maybe, folks will speak dramatically about how the Dodgers helped set up the homer by scoring five runs in the first inning.

That meant they would certainly pitch to Bonds in the bottom of the first because, after all, he couldn't hit a five-run homer.

Maybe people will remember how Chan Ho Park was as noble in allowing the home run as he has been in many of his strikeouts.

When the first inning began, Park summoned the trainer to the mound to examine what appeared to be a foot injury suffered when he rounded first base in the top of the first inning.

Many thought Park, fearful of being caught in history's underbelly, would leave the game before Bonds came to the plate as the third batter that inning.

But he did not. He stayed and fought. He threw Bonds a low breaking ball, then challenged him low again.

It was close enough for Bonds to connect as he has amazingly connected all summer on virtually every pitch in the strike zone.

Bonds may finish with perhaps the great slugging season ever. His power is historic. His timing is unreal.

He even had the dramatic sense to pile on with his 72nd homer in the third inning against Park.

There were bobbing signs that read, "Barry, thanks for making us smile again."

There were hoarse chants of, "Bar-ry, Bar-ry, Bar-ry."

There were flash bulbs and flapping flags and fans who came early and wouldn't leave.

If only there were goose bumps.

On a night swaying with the breeze of history and filled with a postseason chill, you missed the goose bumps.

February 22, 2002

High School Kid Restores Joy to the Games

SALT LAKE CITY — A prone, clammy, gasping, Winter Olympics was resuscitated Thursday by a high school kid with the nerve to simply skate to the middle of its chest and start pounding.

Pounding through the cynicism.

Pounding through the crybabies.

Pounding so bravely and brilliantly, nobody could argue.

Sarah Hughes is the 2002 Olympic women's figure skating champion, and, pardon the language, there's not a damn thing the Russians can say about it.

Nor the Canadians. Nor the South Koreans. Nor any other nation that turned what should be the height of sport into a darkened whine cellar.

Sarah Hughes is the Olympic champion, and these Games stand united today, finally, behind a 16-year-old kid who showed there is still room here for giant leaps in final moments that even fur-lined judges cannot ignore.

She didn't just snatch away a gold medal.

She snatched it minutes before officials pulled it out of the box, snatched in the middle of a triple flip while reaching over the shoulders of arguably the three best women skaters in the world.

She grabbed like nobody has grabbed it before, maybe the biggest upset in Olympic figure skating history, fourth to first in four breathtaking minutes.

We'll let her say it. Immediately after her long program, she mouthed the words in the middle of the Salt Lake Ice Center while a blizzard of flowers and animals and gratitude fell to the ice around her.

She said it better than anyone.

"Oh my God."

Were you watching her? Were you crying?

People in the press box were crying. Fans in the stands were crying. Hardened skating officials were crying.

Unlike the many maudlin stories of these Games, those weren't tears of sadness or joy, but of renewal.

That somebody barely in fourth place after the short program and seemingly out of medal contention could skate like she still believed she could be a champion. . . .

That a kid with a floppy haircut and goofy grin would be unafraid to stare down the judges and their preconceptions and their scams. . . .

That somebody would challenge the system on its biggest and brightest night. . . .

Now that was something.

Hughes said it to those judges again and again, four minutes solid, with the first pair of triple-triple combinations in Olympic history, with a spinning finish that turned her into a perfect violet blur.

You want to prove you're impartial? Then make me your champion.

Amazingly, people were crying even though the top three skaters after the short program had yet to skate.

Hughes was that good.

And the final three skaters were not even close.

Sasha Cohen, the Laguna Niguel teenager who had never been in this position in a world-class event before, finally showed it.

She was clearly uncomfortable during a warmup session that looked more like a skating lesson, picking her way carefully and slowly around the ice.

When it was her turn to skate, she lasted less than a minute before hitting the ice on a triple-combination, and that was that.

Meanwhile, watching on television in the bowels of the arena, holding hands with coach Robin Wagner, the Long Island kid was surely thinking what the 15,000 fans were thinking.

One down and two to go.

Next up, Kwan, who was cheered like a champion, but who immediately showed the same caution that seemed ominous in her first-place short program.

You know what those in other sports always say about injuries occurring more often to those who play it safe?

In a different sort of way, it happened here.

Forty seconds into her program, she doubled-footed a triple jump. Then, at 2:19, she missed on a triple-flip and hit the ice.

She finished strong, even threw in an unplanned triple jump at the end, but it was too late, and she knew it.

"It was the worst I've skated in a while," she said.

Stunned by a teenager for the second consecutive Olympics — remember Tara Lipinski? — Kwan's night went from worst to worse as she tearfully crossed the ice after the event to stand on the bronze-medal podium.

Although she mostly choked them back, they were clearly tears of sadness. But she kept her cool and showed her trademark class, graciously congratulating the top two skaters.

The final skater, Russia's Irina Slutskaya, was not nearly so gracious.

She was probably the best skater in the short program. But clearly, on Thursday, she never found the same groove.

She made several mistakes. Her program didn't flow. Several times she seemed off balance or uncertain. She didn't grab for the gold.

This being the biggest moment of the life of a skater who has never won a world championship, such tentativeness is certainly defensible.

But her behavior afterward was not.

Mere hours after a Russian delegation threatened to pull its team out of town if members weren't treated fairly, Slutskaya unfairly and cheaply stoked the fire.

She thought her presentation marks were low, and wouldn't stop talking about it.

"Interesting thing about these Olympic Games, I'm obviously not the only Russian who has suffered here," she said immediately after her skate.

Later, she added, "I have a shock . . . it's a shame."

When asked about her delegation's charges of overall unfairness, she said, "That's very interesting too."

Slutskaya needed to close her mouth and listen to the philosophy of a champion.

"I didn't think I had a chance of a gold, much less a medal," Hughes said. "I didn't even think about the medal. I skated because I love to skate. I just let everything go."

In other words?

You know the words.

Faster, higher, stronger.

June 20, 2000

Long Wait for Winning Feeling

So this is how it looks.

The big man hugs his mother and weeps. The bright kid jumps on a table and bounces. Through a fine mist of a purple-and-gold confetti snowstorm, a city dances around them.

So this is how it sounds.

A train rolling through Staples Center, an airplane landing outside, different accents, varied tongues, one three-hour, deafening, glorious noise.

"I love L.A.," croons the singer.

"We love it!" shouts the town.

So this is how it feels, after 12 long years, to again live in a place where a professional sports team takes the very best of that place and captures the globe with it.

From a kneeling Orel Hershiser in 1988 to a leaping Shaquille O'Neal on Monday, the faintly flickering torch has been passed.

Today it burns deeply again in the spirit of a town that has been brought together through two words that work in any accent, any language, any neighborhood.

World champions.

So describes the Lakers after their 116-111 victory over the Indiana Pacers in Game 6 of the NBA finals gave them a four-games-to-two series win.

It was this city's first professional sports championship since the Dodgers won the 1988 World Series.

World champions.

Idiots tried to ruin it afterward as idiots usually do, with a disturbance in the streets. But it is hoped those images do not last, and will not stain a triumph for the other 99.9%.

With 18,997 screaming in the Staples Center, and thousands more watching on a giant screen outside, the Lakers created a new reality for a place usually brought together under vastly different circumstances.

This time, the earthquake was O'Neal, who bulled through the Pacer defense for 41 points before tenderly embracing mom.

"Those were tears of joy," he said later. "I just want to thank this city for being so patient with me."

The mudslide was Kobe Bryant, whose intensity blanketed the Pacers before his 21-year-old boyishness landed him on a table.

"Man, I didn't know champagne hurt so much when it got in your eyes," he said smilingly, typically.

And the smog? It was everyone else, a group usually considered bit players, but on this night penetrating everywhere, with important 3-point baskets from Robert Horry and Rick Fox and free throws from Glen Rice.

"This one is for the city," said guard Derek Fisher. "They have been through so much with us . . . from the top of the mountain to the bottom of the San Fernando Valley. This is for them."

In the end, it was a team very much like its city, talented but growing, sometimes brilliant, sometimes confused.

It began the playoffs as the team with the best record in the NBA, but was pushed to a fifth game in a five-game first-round series with the Sacramento Kings, then later pushed to a seventh game in the seven-game Western Conference series with the Portland Trail Blazers.

After overcoming a 15-point deficit in the final 10 minutes to defeat the Trail Blazers and advance to the NBA finals — one of the most dramatic comebacks in NBA playoff history — the Lakers walked into what was expected to be an easy series against the Pacers.

"But you know we never do anything easy," Fisher said.

And so they ended up in a sixth game, the score tied with 5:16 remaining, moments from allowing the Pacers to force a seventh game, knowing that they had probably run out of miracles.

So what happens?

Robert Horry makes a flying shot down the middle.

Ron Harper steals a pass.

O'Neal hits a hook shot.

O'Neal forces a wild layup by Jalen Rose.

Bryant hits a jumper over Rose.

The Pacers, suddenly trailing by six, call time out. Bryant struts back to the bench while patting his hand against his chest as if to say, this one is mine.

And that was that.

"The crowd took over from there," Coach Phil Jackson said. "It was quite a night."

For plenty of people.

This is, first, a championship belonging to Jerry Buss.

He is not the perfect owner, but he's in the perfect town for it.

He's flashy and fun loving, an entertainer who likes to do it big, and do it right. And especially likes to do it when everybody says he can't.

A year ago, there were cries for him to sell the team after he eccentrically forced Dennis Rodman upon us, and tentatively agreed to let Kurt Rambis hold it all together.

Buss was criticized for lacking vision, for losing his touch.

But like his town, he can take a punch.

He rid himself of Rodman, reassigned Rambis and spent plenty of his money on the one toy that would make all this work, a guy by the name of Phil Jackson.

This is, second, a championship belonging to Jerry West.

The team's vice president and creator spent the postseason hidden in front of a TV, or in a room next to that TV, buried in fears that his creation would disintegrate as it had in the last four seasons.

After all, he brought O'Neal and Bryant together when folks

said it might not work. He traded for Rice and Horry when folks said they were finished.

He took as many daring chances with this team as he did as a player.

And, of course, on Monday, that shot dropped.

His Lakers brought this city a championship by mirroring the best parts of this city's soul.

Easy to look at, but tough as traffic.

Flashy, but fundamental.

And a daily celebration of diversity.

They are a 77-year-old white assistant coach, and a black superstar guard who just should be graduating from college.

They are a quiet, aging forward who wears a stuffed bear on his head . . . and a rollicking young center who has a Superman tattoo on his bicep.

They have a radio announcer who has not missed a game in 35 years . . . and a head coach who has been with them for just one.

Their offense was officially known as a triangle, but they pounded through it like cymbals.

They did yoga during practices, and rapped afterward.

They grew up in the Bahamas, and Salt Lake City, and Newark, and even the exotic confines of Portland.

At times they were a Rocky Horry Picture Show . . . and other times they were a Harper's Bizarre . . . but mostly they will be remembered for that alley-oop pass from Brian Shaw to the big man that was known as the Shaw-Shaq Redemption.

"Hard work pays off," Bryant said. "If at first you don't succeed, you keep pushing, because you're going to get there eventually."

When did he know the game was wrapped up?

"The opening tip," Bryant said.

Whatever.

The organization is still Magic — Earvin Johnson was on the sidelines and hugging players afterward.

But today, it is once again majestic.

So this is how it feels.

Twelve long years, and worth the wait.

September 23, 2000

Melting Pool

SYDNEY, AUSTRALIA — America, the beautiful.

Two guys from different neighborhoods, with different skin tones, in different shoes.

Two guys winning the same Olympic race, at the same time, for the same flag.

Our country doesn't always work so well.

But when it does, when it churns and swirls and pushes breathlessly toward the edges of achievement and imagination, our country sings.

America, the beautiful.

That's how it looked when a wacky white kid from Phoenix and a quiet kid of African American heritage from Valencia fell into each other's dripping arms.

That's how it felt when they walked with each other, laughing and high-fiving strangers, to a medal stand.

That's how it sounded when they climbed solemnly to the same spot at the top of that stand, together.

Swimming 50 meters in separate lanes but as one body, Gary Hall Jr. and Anthony Ervin touched something beyond the end of the pool.

Finishing in a dead-solid tie for first place at 21.98 seconds, their Olympic victory wasn't about only the medal, but the montage.

"It was amazing," said Gary Hall Sr., the father. "Two guys with such diverse backgrounds. They look different, they act different, but then they merge their talents together and both come away victorious."

Sound like anybody you know?

Sound like, maybe, us? At our best?

At the conclusion of the race, with fans audibly gasping like the swimmers, Ervin grabbed Hall.

"It couldn't have happened any better," Ervin said.

"You're right," Hall said.

Well said.

When it works, our country is about nothing if not the melding of cultures, the hurdling of stereotypes, an unending search for a common thread.

Ervin and Hall have searched as we have searched.

Mostly underwater, mostly holding their breath, working mostly by touch.

Ervin, whose father, Jack, is 75% African American, is the first swimmer of that heritage to compete for the United States in the Olympics.

Hall, whose father was also an Olympic swimmer, is the last person anyone expected to see on a medal stand after battling diabetes and a marijuana suspension.

"In their own ways, both of these guys are overcoming preconceived notions," said Mike Bottom, their coach at the Phoenix Swim Club.

Ervin, 19, is quiet, reflective and spent the moments before the race staring at the water and "thinking about nothing."

Hall, 25, is loud, playful and spent the moments before the race flexing, kissing his biceps and shadow-boxing for the crowd.

"It's easier for me to tell you the ways they are alike," Bottom said.

Yet when Ervin joined Hall in Phoenix last summer, none of that mattered.

They lived in the same apartment complex, played video games together, did unconventional workouts together, and learned together.

As Hall was leaving the pool with Ervin and the gold medals, he laughed.

"Just another day of practice," he said.

He later added, "In the pool, on the field, with the punching bag, we pushed ourselves to limits that we otherwise would not have reached."

They pushed themselves to a point where, during the pre-Olympic training camp in Pasadena, they became roommates.

"This wasn't a Dara Torres and Jenny Thompson sort of thing," said Hall Sr., referring to the icy third-place tie of U.S. women.

"These guys really did come to like each other."

Hall liked that Ervin joked about Hall's tattooed leg or his flowing hair or 1996 boasts that didn't help him.

Ervin liked that Hall didn't ask about Ervin's heritage.

While Ervin doesn't back away from his African American roots, he doesn't want to be packaged by them either. When asked to mark his ethnicity on census boxes — his mother is Caucasian — he has marked them all.

"I just try to do the best for myself," he said. "I feel like people are trying to pin me down, but for me it's never been an issue. I would think in American society, something the nature of diverse blood would not be that big of a deal."

It's not. That's the point. That was part of the beauty.

Other countries' Olympic stars share common features and names.

The U.S. team is a little bit of everything.

A backstroker from Ukraine. A Mexican American softball shortstop. An Italian American baseball manager.

And, for one splendid evening, Anthony Ervin and Gary Hall Jr.

Their first-place finish wasn't as much amazing as appropriate.

In a span so short that the two swimmers took one breath combined, it was nonetheless a chance to see how far we have come, and where we should be going.

"That's what the Olympics are about," Bottom was saying. "Athletes achieving excellence, and somebody out there saying, 'Yeah, I can do that.'"

In the end, just before they stepped on a medal stand, Gary Hall Jr. handed Anthony Ervin a flag.

Ervin looked at it like, what kind of flag is this?

It was small, wrinkled, a bit faded.

Sort of like us, sometimes.

Ervin paused, shrugged, and waved it anyway.

October 22, 1998

Easy as Big Apple Pie

SAN DIEGO — Best baseball team in history? A question nobody can answer.

Best baseball team you've ever seen? A question everybody can answer.

At 8:24 p.m. Wednesday, that answer came as quickly as 24 gray-shirted men with no names on their backs collided in a joyous pile on a pitching mound, hugging and crying and praying.

If you were watching this week, this month, this summer . . . even if you are 80 years old and once watched Babe Ruth and Lou Gehrig . . . that answer is easy.

The best team you've ever seen? It is surely the 1998 New York Yankees.

To an unreal season they applied a surreal touch on a night that was celebrated with champagne and cigars, but felt like beer and pretzels.

With no stars and devoid of glitter, the Yankees swept the San Diego Padres out of the World Series in four games with a 3-0 defeat that ended their season-long race toward history with a sort of triple crown.

They beat the Padres' best pitcher in the biggest game of his life.

They beat the Padres' best pressure hitter with the bases loaded in the eighth inning.

They beat the Padres in San Diego in front of the largest baseball crowd in the city's history, 65,427 at now-dormant Qualcomm Stadium.

"We had high expectations from the fans, the media, our owner . . . we had nothing to do but lose," said Chili Davis, pausing to savor a sip and a puff.

"But we didn't."

Not when it counted. Never when it counted.

Their 125 victories are the most for one calendar year in major-league history. Their 11 victories in 13 pressure playoff games may be the most impressive in major-league history.

There's even magic in their winning percentage, derived from an overall 125-50 record.

Yep. It's .714. On the 50th anniversary of Ruth's death, you have to think the big lug would be proud.

"You've got to be kidding me," Manager Joe Torre said. "I'm going to wake up in the morning and look at that record in the newspaper and think, it can't happen."

The ending was as perfect as the entire summer for a team that only worked well when it worked together.

They scuffled for five innings against Kevin Brown, then scratched him for three. They staggered briefly when the Padres loaded the bases in the eighth inning, but then Mariano Rivera retired Jim Leyritz on a fly.

Finally, two outs in the ninth, Scott Brosius picked up a grounder from Mark Sweeney, threw it to first baseman Tino Martinez, and within moments the entire team was one indistinguishable pile.

The same indistinguishable pile they have been in since their season began in Anaheim, appropriately, on April Fool's Day.

Appropriately, because that was one of the few days they lost.

"I don't know if we have any Hall of Famers on this team," Torre said. " But I do know we play as a team."

And so in the final chapter of one of its finest seasons, baseball offers the sort of lesson that will last us until next spring.

After the players unpiled, they remained on the field and did an unusual thing for million-dollar New Yorkers. They hugged each other.

Not those cheap, high-fiving half hugs, but real hugs, burying their faces in each other's shoulders, all of them, two by two.

Chuck Knoblauch hugged Derek Jeter. Joe Girardi jumped into the arms of Paul O'Neill. Tino Martinez grabbed Rivera.

And so it went until they adjourned to the clubhouse where, after their initial champagne showers, they joined in their first chant as champions.

"Straw-man, Straw-man, Straw-man," they chanted, hoping the

words would carry over a TV microphone and into the living room of ailing teammate Darryl Strawberry.

"Darryl is one of the reasons we're here, and as soon as I can find a phone, I'm calling him," Jeter said, fighting through the mob.

The biggest reason they are here, of course, is them. All of them.

The 1998 New York Yankees have the face of Brosius, nondescript but not easily fooled, not respected even Wednesday when Martinez was twice intentionally walked so Brown could pitch to him.

The second time, his single made it 2-0, and this morning he is the World Series MVP who said his biggest moment had nothing to do with his two homers.

"The third out, throwing the ball and knowing it's going to end the game and the season," he said, typically.

They have the body of Bernie Williams; long, sleek, perfect for running out every grounder, taking every extra base.

They have the patience of Joe Torre, the expressionless manager who was stunned when his players actually thanked him.

They have the courage of Orlando Hernandez, whose experience as a Cuban refugee allowed him to shrug as he pulled them from the brink in Game 4 of the American League Championship Series against the Cleveland Indians.

They have the will of David Wells, unafraid to fight everyone from George Steinbrenner to his teammates, finally rendered as awe-struck as a child.

"My career could end today," he said, standing drenched in the middle of the field long after the game ended. "This is the storybook ending I've been waiting for all my life."

They have the class of O'Neill, who dislikes the limelight but accepted its burden throughout the playoffs, answering questions that teammates couldn't, supporting and pushing them at the same time.

"We better enjoy this," he said, chewing on a cigar. "Because this will be the best team any of us have ever played on."

And they have the fire of, yes, Mr. Steinbrenner, once again The Boss of all baseball.

Standing in the middle of steamy clubhouse, spreading his arms beneath a white turtleneck drenched brown, he proclaimed, "This is the greatest team that's ever been."

For once, I'm not telling him to shut up. You?

The Master of All

AUGUSTA, GA. — To my great-grandchildren:

I am writing this with sore legs and a sweat-soaked shirt, neither of which can stifle my urge to run across a closely cut lawn while pumping my fist.

Please don't find me a sentimental old fool. But I have just spent an afternoon walking with history.

It is a history you certainly already have seen in books, but I was there. I bumped against it and shouted for it. I melted in its heat and shivered at its triumph.

Just as somebody once told me about Babe Ruth, I want to tell you about Tiger Woods.

You know by now that he was the greatest golfer who ever lived.

Today, through meandering old woods known as August National Golf Club, he first set foot on the edges of that superlative.

Today, April 8, 2001, he won the Masters golf tournament to become the first golfer in history to hold the titles of all four major championships at the same time.

As you surely know now, it hasn't been done before, or since.

Maybe you even have read about what Woods achieved today, by shooting a 16-under-par 272 and finishing two strokes ahead of David Duval.

How he talked about putting all four major trophies on his coffee table. How there was talk of this being the greatest individual sport achievement ever.

But still, you must wonder. A golfer? A national hero once was a golfer?

Now that people are hitting balls for miles off the moon, what is the big deal about hitting a crooked 300-yard drive?

And all this fuss over somebody who was just 25 years old? How can somebody make a lifelong impact while virtually still a child?

I'll admit, I was thinking about this too, until I watched Tiger Woods walk down the 18th fairway into a thunderous standing ovation that quieted even the birds.

Then, as I accidentally brushed my pen against a white shirt in front of me, while accidentally elbowing a woman to my left, steam rising from the mass of people in 85-degree heat, I had some thoughts.

Here was a black man, walking into the teeth of a nearly all-white crowd at an exclusive club that didn't accept its first black member until 1991.

And they were standing for him.

Including a guy named Hootie.

"You're the greatest," said club chairman Hootie Johnson.

Here, also, was a young athlete in a baggy red shirt and a scowl, walking through a group of older colleagues in saddle shoes and shrugs.

And they were cheering him.

"Under these circumstances, with what he was trying to accomplish, to shoot 68 and win the golf tournament in the manner that he did, is outstanding," Duval said.

Here was a guy unafraid to be unlike anybody else in his sport, a guy who took those differences and turned them into fuel that burned him into another atmosphere.

You know what he said was his favorite shot today? It was a soaring, hooking tee shot on the dog-leg No. 13 that led to a birdie. It occurred just one hole after he botched a six-foot putt for a bogey that dropped him into a first-place tie.

You know why he liked the shot?

"It's a shot I've been practicing the last couple of months, knowing the fact that I'm probably going to need that shot," he said.

Tiger Woods reminded us it was cool to practice, cool to work.

Do you know how many times I saw him smile at the crowd during today's round? Not once.

His playing partner, Phil Mickelson, a nice man whom you'll remember as being famous for final-round putting yips, smiled and waved throughout.

Not Woods. He threw his putter on his bag. He flipped his putter behind him. He defiantly swooped his ball out of a cup after matching a Mickelson birdie.

He yelled at his shots — "Stop! Stop! Stop!"

He yelled at the crowd — "No cameras, amateur or professional!"

Tiger Woods reminded us it was cool to be in a zone.

Then he reminded us when it was cool to step out.

After his final fist pump for his final birdie on the final hole that clinched the tournament, he suddenly took off his black cap and buried his face inside.

He later admitted he was crying.

"For some reason, my emotions started coming out and I started experiencing and reflecting on some of the shots I had hit," he said. "A lot of different things went through my head at that moment."

But then, he reminded us it was cool to be polite.

"I had to pull myself together, because Phil was finishing his round, and I had to congratulate him," he said.

Everything that Woods represents can be found in other sports, of course. But rarely in one person. And only in golf can these lessons be so clearly individual and openly inspirational.

He was the right person, in the right place, at a time in our sports evolution when we needed him most.

I know you probably have debated with friends about whether Woods' holding all four major titles — Masters, U.S. Open, British Open and PGA — is the best individual sports achievement in history.

There was no debate today.

Walking with what seemed like 40,000 fans here — the media

is not allowed inside the restraining ropes, unlike at other tournaments — it was impossible not to feel the celebration.

People were lined up 10 deep to see Woods tee off. People were
jumping up and down behind long lines to see him putt. People
were sliding down hills and hanging on to dogwoods just to watch
him walk.

Woods paused several times to cover his sweaty face in a towel.
Another time he held up a shot to chase away a bug.

His gallery, though, stayed hot and bothered, standing
sweaty and motionless from shot to shot, never requiring a mar-
shal to quiet them, huddled together to cheer the moment and
the man.

Among those in the crowd was Woods' mother, Kultida, who
somehow wedged her way in front of small trees or bushes to
watch every shot.

The first family member Woods hugged afterward was his
father, Earl, a loud man who celebrated his son's final putt by jab-
bing his finger into the air in a major-league "I told you so."

Everyone seemed to understand the history here today except,
as usual, Tiger.

After all, when he was asked what he would say to the late legendary golfer Bobby Jones if they met today, Woods smiled and
said he would ask but one question: "How did he come back?"

You may wonder then, children, did Woods appreciate what he
was doing? Did he enjoy it as we did?

Perhaps the answer is that such unprecedented focus on the
course doesn't easily translate to romance in the interview room.

After spending an afternoon thinking about only the next shot,
it may be difficult for Woods to place that shot in history.

But he does know this much: His buddy Michael Jordan won
six major championships. On this day, Woods tied him.

"This will probably go down as one of the great moments in our
sport," Woods admitted. "I cannot imagine accomplishing something greater."

I will end this letter by reminding you that some people actually tried to downplay Woods' four consecutive titles because they

didn't occur in the same calendar year, taking special pains to note that he did not win the elusive prize known as golf's "Grand Slam."

Like greatness ever needs a name. Like greatness ever needs to be anything other than something to embrace, something to share.

His name was Tiger Woods, and here's hoping his memory can touch you like his presence once touched us.

Love,

Great Granddaddy.

February 4, 2002

Emotions of This Game Make Everyone a Winner

NEW ORLEANS — On an untiring, unimaginable, appropriate evening, the Super Bowl champions weren't a football team.

They were a flag.

A single mass of red, white and blue unfurling across the Superdome floor.

Flapping, clanking, rattling, twisting, then flapping again.

So much strength from a cloth so thin. So much surprise from an ideal so old.

Today it is not just the New England Patriots who fly, but so, too, the belief that sports is all about fabric.

High they wave, as high above the St. Louis Rams as Adam Vinatieri's 48-yard field goal in the final seconds that gave the Patriots a 20-17 victory.

Afterward, hidden at midfield underneath a blanket of confetti, they danced like Buster Douglas once danced, whooped like Villanova once whooped, and it's OK if you were howling with them.

This was not only the biggest upset in the 36 years of Super Bowl history, with the best finish in Super Bowl history, but all of it happened with the most timely backdrop.

From the pregame songs of John Phillip Sousa to the halftime unveiling of the names of those killed in the Sept. 11 tragedy, the theme of this game was the resilience of a unified America.

The Patriots became that theme.

Three colors. One cloth. This, from the time they took the field during the pregame introductions, all together, refusing to be introduced separately, another Super Bowl first.

The Rams danced to the field separately. The Patriots rolled out together. The game turned before the opening kickoff.

"I'm sure the TV networks didn't like it, I'm sure the league is going to fine us, but I don't care," said cornerback Ty Law.

"We weren't going to come hopping and shaking out there as individuals. We were going to show everyone we were in this together."

Together, through a game-long series of hits that pounded the Rams into stripes, backed by a strategy that made Coach Mike Martz see stars.

Together, through a 14-point lead, then a 14-point blown lead, on toward what was certainly going to be the first overtime in Super Bowl history.

But together, finally, while holding the ball on their own 17-yard line with 1:21 remaining and no timeouts.

Drew Bledsoe, the Patriot quarterback who lost his job to young Tom Brady yet never complained, grabbed the kid as he was leaving the sidelines for the huddle.

"Drop back and sling it," he told Brady.

"Go win the game."

Few thought Brady, who had only 92 passing yards before that drive, would actually follow that advice. Most thought the Patriots would play it safe, avoid a turnover, and take their chances in overtime.

But then again, most thought the Patriots would lose by two touchdowns.

"Why not go for it?" asked Brady afterward.

"With that much time left, why not? You never know. And this is evidence."

Evidence, indeed.

A nine-play drive that turned the 199th player selected in the 2000 draft into a Super Bowl MVP.

A drive that ended with the making of a New England hero who, right this minute, is bigger than Carlton Fisk.

So, Adam Vinatieri, were you praying?

"I've been praying all day," he said with a grin.

As for Ram quarterback Kurt Warner, even in defeat, his biblical references remained consistent.

"It says in there, 'When the winds and rain come,'" he said, shaking his head. "There's no if. It's a when."

This latest storm will surely shake the NFL in the same manner as the Baltimore Ravens' championship last season.

A team can win the battle of total net yards, 427-267, and lose the game?

A team can have 11 more first downs, hold the ball for seven more minutes, and lose the game?

If that team gets outhit, it can. If that team gets outschemed, it can.

The Patriots proved for a second consecutive season that the best team is not the most talented team, but the most together team.

Talk about your well-timed public-service announcements.

"I hated it this year when people called us a team of destiny, because that implied luck," Vinatieri said. "But then you look at all that happened to our country, and all the patriotic stuff before today's game, and you look at our name and our attitude . . . and you say, maybe something up there is helping us out."

Remember, this is the team that, in the second round of the playoffs, defeated the Oakland Raiders only because a replay official changed a Brady fumble call in the final moments.

This is the team that, in the AFC championship, defeated the Pittsburgh Steelers only after their quarterback, Kordell Stewart, threw two horrible passes on their two final drives.

This is a team that, even if the point spread wasn't as great, began this game as bigger underdogs than the New York Jets in Super Bowl III.

The Jets were 18-point underdogs because, being from the renegade American Football League, few folks knew of their great talent.

The Patriots were 14-point underdogs because they simply weren't as good as the Rams.

"If we're playing next week, we'd probably be the underdogs," Coach Bill Belichick said.

They took the field a couple of hours before the game, bumping heads and pounding pads, determined to get into the sort of hitting mood that would swing the odds.

Then the NFL shooed them off for a show that featured taped speeches from past presidents, the Boston Pops, and emotional renderings of America the Beautiful and the national anthem.

It was arguably the most compelling pregame display in American sports history.

And it drove the Patriots bonkers.

"I hope you enjoyed it, because we hated it," Brady said. "We were ready to play, but we had to go back and sit in our locker room for an hour."

Yet it worked for everyone. When the game started, the Patriots were more restless than ever. And the 72,922 fans in the Superdome had decided upon their favorite team.

On the second play of the game, the Rams' Torry Holt made an 18-yard catch, but the Patriots' Tebucky Jones hit him so hard, one could probably hear it while retching on Bourbon Street. The crowd roared.

Moments later, Holt was bumped by Law on a long ball that he couldn't catch. The crowd roared again.

"We heard all this talk about how they were track stars, but it's hard to run a 100-yard dash with somebody standing in your way," Law said. "We wanted to hit them, and keep hitting them."

Law's 47-yard interception return for a touchdown came after Mike Vrabel smacked Warner with a right jab.

The Patriots' second touchdown came after Ricky Proehl fumbled when he was smacked in the chest by Antwan Harris.

The Patriots' first field goal came after an interception caused when Holt was shoved away by Otis Smith.

"Yeah, they were tough," Warner said. "Real tough."

The Patriots preferred a different word.

"Patriots," owner Bob Kraft said. "Today, we're all Patriots."

Are we ever.

CHAPTER TWO

Hall of Famers

April 26, 1998

Inside Vin Scully

Hi, everybody, and a very pleasant good morning to you wherever you may be. It's a beautiful morning here in Pacific Palisades, the sun shining, a soft breeze sneaking through the trees. Glad you could join us; let's set the scene: The man voted the most memorable personality in Los Angeles Dodger history is on his knees, sleeves rolled up. This most memorable personality is giving infant Jordan Kyle Schaefer a bath.

And oh, what a marvelous time they are having. He washes behind his ears . . . rinses his hair . . . pulls him out of the tub . . . sits him up on the counter . . . and begins massaging his little back while the baby shakes his head, giggles and says something that sounds like "hee-hee-hee-hee."

Friends, at 8:15 in the morning on this sweet spring day, you are looking at more than a baseball announcer, more than a baseball legend. You are looking at a grandfather.

■   ■   ■

Hello, this is Vin Scully. . . .

When calling on the phone, even to people he has known for 25 years, the voice of our city fully identifies himself. Never presuming a familiarity that exists with millions. Never taking their admiration for granted.

"That's all you need to know about Vin," says close friend Dan Cathcart. "When he calls you on the phone, he always gives you his full name when, really, all he needs to do is just say hello."

Hello, this is Vin Scully. . . .

For 40 years in Los Angeles, have any five words been more comforting? Returning travelers turn on the car radios after arriving at LAX, hear those words, know they are home. The lonely turn on their TVs, hear those words, know that they still belong. The Dodgers have a new owner, an ever-changing stadium, increasingly distant players, and yet people throughout Southern California have turned on their radios this month, heard those words and known that it is spring. The sky may be falling, Tommy Lasorda has retired, Peter O'Malley has been bought out, but Vin Scully is talking, so it is spring.

Hello, this is Vin Scully. . . .

That's how he greets this longtime acquaintance on my answering machine, to talk about an interview. For once, I am glad I am not home. I now have the voice on tape, without static or organ music or applause, just Scully talking to me in that soothing tenor.

"Please," I announce to everyone within two square miles. "Do not erase this message."

One problem about the interview. The longtime Dodger announcer — who also happens to be the best announcer in baseball history, no question, don't even think about it — doesn't do these kinds of stories. He hasn't done one in 13 years, to be exact.

After 49 seasons of sitting gracefully in the easy chairs and front porches of our homes and lives, to say nothing of the time he's spent riding shotgun in our cars, Scully has become an intensely private man. Few people, not even 22-year partner and friend Ross Porter, have been to his home. He is almost invisible with the ballclub on the road, preferring to spend his spare moments reading — most recently "The Perfect Storm," by Sebastian Junger, and Tom Dyja's "Play for the Kingdom," a novel about a sandlot baseball game between two Civil War regiments. "Call me in the hotel," he'll tell friends from home. "I'll just be sitting there, killing time."

Scully talks about the Dodgers and baseball and life with such elegance that it sounds like a concerto with words. Yet he is wary of talking about himself. "I know myself to be a very ordinary man, really I do," he says. "I would just as soon go quietly."

That is the worrisome thing, that "go" part. He turned 70 in November. Even though last season was arguably his best ever — when the Dodgers collapse, their lead announcer only gets stronger — he increasingly worries about the time spent away from home.

He says he still gets "goose bumps" when he hears the crowd; he is inspired enough to broadcast games for the next 20 years.

But while he still does all the TV games — 88 this year — he is giving more of the radio innings to Porter and Rick Monday. And
while he says he is excited about working for the new Fox Group
owners — whew, admit it, his premature departure was everyone's
biggest fear — there is a sense that these are his final years.

Next season will be his 50th. The year 2000 would mark the
beginning of his sixth decade as a Dodger play-by-play man.
Maybe he will retire then. Or maybe he will wait until some later
moment that he deems, with his impeccable sense of timing, to be
dramatically correct. No matter. When Vin Scully retires, it will
not be quietly. After listening to him for all these summers, this
town will finally put down its foot and say, "Listen to us." There
will be tributes, parties, retrospectives, and no matter what Scully
says, he will be too darn polite to turn any of it down.

Before that happens, though, it would be nice to collect some
snapshots. Nothing big or deep or pretentious, just a few pictures
of a legend silhouetted against the late afternoon.

Hello, this is Vin Scully. . . .

When you come right down to it, it's not really a voice. It's a
monument. It's a landscape. Like the Hollywood sign, only bigger.
Like Griffith Park, only safer. Like a 70-degree January day in
Pasadena, only more believable.

Yes, that's it. That's the platitude we're looking for. It would
come so easily for him, he would figure it out in 10 seconds. It's
taken me nearly two dozen paragraphs.

I tell Vin Scully over lunch. I tell him we want to do this story
because he has become the most trusted person in Los Angeles,
period.

"Who," he says. "Me?"

∎ ∎ ∎

Hi, everybody, and a very pleasant Christmas Eve to you wherever you may be. It's warm and cozy here around the Scully family
tree. Glad you could join us, let's set the scene:

Sandi Scully, the lovely wife of the Dodger announcer, is crying; tears are dotting her cheeks like so many raindrops. She has
just unwrapped a cassette tape from her husband, and she cannot,

for the life of her, believe what is on that tape. Vin Scully's greatest Dodger hits? Nooo. Famous home run calls of the 20th century? Nooo again.

The tape causing so much emotion is of Vin Scully serenading his wife with the song "Wind Beneath My Wings." And what do you know about that? He sang it and recorded it — on a home-made karaoke machine with help from his daughter — while his wife wasn't looking.

Merry Christmas, Mrs. Scully. Merry Christmas indeed.

. ▪ .

Perhaps the most important thing to recognize about Vin Scully is that, for all these years, there have been two of him.

There is the Scully whose voice wafts through our town for a couple of hours every summer night like a delightful aroma, the Scully who turns pitchers into bullfighters, outfielders into mountain climbers, managers into scientists, baseball into theater.

This is Scully the bard.

"He gives you the imagery you need to paint the picture," says David Hunt, Scully's brother-in-law, who is blind. "Try closing your eyes and listening to other announcers. They leave a void. Vin leaves no void."

The other Scully is the one who goes home to a wife, five children and five grandchildren. That Scully has dealt with the deaths of his first wife, his mother, his father and stepfather and, most recently, his 33-year-old son. From home, he has made the decision to move forward bravely and without regret. At home, one can hear him sing. "Sings all the time," says Sandi. "Singing when he wakes up. Sings before lunch." Then he gets into the car on the drive to work and really sings.

You wonder, to what radio station does this town's foremost radio personality listen on his way to work? He doesn't. He plays compact discs that contain Broadway tunes and movie scores. Some days "Ragtime." Other days "The Music Man." And yes, as he plays them, he sings.

"That way, when I get out of the car at the stadium, I'm feeling good," he says.

He also has stereo speakers hooked up throughout his house so, at the touch of a button, the place is filled with music. When some of his children or grandchildren come over, it is also filled with laughter. "Pee-paw," as one grandchild calls him, will be chasing the kids around on the floor. The music will be from a recent Tony Award winner. The TV will be tuned to a classic movie.

This town's most famous TV sportscaster does not usually watch sports on TV. It's not that he doesn't love sports, he says, shrugging. He says he just loves his family more. This is also why he rarely does personal appearances, or TV talk shows, or anything that would give us another little bit of him that he feels his family deserves. If you feel like he disappears once the baseball season ends, you are right. That is exactly how he plans it.

"I have realized the most precious thing in the world you have is time," Scully says. "I should be utilizing the time I have with the ones I love."

How does this happen? In an age when many famous announcers have started acting like famous athletes, making millions and behaving like children, the Marv Alberts of the world, how does this trend miss the best one of all? The era of arrogance and entitlement has somehow blown past Scully while he stands around in his perfectly pressed blazer and sheepish smile, signing all autographs, sending thank-you notes to those who say nice things about him, refusing to write a book because he doesn't understand why he's a big deal, working on a one-year contract year after year.

"The game is the thing, not me," Scully says. "I am just a conduit for the game. I am the guy between the expert and the fan. I am not the expert."

How does this happen? How does such a rags-to-riches story end up with the rich guy being so nice?

Scully was born in the Bronx, the son of a silk salesman. His father died of pneumonia when Scully was 7, and his mother moved the family to Brooklyn, where her red-haired child grew up playing stickball in the streets. Later, he made the baseball team at Fordham University and worked for the school paper and radio station.

Scully tells a story about what followed. Actually, as with all of his stories, he doesn't tell it — he paints it. It is Brooklyn, 1950, his first season, just one year out of Fordham. As he is leaving Ebbets Field after a rainout, there are hundreds of autograph-seeking children standing across the street behind a barrier, waiting for the players. About the time he steps into the street, the barriers break and the children rush toward the stadium door, surrounding him. Someone sticks a pen and piece of paper in front of his face. He signs it. From the back, there booms a voice, "Hey, who's that!" The kid who has just gotten the autograph looks carefully at his paper and replies, "It's . . . it's . . . it's Vin Scully."

"Hell," shouts the guy in the back. "He's nobody."

Scully finishes the story and shrugs.

"I heard the guy and thought to myself, 'You got that right.'"

∎ ∎ ∎

Hi, everybody, and a very pleasant good evening to you wherever you may be. It is a stressful night in Los Angeles, about 35 years ago, and let's set the scene:

The Dodger announcer has just read the surgeon general's report that smoking is bad for your health, so he has decided to quit. But he needs help. So he turns to the one place of stability in his life. He turns to his family.

In his shirt pocket, where he used to keep his cigarettes, he places a family photo. Whenever he feels like he needs a smoke, he reaches into his pocket and pulls out the photo. He says it reminds him of why he is quitting. For eight months, struggling constantly to break his habit, he reaches into his pocket and touches that photo. It frays and fades, but it never leaves that shirt pocket, never leaves his reach. And after eight months, wouldn't you know it, it works. It really works. Vincent Edward Scully, bless him, never smokes again.

∎ ∎ ∎

Snapshot: Vin Scully's youngest daughter, Catherine, is learning how to swim. Under one condition. She will not jump into the pool unless he announces her name as if she were a baseball player. So every afternoon, before leaving for the stadium, he stands in the shallow end, raises his arms and makes his first call of the day: "Ladies and gentleman, now presenting the infamous 'Catherine Anne Whale.'" Giggling, she leaps into his arms. Twenty years later, she still remembers the laugh, can still feel the splash.

Snapshot: It is daughter Catherine's wedding day. Like all brides, she is nervous about how she looks in her wedding dress. Walking her down the aisle, Scully leans into her ear and begins singing, "Here comes the bride, all fat and wide. . . ." She spends the rest of the procession biting her tongue to keep from laughing. At the altar, when her father gently pulls away her veil and gives her a kiss, his face changes. "He turns away. I look close, and I can see his eyes filled with tears," she says. "The range of emotions he showed that day, that totally describes my father. He is not some myth. He is real."

Snapshot: Nearly 25 years ago, Scully runs into actress Florence Henderson at Dodger Stadium. "Miss Henderson," he tells her, "I have my own Brady Bunch. And I have news for you. Our problems cannot be solved in 28 minutes."

In 1972, Scully's first wife, Joan, died suddenly. The coroner's report said it was an accidental overdose of cold and bronchitis medication. Joan left him with three young children.

Two years later, he met Sandi, a secretary for the Rams, who had two young children from a previous marriage. Before their first date, one of her children was sick, and she could not reach Scully. When she did not show up at their designated meeting place, he thought he had been stood up. He promptly sent her a photo of him standing forlornly in the otherwise deserted parking lot. She agreed to a second date, beginning what may have been the most respectful courtship in history. "It was three months before he even kissed me," she says.

Less than a year later, they married. They cut short their honeymoon because they were worried about the children; later they took another honeymoon, with all their kids in tow. Scully recently gave his wife a medal for running a family that, with Catherine's birth in January 1975, had grown to six children. A real medal — diamonds and everything. "Everyone says their wife deserves a medal. Well, I figured, why not just get her one?" he says.

It is during these times, during the early years of Tommy Lasorda, that the town began to truly trust Scully, to realize that while he was paid by the Dodgers, he really worked for the fans.

During Lasorda's turbulent early reign, Scully remained unafraid to criticize a bad play, point out a manager's unused options or praise an opponent. Guess it's impossible to be phony at work when everything else in your life is so real, when you change diapers before leaving for the park, talk to teachers from hotel rooms, hurry home from airports to play catch.

"Vinny is the class of the Dodgers, the head of the list," says former owner Peter O'Malley, a longtime Scully confidant. "His honesty and integrity come through every day. He wants the Dodgers to win as much as I do, but he tells it like it is, even if it means criticizing the owner."

Says Scully: "Red Barber instilled in me that you always go down the middle. I like to think that if I say that somebody made a good catch, the fans will believe me, because I will also say so if he butchered the play. . . . I don't want to see things with my heart, I want to see them with my eyes."

You can hear that even today. Next time you're at Dodger Stadium, in the late innings of a close game, and a Dodger hits a ball into the air, listen to Scully. The crowd starts screaming the moment the ball is hit, hoping that it will be a home run. Scully's voice will not change until the moment it is.

■   ■   ■

Hi, everybody, and a pleasant good afternoon to you wherever you may be. It's a wondrous afternoon in a West L.A. hospital, glad you could join us; let's set the scene:

Catherine, daughter of the Dodger announcer, is having her first baby, and, oh my, it is coming quickly. At the same time, poor granddad is in Palm Springs beginning a golf telecast. The family telephones the granddad on the course. The start of the telecast is delayed for a few seconds while he whispers encouragement into his daughter's ear. Then, as you might guess, the family brings a TV into the delivery room. Sure enough, while the baby is crowning, the Dodger announcer's face coincidentally comes on the screen. With every push, his daughter leans up and sees his smile, and is comforted.

Ah, but there is a problem. The announcer is so good that the doctor is also paying close attention to him. Too close, actually. The doctor is watching the golf and not the delivery, and, finally, some family members say, "Uh, doctor? The baby?"

And out she comes, bright, bubbly MacKenzie Jean Luderer. That's one round the proud grandfather will never forget.

■ ■ ■

Unfortunately for Scully, four years ago there was another round he'll never forget. He was on the 11th hole of the Bel-Air Country Club when he got the message. Michael Scully, the son who shared his father's blue eyes, whose engineering career at Arco had been bolstered by his father's advice, had been killed at the age of 33. He and a pilot were inspecting pipe damage in central California after the Northridge earthquake when their helicopter hit unmarked power lines.

It was the afternoon of Jan. 20, 1994. Several hours later, Michael Scully's wife, Cathy, gave birth to a son. For once, Scully was visibly devastated, yet he and Sandi were at the hospital the morning after, feeding the baby before going to the funeral home to pick out a casket. That spring, he was back on the radio. He hurt, but we could not tell. At home, it was impossible for him to sing, but we never knew. It was like that when his first wife died. It was like that when, last December, his mother died.

Vin Scully is the most trusted man in Los Angeles, because, when he comes into our homes, he never tracks anything inside.

"To lose a son, there is no way you can ever imagine . . . even to this day, it is so overwhelming you can't get a grip on it," Scully says. "But that is where your work will help you. For a couple of hours a day, you can work through it."

His voice is not only landscape, it is armor. He thinks we all have our problems and don't want to hear about his. That is fine. That is enough.

The voice is enough, as it was many years ago, on a Sunday

afternoon when the Scully family was sitting by their pool with a Dodger game beginning and Vin on the radio. "Hi everybody, and a pleasant good afternoon to you wherever you may be," he said, like he always says. "Pull up a chair and stick around a while."

Catherine, then age 4, walked over to the radio and said, "OK, Daddy, I think I will."

For as long as he's inviting, we all will.

August 18, 1998

There Will Never Be Another View of L.A. Like This One

When people realized I worked with Jim Murray, the first thing they asked was, "Can he still see?"

"Read his columns," I answered. "You tell me if he can still see."

I have covered events with Murray, who was driven to the stadium, pored over a computer with his Coke-bottle glasses, then was driven home.

I would pick up the paper the next day and realize, he saw more of that game than I ever would.

In a sports world that takes itself so seriously, he saw humor.

In victory, he saw humility. In defeat, he saw hope.

In a busy town of big shots, he saw the lone guy walking to the newspaper box with the quarter in his hand, the guy who had no choice but to trust him.

This morning, when that guy pulls open the rack, he will discover another favorite hangout closed, another landmark lost.

Jim Murray is gone, and you know what the worst of it is? We don't have Jim Murray around to somehow make us smile about it.

We can keep running his columns, you know. Every Sunday,

every Thursday, why not?

What he said is still worth hearing. What he taught, we can always stand to learn.

Murray was history during a time when our memories don't extend beyond last night's "SportsCenter."

He was creative thinking in a world that still sees black and white.

He was dignity and class to all of us who scream from the cheap seats.

More than anything, Jim Murray was Los Angeles for a Los Angeles still struggling to understand itself.

He was the city before there was a city. Smart, funny, a bit cynical, a bit sentimental, strong enough to not care what anybody thought about it.

When sports was playing its small part in helping us define ourselves in relation to our more established East Coast rivals, he gave that pride a voice.

Even if, by the time you finished reading him, you were howling too hard to talk.

Any other writer in these parts ever make you laugh out loud over breakfast?

Didn't think so.

Anybody else convince you that something needed to be changed, a wrong righted, a justice served, without ever actually writing it?

Convinced you by making you convince yourself?

Didn't think so.

If we keep running his columns, I guarantee you one thing: Jim Murray will still cover the Masters better than anybody in the building. Same goes for the World Series, the Super Bowl, the Kentucky Derby.

And nobody will ever be as trusted.

Some area columnists have been writing constantly that the NFL needs this town more than we need the NFL.

The other day, Murray wrote essentially the same thing — well, OK, with maybe 1,000 times more grace.

"Finally," one reader immediately wrote, "somebody finally

stands up and writes that the NFL needs this town more than we need the NFL."

Jim Murray was somebody, all right.

He was a giant who walked around like the guy next door, who looked as harmless as Wally Cox, but whose one-liners stung like Muhammad Ali's jabs.

In the beginning, he was this town's older brother, explaining things it didn't understand, defending it against outside criticism, taking on the likes of New York, Cleveland and boxing.

Later, he became a favorite uncle, walking through the door just in time to lend perspective to a Laker loss or neighborhood victory.

In the end, he was our grandfather, beckoning us to his feet twice a week to spin his yarns, particularly the tale that those who don't understand history are doomed to repeat it.

How I wish I had listened to more of those stories. How I wish I had not been too intimidated to call him at home, ask him to lunch, then sit there and listen to a couple of hours' worth of those stories.

During one of his rare trips to the office recently, he started talking about some old team and famous player. Soon, five of us were, literally, sitting at his feet, asking for more.

Jim Murray was somebody, all right.

I remember the time then-Dodger outfielder Kal Daniels refused to talk to Murray.

Murray shrugged, walked away, and four people immediately descended on Daniels to scold him.

Not four publicity or newspaper people.

Four players.

Athletes loved Murray, lined up to meet him. Many grew up reading him, learned to love their games because of him.

Once, when a colleague greeted Murray in a World Cup press tent, one of the workers heard Murray's name, rushed up to him and told him how her late father used to read him every day.

By the time she finished the story, she was crying. She said Murray reminded her of her dad.

Which, in the end, is why his column will stand as the most enduring sports monument in this town's history; prettier than the

Rose Bowl, more magnificent than the Coliseum, more fabulous than the Forum.

Those places were always about someone else.

In the end, Jim Murray was about us.

Could he still see? A lot better than this city and this newspaper, plunged today into the darkness of a great and terrible void.

October 14, 2000

Lifetime Achievement

He will awaken today in a condominium where time has not budged for 27 years.

There is shag carpet on the floor, crushed velvet furniture in the corners, his late wife Nell's enduring vision on walls filled with aging clocks and plates and photographs of men in basketball hot pants.

He won't turn on his cell phone, because he doesn't have one. He won't jump on the Internet, because he doesn't own a computer.

He will not watch the TV in his bedroom, because it hasn't worked for years. He will instead look at the photo of Nell that is propped up on a pillow above where he sleeps, and another one on the side where she slept.

If he decides to drive, it will be in a 1989 Ford Taurus. If he decides to get his hair cut, he will drive to a barber he has used since he was in possession of all his hair.

John Wooden will awaken today in a world unchanged since he became a sports icon and city treasure.

Unchanged, except for him.

Today, John Wooden turns 90.

America's oldest working coach.

"I'm hanging on," he says with a laugh. "I used to be hanging in. Now I'm hanging on."

It is the day before his birthday, which occurred 90 years ago in the bedroom of a farmhouse in the middle of Indiana.

Yet the grip this shuffling old man with the bad hip and aching knees holds on us is tighter than ever.

His modest San Fernando Valley condo, in the shadow of a freeway and with a view of a parking lot, is besieged by gawking florists and mailmen who toss piles of packages onto his porch from the alley below.

His name is on a little stenciled plate in the glassed-in directory by the front door like everyone else in the building.

His phone number is listed.

That phone rings. A familiar voice is heard on the answering machine singing, "Happy birthday to you, happy birthday to you, happy birthday from Australia. . . ."

"Oh," the former UCLA coach says with a smile. "That's Bill Walton."

Wooden rises slowly from his hard-backed chair and walks halting down the hall toward the phone, while Walton makes idle conversation on the machine, as if he knows his old coach is going to eventually pick up.

Wooden finally reaches the receiver in a cluttered office. He sits carefully on another hard-backed chair. He cradles the receiver.

"Bill, Bill, I love you too," he says to Walton. "Yep, it's me, I'm here."

Fifteen minutes later, Wooden shuffles out the room with a smile.

"Bill calls me twice a week, and I love talking to him," he says, his eyes twinkling. "Although, it is safe to say, I don't do much of the talking."

There will be a family party at his granddaughter's house today, with loads of children and maybe a special lemon cake and only one rule.

No presents.

"I said it, and I meant it," Wooden says. "I told my family, their presence is my presents."

The way Wooden views it, every day is a gift for a teacher who is continually allowed to teach.

The other day he agreed to speak to a wheelchair basketball

team at the airport before it departed for the Paralympics in Australia. Because of typical LAX parking problems, he was required to walk a long distance to meet the team. During the walk, he could feel his ankles swell and his legs stiffen.

"I was thinking, why did I get myself into this?" Wooden recalls. "Then I finally get there, and see all these beautiful girls in wheelchairs, all of them so happy to see me, just thrilled at anything I would say. . . ."

He shakes his head.

"And here I was, bemoaning my situation? I was ashamed, just ashamed."

Wooden told the team what he tells many teams these days, that the journey is more important than the result, that they are winners by just trying.

Some days, he not only says those words, he must live them.

Although he is in generally good health, a couple of times in the last few months he has become suddenly dizzy and fallen at home.

Because his bad artificial hip makes it impossible for him to stand up from a sitting position without support, each time he has crawled down the hall on his belly to a chair, and lifted himself into a sitting position.

"Felt like I was crawling for two hours," he says, smiling. "Although I'm sure it was only minutes."

Neither time would he call for help.

"What for?" he says. "Once I sat down, I was fine."

He still attends nearly every UCLA home basketball game, sitting in the same place in the corner behind the UCLA bench, enduring the same autograph sessions during halftime, an autograph for which he has never been paid.

"It's like I always told my players, if they want your autograph, in a sense they are honoring you," he says.

He has yet to attend a sports event at Staples Center, and while he cheers for the Lakers, he still thinks college basketball beats the knee-length pants off the NBA.

"All that traveling, the post play is wrestling, so much showmanship," he says.

In fact, he even thinks the WNBA can be, at times, better than the NBA.

"Technically, the better women in that league are better than the men," he says.

Though, even with his record 10 NCAA championships and 88-game winning streak and career .813 winning percentage, he can't believe anyone cares what he thinks.

"I am not a famous man," he says. "I hate being called a wizard. I am not a wizard."

He pauses.

"I think being famous is somebody who did something good for mankind," he says. "Mother Teresa was famous. Nobel Prize winners are famous. Basketball coaches aren't famous."

He looks out the window over the parking lot, and beyond to the plain doors of a neighboring apartment complex.

He has given away all but one of his championship rings. Of all the gaudy trophies that sit haphazardly on his floor, his most prized award, he says, is stuck back on a shelf in a little black box.

It is a bronze medallion for academic-athletic achievement he earned in 1932 as a senior at Purdue.

"I was a person who was a teacher who happened to be in the public eye," he says.

And still teaching. Just ask Lindsay Benko, an Indiana-based competitive swimmer who was the granddaughter of one of Wooden's former pupils.

When she was struggling during the Olympic trials, Wooden phoned her with a pep talk.

When she made the Olympics, she credited her closing strength to that talk.

When she won a gold medal as part of the U.S. 800-meter freestyle relay team, Wooden felt young again.

"The greatest joy you can get is saying or doing something that helps another person," he says. "That joy is reward in itself."

Good thing, because Wooden's annual income never exceeded $38,000, including basketball camps.

That is why, during his final years at UCLA, he and Nell settled in a condo that looks more like student housing than legend housing.

But that is not why he stays here.

He stays here, in a place darkened by piles of books and trophies and photos, because Nell is here.

"My children have wanted me to come live with them, but everything here reminds me of Nell," he says of his wife of 53 years, who died in 1985. "Everything on the wall, she put there. The bookcases were her idea. The white carpet, she picked out."

It is well known that Wooden refused to attend a Final Four for nearly a decade after Nell's death, because they always attended together. The Bruins' 1995 appearance, and national championship victory, finally drew him back.

He continues, however, to write letters to Nell on the 21st of each month, the day she died. The love notes have been carefully bundled together and rest on her pillow next to his.

"I haven't been afraid of death since I lost Nell," he says. "I tell myself, this is the only chance I'll have to be with her again."

As the midafternoon shadows creep across the plain windows and into a room brimming with nearly a century of wisdom, John Wooden begins reciting a poem.

"If death should beckon me with outstretched hand, and whisper softly of an unknown land, I shall not be afraid to go. . . ."

He finishes, taps his bare fingers on his nose, smiles.

"But you know, I'm still having fun," he says. "It's been a really good life."

Happy 90th, Coach.

Aug. 6, 2002

We Lost a Friend as Well as an Icon

We didn't only lose a voice.

We lost a guy who rode shotgun with us on harried winter afternoons.

We lost a neighbor who sat in our living rooms on tortured spring evenings.

We lost a friend, darn it, an old friend, a dear friend, a curmudgeonly, eccentric, funny, couldn't-wait-to-see-him-again friend.

A trusted friend.

Besides Vin Scully, do Los Angeles sports fans have any of those left?

Chick Hearn is gone, and it's hard to even write the words.

He was 85, he barely survived last season, the last time I saw him he was slowly moving through a New Jersey gym, his face pale, his hands clutching a walker.

Yet it's still as difficult to fathom as the idea of someone broadcasting 3,338 consecutive games.

Chick Hearn is gone.

The Jell-O has stopped jiggling? The butter is melting? The eggs are broken?

His death feels like a fire that razed that wonderfully creaky antique house on the corner. We didn't only lose a voice, we lost a little piece of our city that can never be rebuilt.

The Lakers are our city's most beloved sports team, yet there was only one who was completely beloved by everyone.

We know everything about the Lakers, yet there was only one of them who acted as if he knew anything about us.

Chick — and I will not refer to him as Hearn, nobody ever called him Hearn — was the amazingly flexible and resilient bridge between the common fan and the movie stars who played basketball for them.

On Hollywood's team, he was our connection.

We growl when the Lakers don't play hard? So did Chick.

We moaned at Shaquille O'Neal's early foul-shooting troubles? So did Chick.

We cringed at Kobe Bryant's crazy shots? So did Chick.

When the Lakers won a close game, it was Chick who wiped his face first, then handed us the towel.

When the Lakers lost a bad game, it was Chick who threw down the program just in time for us to kick it across the floor.

Perhaps my favorite Chick moment occurred when he was honored during halftime of one of their home games.

The Lakers had struggled in the first half. Chick was brought to midcourt for the ceremony. He was handed a microphone. Maybe you can guess what happened next.

He didn't say he was thankful to the Lakers for honoring him.

He said he was angry with the Lakers for dogging it.

The crowd roared, as it always roared for Chick, the only Laker who consistently garnered a standing ovation before every game.

Appropriately, he was introduced as he sat in his unusual seat, which wasn't along press row but halfway up the lower level, smack in the middle of the stands above midcourt.

Appropriately, the cameras would always catch him surrounded by gawking and gesturing fans.

When I first came to town, I wondered why Chick never asked for a better seat. But as the years passed, I realized, for him, that was the best seat. He could see the entire game, and he could do so among friends.

In 42 years, the Lakers became huge, their salaries became incomprehensible, the gym moved downtown, a bunch of guys running ball in Inglewood became a group of international heroes that sometimes felt too large to embrace.

But Chick never changed.

A guy making $20 million a year could still get faked into a popcorn machine.

If a platinum rap artist lost the ball, the mustard was still off the hot dog, even if that hot dog could now afford to buy the entire slaughterhouse.

The language of the league changed, but Chick kept talking the same way.

The work ethic of the league slackened, but Chick refused to buy into that either, setting a standard that will be best illustrated by the Lakers' attempt to replace him.

I have been told they may have to hire two people. One for radio, one for television.

And, yeah, like one of them will start next season and not miss a game for the next . . . 36 . . . years. No matter how much that record is celebrated, it can never be fully appreciated, because it can never be fully comprehended.

Did you know that Chick invented the term "air ball?" Or that he was the first to use "dribble drive?"

Like any good friend, Chick eventually changed the way we spoke. He changed the way we saw.

For nearly half a century, he sat with us and laughed with us and cheered with us until, instead of simply broadcasting the Laker experience, he defined it.

It will be impossible to think of anything but him this fall when the Lakers win their first game in a quest for a fourth consecutive NBA title.

Ten o'clock at night, and half of L.A. will be running to the refrigerator.

January 4, 1997

There's No Place Like Home

SOMEWHERE ON ROTTEN BAYOU, MISS. — Marty Robbins on one radio station, a gospel song on the other, the rental car twists through rows of tall pine trees, past shadowy swamps.

Above a desolate crossroads, where the street turns from pavement to dirt, stands an official-looking green sign.

Irvin Farve Road.

It is named after the only family that lives there.

And yes, it is misspelled.

You drive half a mile farther through more tall trees, until the dirt becomes pavement again, circling through the woods and into a clearing of three modest wooden homes and a trailer.

There is murky water on three sides. Trees dipping into the water, cackling sounds coming out of it. The air is thick enough to taste.

A hornets' nest hovers in a tree. Is that a snake coming out of the bush? Maybe this was not such a good idea.

One knock on the front door and it is too late.

Out pops the mother of the NFL's best player, a cat nipping one leg, a dog nuzzling the other.

Sorry to drop by, you say. But you are in search of something.

"Don't worry," she says. "Third time it's happened this week."

Third time this week? And what have you done before?

"Just like I'm doing now," she says, shrugging. "Walked outside and said, 'Hey.'"

■   ■   ■

It is the eve of the first playoff game for the NFL's best player, and you have come to the Mississippi bayou in search of something solid.

You are in search of that player.

He is Brett Favre, quarterback of the Green Bay Packers, not long ago celebrated as our last unaffected hero.

His face dotted with beard stubble, his voice rich in southern Mississippi twang, he regaled America with tales of footballs eaten by alligators, of writing his name on his underwear, of the wonders of life in a town of several hundred folks just like him.

Then last summer, after winning his first of consecutive MVP awards, he was treated for an addiction to painkillers. He was accused of drinking too much. A brother and sister later had legal troubles.

Suddenly, our beloved hayseed was holding secret weddings and hiding from fans and talking about retirement.

On the eve of his return to the national spotlight against the San Francisco 49ers, you have driven an hour east of New Orleans to see if any trace of Brett Favre still exists.

To see if, somehow, the monster created around each of this country's sports superstars has not yet swallowed him whole.

Your destination is the home where he grew up and hangs out during the off-season.

"You have never witnessed anything like you are fixin' to witness," says Al Jones, a family friend, before leading you to the Favre compound.

You quickly discover that he is right.

And that you are not alone.

"People come here from all over the country," Bonita Favre says, popping the top on a cold can of Coke. "A lot from up north, people just driving right up in front of the house."

And what do they want?

"Just want to see if this place really exists, I guess," she says.

Not only have the Favres refused to build a security gate, but some visitors even end up like that lucky elderly couple from Green Bay recently.

They pulled up during a Packer game, which Favre's family and friends watch during weekly parties here.

"They poked their heads inside, looked at me, and I thought, what the heck," Bonita recalls. "I yelled, 'Put a couple of more burgers on.' What were we supposed to do? We are not rude people."

That couple came to the unexpected realization of every visitor here.

The mixture of strength and flexibility that Brett Favre uses to survive his constant NFL storms was learned at home.

Wherever that is.

The Favres' mailing address is a small city called Pass Christian, but they don't live there.

Favre tells people he is from "The Kiln," a town of a couple of thousand, pronounced "The Kill." But that is only the location of the nearest bar; a one-room, wooden-floor, wood-stove joint called "The Broke Spoke."

In reality, the Favres live in a little speck called Fenton.

But who's counting? They are 12 miles from the Gulf of Mexico, and one long leap from Rotten Bayou, and around here, not much else matters.

"They still have our name misspelled on the road sign?" Bonita asks. "You know, I never really much notice."

.   .   .

Rotten Bayou is really a small river that runs along the front of Favre's house. According to legend, it was given that name when the Indians dumped their old pelts there, causing it to stink.

Irv and Bonita Favre had a rule that none of their four children could swim there.

A tribute to Brett is that rope still hanging from a nearby tree, a perfect location for someone to swing his way into the muck.

"Any time one of our children were gone, I would run to the bayou, thinking it had taken one of them," Bonita says.

The bayou left the children alone, choosing, among other things, to swallow errant Favre throws during pickup football games in the 50-yard field alongside the main house.

Favre told some it also may have taken a favorite dog last year when that dog, inappropriately named "Lucky," was chasing one of those balls by the drink.

If the threat of the bayou didn't make Favre strong, then the beast that his family once pulled out of it certainly did.

"We lured an alligator out of there and tied it to a swing set," Bonita says. "We put it back in only after we found it was a $500 fine."

Recently, officials discovered a dead body in the middle of the forest on the other side of the bayou.

"I told somebody, 'If they are going to be dropping bodies there, I can go somewhere else,'" Bonita says.

There is a story with every nook of this family compound, built by Bonita's father in 1943 with money he was making as the owner of Benny French's Tavern.

Across the clearing from the main house is a trailer where Favre's grandmother lives.

She's "Mee-Maw."

Next door to the trailer is a tiny house where Favre's aunt lives. That's "Kay-Kay."

At the end of the clearing is an even bigger testament to the Favres' sense of family.

The quarterback built a "party house" where his friends and family can watch him play.

There is a reason that TV cameras at Packer games may pan the stands for Favre's dad, but never his mom. She's rarely there.

She stays home to supervise those parties.

"Excuse me a second," she says on the eve of the 49er contest. "I have to tend to my red beans. Fixing them up for tomorrow."

The parties are never official, nobody is ever invited, no plans are ever made.

Everyone in the family circle just shows up.

Somebody brings crawfish, somebody else brings redfish, somebody fires up the grill, and Bonita brings out the red beans and rice.

The usual games draw 30-40 folks. The bigger ones attract as many as 200, with acquaintances from all over the area showing up.

"That party in these parts has as much tradition as 'the frozen tundra' in Green Bay," Al Jones says.

Lest anyone think she is a pushover, however, Bonita always demands a seat directly in front of the TV behind the bar.

And lest anyone think all of this down-home stuff makes her a simpleton, she taught for nearly 20 years and earned her master's degree while raising four children.

"Where we come from, family is just important, that's all," she said.

So important that Favre was recently quoted as saying he would think about returning to southern Mississippi full time if the Packers won the Super Bowl.

Later, he amended that comment to, "a couple" of Super Bowls.

"I don't know what's gotten into him lately," Bonita says. "He's been calling four or five times."

A week?

"A day," she says.

The last time Favre was in town, during the Packers' recent bye week after the regular season, he risked wrist injury by shucking oysters at a friend's party.

But, unlike his appearance would suggest, that's about as rough as he plays.

"I remember Brett walking out of those woods once, and a deer was walking the other way, and they scared each other half to death," Bonita says. "Things were a lot more simpler back then."

Not like they are now, when not only Favre, but his family, makes news with every move.

In August, older brother Scott was charged with a felony count of driving under the influence during an automobile accident that killed a close family friend.

A month later, younger sister Brandi was arrested for allegedly taking part in a drive-by shooting at a Louisiana motel. She was not charged with actually firing the shots.

"I'm not saying anything anybody did was right," Bonita says. "But to have everything always in the press because of the Favre name, that makes it hard."

She sighs. "It's been a tough year for all of us. But what family do you know doesn't have trouble?"

And how have the Favres handled theirs? By refusing to hide, refusing to point fingers, refusing to do anything but keep walking to the front door every day to say, "Hey."

"The way we look at life, you just keep doing it," Bonita says. "You don't think about it, you just do it."

As you are walking through the dirt and brush to your car, you thank the mother of the NFL's best player.

She doesn't know what you were searching for, but senses you have found it, and smiles.

"Well, now, maybe it's time you visit some of the casinos down on the gulf," she says. "You know, they have great entertainment down there. Mickey Rooney is even coming to town."

Mickey Rooney?

"I thought he was dead," she says. "But, shoot, now I'm going to have to buy Mama some tickets."

August 30, 1998

Standing by Their Man

FARGO, N.D. — Grilling burgers in the parking lot behind the high school once attended by the most famous athlete to walk these plains, old men pray.

"I don't know," Orv Kelly says. "Maybe Mark McGwire will slide into second base and twist an ankle."

"Or maybe," Wayne Blanchard says, "he'll get hit with a pitch, break a finger."

"Not that we want him to get hurt," Kelly says.

"Nah, nah, of course not," Blanchard says.

"We just wouldn't be up all night crying if it happened, know what I mean?" Kelly says.

"Yup," Blanchard says.

Sitting in a downtown bar a couple of blocks from where this town's most famous resident lived in a tiny apartment, young men curse.

"The strike zone is as small as a dime," Jeff Montplaisir says.

"Expansion has filled the league with a lot of bad pitchers," Craig Montplaisir says.

"Hell," Joel Christianson says. "I've seen every McGwire home run replayed so many times, you'd think he'd hit 5,000 of them, already broken the damn record."

Down the road, in a small house by a lake, one of the famous man's best friends holds a nightly vigil.

Bob Wood sits on the corner of a leather couch in front of his TV, with his jelly beans and peanuts and remote control. When he finds a baseball game, he will watch it in hopes of catching information about the home run progress of McGwire and Sammy Sosa.

If there is no game, he will flip to the stations that display constant scores, Channel 35 to 30 to 25, back and forth, watching the clock and the TV, knowing that no news is good news.

At the end of each night, he will look at the calendar and wonder if he and his friend can make it through another day.

"Who knows, maybe those guys can go 30 days and not hit another home run," Wood says. "I mean, who knows?"

When McGwire and Sosa hit their home runs in the final weeks of their wondrous chase for baseball's single-season record, the balls will soar high and wide, from coast to coast, thrilling and touching millions.

Except here. Not here.

Not in this rich, flat land marked by the mountainous resiliency of the home run hitter raised and buried within its borders.

Not in the last place on earth unafraid and unashamed to defend the honor of Roger Maris.

▪   ▪   ▪

He didn't move here until the seventh grade. He stopped living here full time shortly after graduating from high school.

But Fargo is where Roger Maris hit his first home run, kissed his first girl, earned his first baseball paycheck.

This is where, he said, he learned to be the type who could survive the pressure of breaking Babe Ruth's hallowed home run record by hitting 61 in 1961.

This is where he returned after that season, and each of his 12 major league seasons, to shoot pool and play cards and hang out at the Knights of Columbus. He said snowy Fargo gave him warmth.

After retirement, when he was living full time in Gainesville, Fla., this was the only place he agreed to display his memorabilia.

After losing a fight with lymphatic cancer December 1985, at age 51, this was where he asked to be buried.

"Evidently, he wanted to come back home," said friend Dick Savageau, smiling, recalling the funeral. "But maybe, he also wanted Mickey Mantle and Whitey Ford to feel what it's like at 20-below."

While a couple of Yankee stars were his pallbearers, so were three of his high school friends.

The nation may have been his stage, but those in this isolated town of 80,000 were his people, right down to the crew cuts and big hearts and intolerance for all things pretentious.

Even today, it seems each of them has a story.

Visit his gravesite at the Holy Cross cemetery in North Fargo. The only diamond-shaped headstone in a grassy patch along a gravel road reads simply, "Against All Odds."

Out of a nearby building walks a caretaker, Doug Dyrdahl, waving your car to a stop.

"I don't want to brag on myself, you know?" he says. "But my mother went to school with Roger Maris."

Visit the Roger Maris Museum, possibly as understated as the man, perhaps because it is a 74-foot display case in a local shopping mall.

On one side is Pet Center. On the other, Spencer Gifts. To reach the museum from the parking lot, you walk through the entrance between Walgreens and Sears.

A recent publication listing America's most unusual tourist attractions cited only two in North Dakota: a big plastic cow on a hill and this.

Pausing in front of the display, with a broom and shy smile, is maintenance worker Brenda Jacobson.

"I wish they would just leave Roger Maris and his record alone," she says. "He and I had the same birthday, you know."

Visit the originally named "Sports Bar," a downtown joint filled with folks who remember Maris from games of cards or golf.

Up at the bar, teacher Christianson laughs.

"My mom once said that when they were both in high school, she saw Roger walking down the street carrying a bat and a ball," he recalls. "I said, 'Ma! Why didn't you hook up with him? Why didn't you show a little leg, chase him down the street?'

"That happens, hey man, maybe I'm not sitting here."

Or visit Roger Maris Drive, a winding road through a city park along the Red River of the North.

Think they are proud of that name around here? Along the 1.6-mile loop, there are 15 street signs.

On a recent afternoon there, retired salesman Carl Hjalmquist slows his bike, shakes his head.

"When somebody breaks that record, for this town, it's really going to be a blow," he says. "This town will be hurt. It will be hurt bad."

Although the city's leader differs — "It seems the record will be inevitably broken, so we wish Mark McGwire well," Mayor Bruce Furness says — the city's pulse confirms it.

While the rest of the country cheers wildly for McGwire and Sosa, the people on the plains are holding their breath and hoping for the worst.

Maris' record is not only his record, it is their record.

It was not only him overcoming the odds, it was them.

Many here claim this town's other claim to pop culture fame, the movie "Fargo," was phony. They say it wasn't filmed here. They say they don't talk like that.

But Roger Maris, he was real. He was them. They will never forget.

"It's the darndest thing," said Steve Bergeson, an official with the Roger Maris Celebrity Benefit golf tournament. "In 1961, nobody but us wanted Roger to break the record. And now, nobody but us wants him to keep it."

■ ■ ■

Things Fargo knows about Roger Maris that you don't:

His name is not really Roger Maris. It is Roger Maras.

That's the way it appears in a 1952 Shanley High School basketball program and a 1953 newspaper account about his baseball heroics.

When he turned pro, hostile fans in small Midwestern minor league towns began serenading him with obscene "Mar-ass" chants.

His father, a proud and tough railroad worker, was appalled. So in 1954, his son's second year in professional baseball, his father changed the spelling of the family name.

"One winter Roger came home, and the name was different, and that was that," Blanchard recalled. "He never did talk a lot about it."

While appearing quiet and detached on the public stage, he was a hellion at home.

Working for a florist in high school, he would hassle his female co-workers so much that the boss would send him to a nearby pool hall between deliveries.

On what is now Roger Maris Drive, Maris and Wood used to park in the dark with Wood wearing a woman's kerchief around his head.

When punks would walk up to hassle them, thinking they were young lovers, Maris and Wood would climb out of the car and whip them.

Maris and Wood once even fought two older boys in the street in front of a storefront where a local radio station was broadcasting live. The announcer stopped the music and gave a blow-by-blow of the fight.

"And did you hear the one about the sister and the pancake batter?" Orv Kelly asks.

It is impossible to spend 10 minutes in Fargo and not hear about the time Maris poured pancake batter in sister Edna's shoes, earning him a week shoveling coal.

When Maris broke Ruth's record, he did not call his buddies back home. That would have been conceited.

When he returned that winter, he did not want to talk about the record and did not want anyone else making a fuss. That would have been putting on airs.

"He took me aside one night and said, 'Why are all these people treating me different?'" Blanchard recalls.

He became so uncomfortable with the attention, he once needed a getaway from his getaway. He took eight of his buddies 90 miles north to a remote and sparsely populated golf course. They ate fried chicken and played in a ninesome.

"That is how I'll remember him being the happiest: standing around the trunk of a car, spitting chicken bones onto the ground, hanging out with the guys," friend Dick Savageau says.

Maris was found to have lymphatic cancer shortly before his first celebrity golf tournament in 1983, yet played that first year without telling anyone but Wood.

The next year, he was too sick to show up.

The year after that, he was dead.

"I remember him telling my wife, who also had cancer, that nobody would ever know how bad it was," Savageau recalls. "And they wouldn't, because he never wanted to burden them with it."

■　　■　　■

Fargo was recently judged one of the least stressful communities in the country. Another survey ranked it the seventh-best place to start a career.

North Dakota has the lowest crime rate in the nation, the unemployment in Fargo is less than 1 percent, the streets here are clean and the traffic nonexistent.

But if there is one thing people in this area do better with their lives than anyone, it is accepting them.

The snow that piles as high as the gutter. The spring flood that carries away the neighbor. The monotony of a land so flat, they say you can watch your dog run away for three days.

"We've come to realize, there's not a whole lot you can do about a whole lot of things," says Kent McCullough, a policeman standing in front of the Roger Maris Museum. "We're just a small speck around here. We do what we can, and try not to worry about the rest."

And so, slowly, they are trying to accept that their most famous son will probably soon lose his chief claim to fame.

They are trying to understand that, as far as the rest of the nation is concerned, Roger Maris will soon be just another George Foster.

They have grudgingly acknowledged that he did not make the Hall of Fame. They endured the years when his home run record was under a mythical asterisk.

They could even understand that, when he broke the record at Yankee Stadium on the final day of the 1961 season, his chase was so unpopular that only about 23,000 showed up to watch.

So, yes, they will handle this, too.

"Little town like he was from, to accomplish what he did, that will never change," Wood says.

The directors of the golf tournament have already raised the question of whether the event — which has raised more than $500,000 for local charities, including the MeritCare Roger Maris Cancer Center — should continue if the record is broken.

"There was no debate, we all agreed it should continue," Kelly says. "This is about more than a record."

The tournament folks have vowed that even the logo that adorns their shirts — "61 in '61" — will not change.

"Heck, he still hit the home runs, didn't he?" Blanchard says.

The local minor league team, the independent Fargo-Moorhead RedHawks, issued a preemptive strike this winter by retiring the number "8" that Maris wore during his first pro season with the local Class-C Twins.

Club officials were alerted by McGwire's 58 homers last year and wanted to act before the record was gone. They didn't know he wore "8" until an intern discovered an old picture in library files. Then they were astonished who had been wearing it since.

"Last year, uh, I wore it," says Josh Buchholz, team publicity director who served as bullpen catcher.

Then there is that unusual museum, Maris' real lasting legacy here, filled with Gold Gloves, slugging crowns, uniforms and a constantly running videotape that curator Jim McLaughlin replaces every four months.

How it came to be located in a shopping mall is a Roger Maris kind of story.

When a couple of guys from the local American Legion convinced him that folks here wanted to see his memorabilia, he agreed to display it under two conditions: It had to accessible to a large number of people; it had to be free.

"We looked around and said, well, the only place that would satisfy those requirements in this town would be the mall," McLaughlin says. "So we said, 'Why not?'"

How did they get all the things from Florida? McLaughlin and a friend drove down a U-Haul to pick them up, of course, opening the museum in June of 1984.

Why the museum will continue to operate — no matter how many home runs McGwire and Sosa hit this year — is another Roger Maris kind of story.

When it opened, Maris signed hundreds of postcards to distribute to the first visitors. But then he signed an extra 100 and told the curator to tuck them away for later.

"He said that after he was dead, he wanted me to give these postcards to people who understand who he really was," McLaughlin recalls.

So McLaughlin occasionally patrols the hallway in front of the museum, looking for people who understand, waiting to bestow a souvenir that is now worth several hundred dollars.

There was the couple from New York who flew here for their honeymoon. McLaughlin drove home and brought them back a postcard.

There was the elderly man from back East who had been begging his son to bring him here. When McLaughlin returned with the postcard, the elderly man cried.

"They can take away Roger Maris' record, but they won't take away what he meant to this town," McLaughlin says, sighing. "Anyway, they haven't broken it yet, have they? I watch every night on ESPN, and they haven't broken it yet."

February 14, 2001

Urban Legend

"What round were you taken in the NBA draft?"

Raymond Lewis held up one finger.

"How many points did you score against Long Beach State?"

He held up five fingers, then three fingers.

"We're going to leave now."

He curled his fingers tightly around my fingers.

But he was too sick. The tubes and tape stuck to his chapped lips and withered body were too much. It was too late.

We left. Everyone left.

Five days after my first and last visit with the best basketball player in the history of Los Angeles, Raymond Lewis died alone.

It was a Sunday morning, bathed in sun, then angry and dark.

The 6-foot-1 guard whose legend brushed every corner of a large diverse community died, at 48, in a sterile hospital room the size of a closet.

The man who'd flown died with one leg.

The man with the rich jump shot and priceless dribble died with no car, no phone and no money.

His burial is being paid by the proceeds of a life insurance policy purchased by brother-in-law James Pilcher.

"I did it because the man is a dignitary," Pilcher said.

The ruler of a kingdom of shadows. The presider over a congress of ghosts.

Every serious basketball fan in this city, playground runners and gym rats, from Compton to Crenshaw to the corner of Central and 109th, regards Raymond Lewis as the ultimate baller.

Yet he never played one minute of professional basketball.

He played only two seasons of college.

He never held a permanent job.

He never left Watts.

In those isolated spots in the rest of the country where Raymond Lewis is remembered, it is only for his stubborn will, his poor choices, his odd behavior.

Here, it's about the jumper.

"Without exception, the best player ever to come out of L.A.," Marques Johnson said.

Here, it's about the time he scored 52 points in a summer league game against Laker rookies while in high school.

"The best high school player I have ever seen anywhere," Jerry Tarkanian said.

Here, it's about the time he took on the city's 30 best playground stars in knockout games of one-on-one and went 30-0.

"How interesting that Allen Iverson won the All-Star MVP on the day Raymond passed away," said George McQuarn, his coach at Verbum Dei High. "Because Raymond was the Allen Iverson of his day."

The legend met the truth Sunday at 11:35 a.m. at County-USC Medical Center.

Lewis, an alcoholic, died after failing to seek medical attention for an infected leg, leading to an amputation from which he never recovered.

He spent his final days at home on a mattress on the floor of his mother's tiny duplex in Watts, his leg rotting, his body failing, refusing medical help, even once shooing away paramedics summoned by his mother's 911 call.

When he finally did agree to leave the duplex last month, he was blind and unable to walk because of an untreated stroke.

Once at the hospital, doctors told him he had 48 hours to live unless they amputated the leg, yet he would not consent.

"I can still go down to the corner and shoot the ball," he told Pilcher. "If my leg is gone, I can't do that."

Desperate, Pilcher and Lewis' uncle, the Rev. Joseph Peay, called the family to the hospital to persuade Lewis otherwise. One by one, relatives visited Lewis, pleading with him to have the amputation.

He finally agreed. But it took them all day.

When Raymond Lewis finally died, it was not as the object of a young man's dreams, but as the victim of a self-fulfilling prophecy of doom.

"My father felt that if he wasn't playing ball, he wasn't worth anything," said his daughter, Kamilah Lewis-Harris.

The tragedy here, for both a man and his community, is that he was right.

If he wasn't playing ball, he wasn't worth anything. He played as long as he could, for whoever would treat him like the star that he was.

Then he curled up on the floor and died.

I got the cell phone call Sunday morning while watching my 9-year-old son's basketball game.

It was from Pilcher, who had held Lewis' hand with me five days earlier.

"Raymond has passed," he said.

At that same moment I looked up to see a little boy hit a 15-foot jumper, then dance downcourt ahead of his teammates, one arm raised to the sky, another arm grabbing his jersey, dancing alone.

■ ■ ■

In his last pickup game, Raymond Lewis challenged James Pilcher for $10 and a six-pack of Coors.

Lewis made 15 consecutive shots.

He was 41.

In one of his last public appearances, Lewis agreed to pose for a shoe company billboard for an advertising campaign about playground legends.

While waiting for the photo shoot, he wandered over to a basketball goal in a nearby parking lot.

Marques Johnson, working in a TV studio nearby, walked up and saw Lewis shooting.

"He's out there in his black slippers and he's firing," Johnson said. "Swish. Swish. Swish. At least 15 straight."

That last vision was an appropriate one.

A parking lot goal, because that is where he was most comfortable.

Jumpers, because that is what he did.

Slippers, because he never left home.

Even when he was given a red Corvette to sign at Cal State L.A. out of high school in 1971, Lewis wouldn't leave the neighborhood.

"I remember talking to one of his friends two weeks after he got the car, and he said Raymond is doing nothing but driving circles around Watts," Tarkanian said.

His decision to attend Cal State L.A. — instead of signing with second-choice Tarkanian at Long Beach State — is generally regarded as Lewis' first mistake.

At the time, he had led tiny Verbum Dei to three consecutive CIF championships. He was so much better than his opponents, McQuarn ordered him not to shoot during the first five minutes of each game, in hopes of teaching him teamwork.

One night in Lewis' senior year, McQuarn took him to dinner with John Wooden.

But the pyramid of success didn't mix too well with the star.

"As soon as we got in the car after the dinner, he said, 'Coach, you know I'm not going to UCLA,'" McQuarn remembered. "It wasn't his type of program."

Seemingly a legend from age 3 — when he kept his parents Ella and Raymond Lewis Sr. awake at night by shooting socks into a plastic hoop by his bed — Lewis wanted to play somewhere that he could still be a legend.

His coach and family pushed him toward Tarkanian, who they believed could let him fly while helping him get to the NBA. He initially agreed.

But when numerous sources say Cal State L.A. offered him the car, and scholarships to several of his friends, at the last moment, Lewis changed his mind.

"I would have loved to have him," Tarkanian said. "I really think if I had him, things would have been OK."

At first, it was still OK. His first year, he led the country's freshmen in scoring at 39 points a game. His second season, he finished second in scoring among all players at 33 points a game.

Walk into any barber shop in the city and somebody there will tell you about his 53 points in a double-overtime victory over Long Beach State that year. Many say it was the greatest game in this city's history.

Tommy Hawkins, the Dodger executive who used to serve as a commentator with Ross Porter on Channel 4's weekly high school telecasts, walked into such a shop last week.

Turns out his barber was one of Lewis' old girlfriends, and the guy sitting in the other chair was a former teammate of Lewis.

"He was an absolute hero to everyone who knew him," Hawkins said. "And an all-time troubled human being."

.   .   .

So many people loved Raymond Lewis. Yet when he needed them most, he chose to be alone.

His first contract negotiations after being taken as the 18th and final first-round pick in the 1973 draft? He was alone.

"I wanted to represent him, but he thought agents couldn't help him," Fred Slaughter said. "It was his first mistake."

The Philadelphia 76ers paid top overall pick Doug Collins

more money per year, $200,000, than Lewis was being paid for three years, $190,000.

When Lewis grew angry about the contract after playing well against Collins in summer rookie camp? He was alone.

When Lewis decided not to show up on time for regular training camp because the 76ers wouldn't renegotiate a deal that had been signed a few months earlier? He was alone.

"The tragedy here is that he received some really bad advice," said Collins, now an NBA commentator. "When you are going to a team that was 9-73 the year before, you just go play. And he could really play."

He rejoined the team during his first training camp just in time for an exhibition game in Collins' hometown, Normal, Ill.

Obviously overshadowed, he left the game at halftime. Alone.

And that was strangely, sadly, the end of the career of Raymond Lewis.

"He was a terrific player," said Gene Shue, then the 76er coach. "But somewhere along the line, something happened to him."

He didn't show up for his second 76er season because he thought he could play for the ABA's Utah Stars. But moments before his first game, the 76ers threatened him with a lawsuit that literally forced him to leave the bench.

He was invited back to Philadelphia one more time, in 1975, for the third year of his three-year contract, but he wasn't the same Raymond Lewis.

"Whatever talent he had, he was a shadow of his former self," said Bill Livingston, a Cleveland columnist who covered the 76ers for the Philadelphia Inquirer. "One day he had a bad back. The next day it was something else. When he got on the court, he didn't have it anymore."

Finished, at 22.

Was it drugs? At times there were drugs. Was it booze? There was always booze.

But talk to those close to Lewis at various times in his life, and they will tell you he abused different things.

He was hooked on the drugs of city basketball stardom, demanding the sort of life where everybody says yes and nobody says pass.

He was dizzy on the liquor of athletic self-importance, believing that his ability to make a no-look pass freed him from the responsibility of looking somebody in the eye.

He bounced around in various tryout situations after the 76er fiasco, but each time he either quit, or the team quit on him.

Although some say he was blackballed, in the end, he finally quit on himself.

"He had a lottery ticket worth $80 million, and it just blew away," Pilcher offered as an analogy. "Now how would you live the rest of your life if it was you?"

By all accounts, there was mostly drinking and hanging out in the plain, dark duplex across the railroad tracks from Verbum Dei.

"My father was very depressed the last few years," Kamilah said. "He isolated himself from everybody. It was hard."

At the time of his death, his wife, Sandra, had long since separated from him and moved the family to Oakland.

His son, Rashad, 21, had not talked to him since being incarcerated several years ago in a California Youth Authority facility for drug abuse.

Only Kamilah, co-owner of an Oakland promotions firm, and her 9-year-old son, Rajon, had kept in touch.

"That's because he taught me to be everything that he wasn't," she said.

And what, in the end, was Raymond Lewis?

A hero? A tragedy? A lesson?

These things will be discussed Saturday at his 11 a.m. funeral at the Paradise Baptist Church, 5100 South Broadway.

It will not be only an ending, but a beginning, considering that there are already plans in the works for a documentary about the greatest who never was.

"He almost had to be silenced by death for this to happen," said the Rev. Peay, smiling endearingly. "If he was on his feet, he would find a way to mess this up."

At the end of my first and only visit with Raymond Lewis, I told him to hang in there. I didn't know what else to say. I never really knew him.

For all those who loved him and the hope he represented, I wanted to hug him. But there was hardly anything there.

December 31, 1999

To Air Is Human, but Babe's the Man

One hundred years' worth of recollections have been culled, widespread polling has been completed, the votes have been tallied, the verdict is in.

Athlete of the century?

For its incredible ability to leap over reality, sprint past history, punch out perspective and flatten common sense. . . . I would like to give that award to the Los Angeles Times.

We win.

Because we anointed Michael Jordan.

No offense intended — well, OK, some offense intended; actually, I'm writing this on my day off because my ears are steaming — but we blew it.

Michael Jordan soaring over everyone on the cover of Wednesday's millennium special section is like Bill Gates soaring over Gandhi.

Jordan is not the greatest; he's only the latest.

His victory in our 14-person poll — as well as his win in ESPN's celebrated 48-person poll — reveals more about our society than our sports.

In a world of video eye candy, we've lost our peripheral vision.

In an era when every tackle is celebrated by every tackler as if he is the only man on the field, we've taken to ignoring everyone but ourselves.

Narcissism over nostalgia. Our time is the best time, the first time, the only time. If it didn't happen on ESPN, it didn't happen.

Nobody should have been surprised that Michael Jordan swept most of these athlete-of-the-century polls.

But everybody should be just a little embarrassed.

The winner, clearly, should have been the guy standing underneath Jordan's armpit on the left side of the special section's cover.

That would be Babe Ruth.

Without Ruth's impact on his sport and society, there might have been no stage for the guy who should have finished a close second.

That would be Jackie Robinson.

Without Robinson's courage and grace, there would not have been the freedom of expression and increased tolerance enjoyed by the guy who should have finished third.

That would be Muhammad Ali.

Without Ali's strength in joining the world through sport, the guy who should have finished fourth isn't anything more than a darn good basketball player.

That would be Michael Jordan.

Don't listen to me, listen to the greatest sportswriter of the century.

That would be Jim Murray.

Before he died, Murray voted on the ESPN Sports Century project, which was brilliantly conceived and produced in everything but the final chapter.

Don't blame him.

On Murray's ballot, Jordan was 15th.

When coordinating producer Mark Shapiro asked him how he could have chosen Jordan so low, Murray responded, "I'd like to see Michael Jordan try to dunk a basketball over Bill Russell."

Case closed.

Murray's first pick was Robinson.

His second pick was Ruth.

Either combination would have worked.

Shapiro, who spent several years with his nose stuck in sports history books while shaping the memorable series, was asked this week about his top selection.

"I haven't said anything until now," he said.

And . . . ?

"No question, Babe Ruth," he said. "Had he not moved to the outfield, he would have been the best pitcher ever. If he had played football, he would have been one of the best football players ever.

"Everything he did, he did bigger and better than anyone else."

ESPN's criterion was only an athlete's ability, not his effect on the landscape.

But how do you vote for an athlete of the century without measuring his impact on all facets of that century? Once you do, Ruth is a lock.

Babe Ruth not only saved a game that was in danger of collapse after the 1919 Black Sox scandal, he forever changed the way all sports were played and viewed.

He essentially invented the home run. He hit 54 in a year (1920) when the player with the second-most home runs hit 19.

He practically invented the autograph. The former street punk was one of the first athletes besieged by children with pens and paper, and the first to sign for almost all of them.

He invented pinstripes. The New York Yankees began wearing them to make him look thinner.

He invented the player agent. He hired a kid who had met Ruth by posing as a bootlegger delivery boy.

He invented the player endorsement deal. He modeled underwear at a time when the public assumed he didn't wear any.

Babe Ruth even changed the language.

That adjective "Ruthian" is universally known as big.

The next time somebody accuses you of being out in left field, you can also thank the Babe.

When Ruth played, because he was a left-handed hitter, all the smart kids gathered in right field to catch his home run balls. The dumb ones were, well, out in left field.

Ask any World War II veteran who was stationed in the Pacific to name his athlete of the century.

When the Japanese engaged the Americans in battle, their rallying cry was, "To hell with Babe Ruth."

He wasn't merely a New York Yankee or a baseball player, he was a symbol for this country during a time when the country was searching for itself.

Winning six NBA championships is nice, but it doesn't compare.

Although Michael Jordan also had a great impact on his world, nearly everything he did, either Ruth or Jackie Robinson had already done.

The difference is, Jordan did it more recently, and on TV, and that's all that matters anymore.

"To a lot of people out there," Shapiro said, "Babe Ruth is still just this old fat guy."

Part of the problem is baseball itself.

The Times' poll was well represented in other areas and included a pretty good baseball person in Ann Meyers Drysdale — she picked Jackie Robinson as No. 1 — but there were no current or former Dodger or Angel employees.

A couple of those people were asked to participate, but declined, proving again that baseball continually requires direction to the big picture.

Another problem was The Times' scoring method. As with the ESPN poll, only one point separated a first- and second-place vote. This meant that Jordan won even though he received only one first-place vote, while Muhammad Ali received six.

That said, maybe my bosses should have intervened. Maybe they should have announced the results of the poll, politely admitted that it didn't work, and given the top spot to the Babe.

Some people might have accused us of being out in left field. But it would have been a Ruthian gesture indeed.

July 15, 2001

Livin' Time

Magic Johnson drives through three defenders for a layup, leaps on a press table to celebrate, his legs quaking to the cheers.

I thought he would be dead by now.

Magic Johnson grabs a ball at the top of the lane, flips it over his head to a teammate for a dunk, smiles at the faces of astonishment.

I thought I'd be writing this column from his funeral.

On a precious Saturday afternoon at the Long Beach Pyramid, Magic Johnson poses and preens and laughs and dances and fills the room with life.

I thought he would be in a casket, and I'm not the only one.

It was billed as a Summer Pro League game featuring a former Laker great making a rare appearance for a team he sponsors.

Yeah, and Magic is just another nickname, and AIDS is just another disease.

What happened Saturday in front of 4,700 fans was a party, a reverent and rowdy remembrance of one of the most important anniversaries in both society and sports.

Ten years after Magic Johnson was diagnosed with HIV, the virus that causes AIDS, he again showed that the virus is losing.

He again took back what the demon had stolen from him.

He again played basketball.

All 6 feet 9, 255 pounds of him. Bigger than ever. Thicker than ever.

"I think you say bigger, not thicker," he said afterward, laughing, his shirt soaked gloriously dark. "I mean, it's not like I'm chunky or something. I just played 30-some minutes!"

In a game featuring former NBA players, NFL stars and even rapper Snoop Dogg, Johnson played 36 minutes, scoring 20 points with 12 rebounds and 10 assists.

A triple double, a decade after many figured he was a goner.

"A lot of people thought I would be dead," he said. "And I know nobody in the world thought that 10 years later, I would be playing on this court, in this game, right now."

Not merely playing, but standing at midcourt autographing basketballs during momentary breaks in the action.

Smiling and cupping his hand over his ear to increase the screams after great plays.

Mugging in frustration when his teammates weren't ready for passes that could have become great plays.

"A lot of them didn't even know they were open," Johnson said. "They were like, 'Man, how did you see me?'"

Man, it was good to see him.

Not that he hasn't been in constant public view since the diagnosis, sometimes irritatingly so, wandering into everything from a TV talk show to the Laker sidelines.

He also makes at least one public appearance on the basketball court every summer in his charity classic, besides playing in frequent pickup games at UCLA.

All of this, and he runs a $300-$400 million business that has helped revive parts of the inner city.

During the last decade, it has been nearly impossible to live here and not at least once bump into Magic Johnson.

But Saturday was different, because this year is different.

On Nov. 7, we will note the precise anniversary of the day Johnson stunned the world with the news of his virus and his retirement.

At the time, the average period of time between the diagnosis of HIV and the onset of AIDS was 10 years.

At the time, Johnson's announcement sounded like a death sentence.

This is the year to celebrate that it was not.

Saturday was the beginning of that celebration.

"The day is going to go well," Johnson, 41, said before taking the floor for the only game he will play in this league. "Even right now, already, I know that it is going to go well."

Just seeing him standing there in a baggy uniform, the day had gone well.

We thought that, at the very least, by now he would be wasted away like all those tragic cases that flicked across our TV screens.

Instead, his biceps are the size of Big Gulps and his neck is the approximate circumference of a beer keg.

"Some of the Lakers look at me like, 'What have you been doing?'" he said.

He could answer everyone by describing how he runs five miles a day, lifts weights and plays basketball.

Instead, though, he says this:

"You go. You do your thing. You live."

Johnson is so active, there is a tendency to wonder whether he is a living example of how, with the best treatment, this disease can actually be cured.

Don't. Because there still is no cure.

In this country, 17,000 people still die annually from complications caused by AIDS.

There are 700,000–900,000 people living with HIV. There are 40,000 new infections annually.

"I wouldn't say it was gone, but I would say it is sleeping," Johnson said of HIV, which he treats with a daily cocktail of medications. "And I'm gonna let it sleep for 20 or 30 more years."

It was snoring loudly Saturday when, by simply playing a game of basketball, Johnson showed that his legacy will be about far more than basketball.

"It was unbelievable," said Ed O'Bannon, the former UCLA star who played with the Young Guns, who defeated Johnson's All Stars, 134-130. "We all thought he was going to get smaller. But he's only gotten bigger."

More than physically.

Through his businesses and charities, his impact on this city has become far greater than when he was just running up and down a waxed floor in Inglewood.

"I took a businessman to one of my theaters the other night, and a bunch of kids ran out to me calling my name," Johnson recalled. "My friend said, 'You know what's amazing? Not one of those kids has ever seen you play.'"

Johnson shook his head. "I never thought about that. But that's nice."

Through his public fight, Johnson has become big not only in the world of AIDS awareness and prevention, but also AIDS acceptance.

Remember 10 years ago, when he thought about returning to the NBA and was met with fear from players who didn't want to touch him?

On Saturday, they bounced off him, climbed over him, fell on him, embraced him.

"The most amazing thing for me is the education," O'Bannon said. "How much has he educated the world on AIDS?"

Ten years ago, Pat Riley, then the coach of the New York Knicks, asked the Madison Square Garden crowd for a moment of silence.

During the silence, in tribute to a very sick Magic Johnson, the tearful Riley read the Lord's Prayer.

On Saturday at the Pyramid, there was no silence, only cheers. There was no sickness, only promise.

Ten years ago, Magic Johnson said, "I think you just have to come out swinging."

On Saturday, a city again stood in awe of the fight.

CHAPTER THREE

Unsportsmanlike Conduct

February 17, 1998

Star-Spangled Banter

"Don't stand there."

"Why not."

"The U.S. team is going to walk right past you."

"So?"

"So, in a few minutes, it's going to be raining."

I laughed. I stayed.

But my friend was right. In a few minutes, as the U.S. soccer team walked off the Coliseum field after its 1-0 loss to Mexico, it was raining.

Raining disrespect. Raining anger. Raining what could easily be interpreted as hatred.

From out of the stands soared plastic bottles filled with water, crashing on the U.S. players' heads, splashing and bouncing at their feet.

What followed was an avalanche of water and beer-filled cups, a lemon, a giant empty box, more water, more bottles.

The garbage covered the U.S. team like an ugly blanket. It was accompanied by a chorus of words screamed in Spanish.

It was enough to make a man want to scream back.

God bless America, land where American soccer players, playing a game for their country in their country, are treated like the enemy.

. . .

"Why would any Mexican living here not like the United States? This country has given us everything our country could not give us."

The question posed by renowned Univision anchorman Jorge Ramos was a good one.

Why, indeed, would about 91,000 of the 91,225 fans in the Coliseum act as though they hated the United States? Why would U.S. citizens and residents blow horns and boo loudly enough to drown out the U.S. national anthem?

Why would those who attend U.S. schools and receive U.S.

medical care feel it necessary to pelt any U.S. player running near the stands with water and beer?

It's one thing to cheer for Mexico, the native country of many of those 91,000 fans.

It's another thing to boo and ridicule the U.S., the home country of those same people.

Ramos laughed. The question, you see, was a rhetorical one.

"Of course those people don't dislike the United States," Ramos said. "This is not about politics, it's about soccer. You have to make that distinction."

Sure, but it's tough when you are sitting in your country watching your country's flag get jeered by fellow countrymen.

"What happened at the Coliseum Sunday is exactly what happens in games at Mexico City," Ramos said. "Throwing things, the violence, that is not good but . . . but being loud and cheering for our team, that is one way we feel truly Mexican."

Ramos, a former resident of Los Angeles who is based in Miami, put it another way.

"When the Dolphins play the Cowboys in Miami, people who cheer for the Dolphins aren't perceived as being anti-Texan," he said. "It is the same thing here. You have to understand, it's nothing against the U.S. It could have been any opponent. This is just sports."

Sure, but it's tough after watching a U.S. player hit with a water balloon while preparing for a corner kick in an American stadium.

"I would have no problem with Mexican Americans who wanted to support the U.S. team," said Kasey Keller, U.S. keeper. "After all, you live in America. Why don't you become American?"

That is the larger question facing everyone involved in Sunday's unsettling afternoon.

When it comes to sports, when do Mexican Americans begin giving more weight to the American part? Or will they ever?

The answer is not as simple as it seems.

Does U.S. citizenship or residence, demand loyalty to everything American? Of course not.

Without hassle, we buy foreign-made cars and watch foreign-made TVs and generally give jobs to the hardest workers, no matter what their nationality.

This is true even in sports. It wasn't that long ago that half the country was secretly hoping the U.S. basketball team lost in the Summer Olympics just to see the expression on the face of pompous John Thompson.

Does living in America mean you must "become" American?

Not necessarily.

Seeking an economic and physical comfort zone, many newly-arrived Mexicans move into Mexican neighborhoods, where they continue living in Mexican culture.

A colleague spoke of Mexican American friends who have lived for years in Los Angeles with established jobs and residences, yet never need to speak a word of English.

For those people to leave home on a Sunday afternoon and drive to a stadium and cheer for the U.S. against the foundation of their daily lives, that would be silly.

This city likes to think of itself as a melting pot. But, as Sunday proved, it is more like an ice tray, the nationalities divided into little compartments, living side by side.

Some days, everyone is popped out and thrown together in a joyful clatter.

Other days, everyone remains frozen in place.

Sunday was one of those other days.

That's not wrong, it's just life in a democracy.

What is wrong is when Pat Orland, who brought her son and his friend from Sherman Oaks to cheer the U.S., can't hear the national anthem.

"It's very strange," she said. "It feels like I'm in a foreign country."

And it's wrong when the U.S. players are subjected to a barrage of potentially dangerous flying objects by U.S.-based fans.

This would be the same if those fans were white, black, brown or green.

To cheer somebody simply because of his nationality is fine.

To ridicule somebody simply because of his nationality is wrong.

You'd think that we Angelenos, more than anybody, would know that by now.

July 9, 1999

There's No Spot for These Crimes

Hearing the news was as nauseating as watching somebody pull into a blue curbside parking spot, then sprint from the car.

Criminal charges were filed Thursday by the Los Angeles City Attorney's office against 14 current and former UCLA football players who allegedly submitted phony applications to obtain handicapped parking placards.

The defendants, arguably the most able-bodied individuals on campus, allegedly claimed fake physical handicaps on the applications, then used the placards for preferred parking.

Six of the players are listed as starters for the fall season.

Three more are key reserves

Each is a portrait of strength.

There's hard-hitting linebacker Ryan Nece, son of NFL legend Ronnie Lott.

There's bruising fullback Durell Price.

There's speedy and strong cornerback Ryan Roques.

You read the names and you remember last season's heroics and you wonder, what handicaps did they allegedly fake?

Did strong linebacker Ali Abdul Azziz claim he was a paraplegic? *Ha-ha!*

Did swift cornerback Marques Anderson claim he suffered from multiple sclerosis? *Hee-hee.*

The list goes on and on.

Until you want to throw up.

These are only charges, not convictions. But Coach Bob Toledo issued a statement giving them merit, saying, "I am embarrassed and disappointed for the young men who were involved. . . . This is not how I expect players in my program to act."

If the charges are indeed true, heaven help those players.

Heaven help them if they ever truly have to endure the hell of parking and then getting into a wheelchair.

"That's sick," said Joe Tusia, 30, a former pro hockey player who is a paraplegic. "If those charges are true, that's really, really sick."

Tusia, of Long Beach, has been confined to a wheelchair since he was shot in a robbery five years ago.

He would like to remind the UCLA players why those handicapped spaces are so important.

It's not only because of their proximity. It's also because of their size.

Folks in wheelchairs need room to assemble the chairs. Quadriplegics need room for the lifts that lower those chairs to the ground.

Tusia would like to take those UCLA players on a little trip with him. To the middle of a large parking lot. With cars crowded on both sides.

"In those situations, you can't get out of your car," he said. "And if you park between two empty spaces, and somebody takes those spaces, you can't get back in your car."

He remembers the time that a handicapped spot was taken by someone without a placard, forcing him to park in the middle of a near-empty lot.

When he returned to his car, it was surrounded, leaving him momentarily helpless.

"I had to wait 15 minutes for somebody to come out, and then I had to ask them to back my car out for me," Tusia said. "Times like that, you really start to feel different. It was kind of embarrassing."

The UCLA football team thought it knew embarrassment.

One game from qualifying for an appearance in the national championship Fiesta Bowl last season, it suffered bad losses to underdog Miami, then underdog Wisconsin in the Rose Bowl.

Later, there were charges that the UCLA defense was distracted against Miami because it was not allowed to wear black wristbands protesting the end of affirmative action in state university admissions.

Then there was an FBI investigation of UCLA players' involvement with gamblers, although no charges were filed and everyone was cleared.

Don't forget the unpleasant sounds of the UCLA offense ripping the defense after the Rose Bowl, or the recent suspension of touted freshman safety Audie Attar for violating team rules.

The UCLA football team thought it knew embarrassment.

If these charges are true, they have no idea.

"I guess these guys, Division I players, big men on campus, they are used to getting the royal treatment," Tusia said. "I'm sure they're thinking, 'Why shouldn't I be in the front row?'"

I was arranging an interview with a paraplegic athlete once when I mentioned that I might be late because of the difficulty parking.

"I don't have to worry about that, I'll just use the handicapped space," she said.

"Lucky," I said.

"Lucky?" she said.

It is one of the most common, and cruel, of vanities. The healthier we are, the more we fail to appreciate the assistance required by those who are not.

We scamper up ramps because they are quicker.

We use handicapped bathroom stalls when no one is around because they are bigger.

And when we joyously drive up to the empty parking space at the front of a crowded lot . . . we curse when we spot the blue wheelchair design that is saving it for someone who needs it more.

It is a sadly human trait of many able-bodied people to take for granted that they are able-bodied.

It is considerably less than human, however, to take clear advantage of those who are not.

If the UCLA football players did this, their punishment should be far worse than the maximum six months in jail and $1,000 fine that goes with each misdemeanor count.

They should be made to spend those six months volunteering at local rehabilitation centers that work with those who will never make a leaping interception or a flying tackle.

Driving their vans.

June 11, 2002

'Biological Didn't Bother'

NEWARK, N.J. — The man who doesn't exist walks larger than life through the dank hallways of the Goodwill Home and Mission, wearing a gold Laker jersey adorned with, "O'Neal."

The man who abandoned his second child awakens every morning in his tiny, windowless room to photos of the boy on the wall and desk, all grown up, giant and famous and gone.

The man who has been purposely forgotten has put a message on his answering machine that shows he will never forget.

"Hi, this is Shaq. . . ." says the voice.

That's not his name. But it was once his shame.

And even as he tries to fix things from his place in the darkest shadow of his son's greatest glory, Joseph Toney realizes it's much too late.

"It's finished, and it's God's will, and there's nothing more I can do," he said softly.

Joseph Toney is Shaquille O'Neal's biological father.

He lives and works in a Newark shelter 15 minutes from the Continental Airlines Arena, where O'Neal will lead the Lakers against the New Jersey Nets Wednesday in what could be a clinching Game 4 of the NBA Finals.

Toney has obtained a ticket on his own and will cheer for his son but will not say hello.

He has never said hello.

They have never spoken.

They have never even met.

This is not by accident.

Wondering how a father could leave his son when he was 6 months old, O'Neal treats him as if he's dead.

Claiming he lost contact only because he was in prison, then on drugs, Toney says he is alive and sorry.

O'Neal's people claim Toney is only looking for money and fame.

Toney's people, who include his Goodwill employers, say he is clean and sober and looking for nothing.

The only thing certain is that these glorious days for a giant hero have been painfully nicked with irony.

This is O'Neal's triumphant homecoming to a Newark area where he grew up and still maintains ties with as many as 200 relatives. Yet his closest blood relation here is not welcome.

This is a time when O'Neal's funky trademark smile is becoming the NBA's logo. Yet the only man in the world who shares that smile doesn't even know him.

When asked about his biological father, O'Neal's smile turned to stone.

"No, it doesn't bother me at all," he said. "Because the man doesn't even exist."

        ▪   ▪   ▪

"You want to see Shaq?"

That is what the weary-eyed man behind the front desk of the Goodwill Home and Mission says when you ask about Joseph Toney. That is what they call him here.

It's a place more about desperate hope than heroes, these brick buildings lodged in a narrow street in downtown Newark, dozens of men wandering around, the air thick with old sweat and mumbled promises.

Lots of men come here claiming to have something special.

Joseph Toney has delivered.

"When I heard he was Shaq's father, I took it with a grain of salt," said Rich Callahan, director of ministries. "You hear a lot of that sort of thing a round here."

But Toney, who checked in three years ago as just another drug-addled soul, always kept a scrapbook. And in that scrapbook he kept a birth certificate.

He's only 6 feet 1, but he does have O'Neal's smile, and his lower jaw, and even his slow gait.

As Toney straightened up and became a member of the Goodwill staff, driving a truck that delivered bread to homeless shelters, his credibility increased and everyone believed.

"It's a pretty amazing story," Callahan says.

Over the years, Toney has occasionally shared that story with the local newspaper, and he did so again last weekend. But with the Lakers arriving in town for the middle games of the NBA Finals, the news was too close for comfort.

Sunday morning before Game 3 here, Phillip "Sarge" Harrison, O'Neal's career Army stepfather, was inside the mission's hallways, rapping on that front desk.

He summoned Toney from his third-floor dormitory room and into the street, where he repeated rules that he had set many years ago.

Recalled Toney: "He was upset and told me to stay away. I told him I didn't want anything. I never wanted anything."

Said Harrison later: "Of course he wants something. If Shaquille wasn't famous, we would have never heard from him. Why is he doing this? Why?"

Toney has asked himself that same question and, now that he has been clean for three years, he says he has an answer.

Said Toney: "Only one person can take a son away from you, and that's God."

Said Harrison: "I wish he'd just be quiet. All these years ignoring his flesh and blood, and he shows up now?"

■   ■   ■

Joseph Toney was a local basketball star. Lucille O'Neal worked down at the local drug store. They dated for three years until she graduated from high school.

Then she became pregnant, just as Toney was turning to drugs. Toney was in the hospital with her when she gave birth to

Shaquille. It was Toney who named him.

But soon, Toney was sent to federal prison in Lexington, Ky., on a conviction involving fraudulent checks.

The way he tells the story: "When I came back home six years later, Lucille had already married Phillip, and I was out of the picture."

Harrison tells a different story.

"When he came back from prison, I saw him in the park, and we agreed that because he already had another child, I would be Shaquille's dad and take care of him," Harrison said. "We even shook hands on it."

Toney said that while he agreed to give up parental rights, "I never said I didn't want to see my son again."

The years passed, O'Neal moved to a military base in Germany, and Toney said all attempts to find him became fruitless.

Said Toney: "Too much red tape."

Said Harrison: "He never tried."

Toney said he had given up, thinking his son would remain in Germany indefinitely, until the day he recognized Shaquille on TV during a high school all-star game.

"I saw a guy dunk and I heard them say his name and I said, 'Oh my, that's him! That's my son! And look how big he is!'" Toney recalled.

Toney said he tried to reach his son, phoning him at the basketball office at Louisiana State. But he said the return call came from Harrison.

"He was really mad, told me to stay away," Toney recalled.

Toney waited a couple of years until O'Neal played for the Orlando Magic. He flew to Orlando, contacted his coaches, and was told to wait for O'Neal near an exit after one of the games.

"While I was standing there, they hustled Shaq out the other exit," he said. "So he was trying to avoid me."

He was. He still is.

Several years ago, O'Neal poured out his hurt in a rap song, "Biological Didn't Bother."

Toney said this obvious pain is why he has finally stopped bothering.

"I understand their situation, I feel for them," Toney said. "Phillip did a great job raising him. Probably a better job than I would have done. Shaq seems to be a nice young man. Things have turned out for the best."

Toney said the only thing he wants is for his other two sons to meet their half-brother. That is what he told Harrison. Harrison said he would consider it.

"I understand, it ain't those boys' fault," said Harrison.

But as for Toney's involvement with his biological son, he has about as much chance right now as the Nets.

His friends may call him "Shaq," but he clearly once made the choice to ignore that name. And now that the sports world is celebrating it, he cannot.

Said Toney: "I still feel that I had a part in creating one of the greatest players in the world."

Said Harrison: "Yeah. But he left him. Think about that. He left him."

December 10, 2001

We Were So Much Better Off With Traditional Bouquet

Give me back my Rose Bowl.

Give me back my gently aging neighbor who never understood politics and can't work a computer.

Give me back golden afternoons in his back yard, a football game between kids, our street against their street, means nothing, means everything.

Give me back Jan. 1, right after the last petals have been swept from the parade.

Give me back 2 p.m., sunlight fading to shadows.

Give me back Granddaddy.

And get rid of that drawling huckster with the comb-over who showed up Sunday to take his place.

Miami against Nebraska?

An undefeated, top-ranked team against a collection of corn chokers who failed to win even their division after losing their final game by 26 points?

Two days after the Rose Parade?

Beginning at 5 p.m.?

No floats, no queens, no streaming January brightness . . . and for a game that might not even decide the national championship?

The Brother-in-Law of Them All.

Maybe it's not too late to change.

Maybe the computer geeks can push a button and give us the game we should have had, Pacific 10 champion Oregon versus Big Ten champion Illinois, each team 10-1.

Both are undefeated since October.

Nebraska lost, when, two hours ago?

Both have players who have spent their entire college careers hoping for a trip to Pasadena and Disneyland and Lawry's.

For Miami and Nebraska, we're just another belt notch.

How about the BCS sends those guys to the Fiesta Bowl, where they can play a prime-time game in a giant bag of corn chips? Or maybe to the Orange Bowl, which has all the charm of an overnight mail package?

What? Too late?

Too bad.

To those Rose Bowl officials who sold out to college football's powers five years ago, we say, nice 88th birthday party.

It will take us another 88 years to rid the icing of the candle wax.

It's not completely Granddaddy's fault, of course.

He was hoodwinked.

He was promised a national championship matchup by human

beings who later made the decision with computers. He shook hands with a man to seal a deal with a machine.

That's the worst part of this, you know.

If real people who live and breathe and watch college football were making the decision, Miami's opponent would be No. 2 Oregon, and that would make sense.

The Ducks lost only by a touchdown to Stanford on Oct. 20, and only then on a couple of fluke special teams plays.

Those who judge by the eyes would take Oregon.

Those who judge by the heart would take Colorado, which finished stronger than any team in the country with wins over highly ranked Nebraska and Texas.

The Buffaloes even scored 62 points against one of those teams.

The team that's coming here.

Remember when they used to throw roses at each of the two participants when they qualified on the field? The only roses the Corn Chokers saw this year were digital.

If this sounds familiar, last season one-loss Miami defeated one-loss Florida State. Yet the computers sent Florida State to the Orange Bowl to play unbeaten Oklahoma.

Then, the BCS got lucky. Oklahoma won. The nation's only unbeaten team was its national champion.

The BCS needs the same thing to happen this year. Desperately. It needs Miami to beat the Corn Chokers so somebody can legitimately run off the Rose Bowl field waving one index finger in the air.

If the Corn Chokers win, then they will have no right to claim anything if Oregon beats Colorado in the Fiesta Bowl two days earlier.

We're number . . . number . . . aw, the heck with it.

Nebraska won't know. We won't care.

For those university presidents looking for one last reason to scrap the entire irrelevant bowl system and institute a playoff that would make them even more money, this is it.

Granddaddy could be part of that playoff. As long as he is still allowed to be, well, Granddaddy.

Give me back my Rose Bowl.

Give me back the Stanford football team marching in the Rose Parade chanting, "Give 'em the ax, the ax, the ax — right in the neck, the neck, the neck."

That was in 1902.

Give me back Washington linebacker Anthony Kelley sounding surprised that anyone would even care about a national championship shortly after the Huskies beat Purdue.

"You have to understand, this is what every West Coast kid dreams about — the Rose Bowl," he said.

That was in 2001.

Until now, a circle that has endured a century.

Until now, a tradition unharmed by technology.

While it's too early to offer a detailed analysis of this season's participants, I have already procured a scouting report on the roses.

They squirt.

POSTSCRIPT: On Jan. 3, 2002, Miami waxed Nebraska, 37-14, in arguably the worst Rose Bowl game in history.

January 26, 2000

A Crying Shame

ATLANTA — Fifteen months later, it is happening again:

An out-of-control vehicle speeding through a red light; an impending collision of an untouchable and an innocent.

The Super Bowl is barreling down on Bill Gutweiler, who falls asleep every night on his living room couch praying he can get out of the way.

"Why does it have to be like this?" he wondered this week from his home in south St. Louis. "You know, it doesn't have to be like this."

Fifteen months after a drunk driver plowed into a car driven by his wife, Sue, killing her, robbing him, Bill Gutweiler is still struggling to find his balance.

And preparing to be flattened again.

Taking the field for the St. Louis Rams in Sunday's Super Bowl, cheered by Gutweiler's neighbors, will be that deadly driver.

He is linebacker Leonard Little.

His blood-alcohol level on the night of the accident was 0.19, nearly double the legal limit to drive in Missouri.

Three witnesses saw his sport utility vehicle run a red light and smash into his wife's aging Thunderbird, crushing the car and her.

Last summer, Little pleaded guilty to involuntary manslaughter, but somehow was sentenced to only 90 nights in jail, 1,000 hours of community service, and four years' probation.

In November, though he still had not served most of his jail time, Little was somehow allowed to return to practice.

Sunday, running downfield on special teams, Little can somehow become a star.

Forgive Bill Gutweiler if he can neither watch nor understand.

"I get a big kick out of their coach, Dick Vermeil, always crying about his team," Gutweiler said. "I could tell Dick Vermeil a little bit about crying."

∎   ∎   ∎

The best thing about sports is that it forgives.

The worst thing about sports is that it forgets.

In no other business can failure be followed so closely by redemption; an inning, two minutes, 10 seconds.

Yet, no other business so blatantly ignores the cost.

The Rams have done a marvelous job of restoring the career of a young pass rusher who flies.

But in doing so, they have forgotten about a middle-aged truck driver who mourns.

"As everything in Little's life has gotten better, everything in my life has gotten worse," Gutweiler said.

It might have done him good to see Little during Tuesday's first Super Bowl interview session. One look at his nervously contorted face revealed that things haven't completely become better, that there were still ghosts in there, maybe always there.

"Nothing will ever overcome what happened," Little said, fidgeting with his baseball cap. "This will be with me the rest of my life. I made a terrible mistake, and I'll always have to live with it."

But then the questioners departed, and Little stood and stretched and mugged for the cameras, and maybe Bill Gutweiler shouldn't have been there after all.

He and Sue were married for 31 years. They could read each other's thoughts. They completed each other's sentences.

They weren't rich or famous. They weren't anything other than a man who delivered magazines and a woman who worked at a mapping agency.

But for most of their lifetimes, they were one.

"She was the chief cook and bottle washer around this joint," Gutweiler said. "She was the boss."

Together, they worked through the death of a 7-year-old daughter who, 20 years ago, was also killed by a car.

Together, they survived the death of Gutweiler's brother in, yes, another car accident.

Together, they helped raise a son, Mike, who was waiting for his mother to pick him up after a concert on the night she was crushed.

The date was Oct. 19, 1998. Together in their modest home, the Gutweilers had just finished watching a rerun of "Seinfeld."

Bill, 52, with an early-morning delivery to make, went to bed. Sue, 47, drove to a nearby concert hall to retrieve Mike.

About two hours later, just after midnight, Mike phoned home, saying his mother had not shown up.

Bill jumped into his car and drove until he saw the flashing lights.

Little had been at a downtown birthday party where he consumed what experts say were about 14 alcoholic drinks.

At precisely the time he was speeding through a red light, Sue Gutweiler was casually driving through a green.

Her car was hit so hard, she was nearly buried in it.

Since then, the Gutweilers feel, the Rams have been piling on.

Not once since the tragedy has Gutweiler received condolences from Little, or the team that continues, against all common sense, to employ him.

Said Little, "Now is just not the right time, but we're working on that. We're going to get together, I'm sure of it."

Said Gutweiler, "I've never heard anything from any of them. Even if I couldn't face Little, it would be nice if he at least tried."

Oh, but Gutweiler has heard other things.

He has heard Vermeil say of Little, "It's been a tough, tough time on that young man."

And he has heard him say, "The Ram organization will support him and help him get through a tough time in his life."

Gutweiler sighed.

"Sometimes when Dick Vermeil talks, it's like a slap in my face," he said.

Forget the apologies and support. The one thing Gutweiler really wants to hear is that the Rams are trading Little, so his family can start to heal.

During a time of community unity, Little's presence on that unifying force has left the Gutweilers feeling more alone than ever.

"Teams trade problem players all the time. Why couldn't they just get rid of him?" Gutweiler asked. "It isn't fair. I would like to root for the Rams like everybody else. I would like to be sitting with everybody cheering for them. But now I can't even watch them."

Vermeil's stance has been that he is doing what is best for the team. He said he has received letters of support as well as criticism.

"I can't control how people think, how they evaluate," he said. "The only thing I can control is what is best for this organization."

And who controls what is best for the widower? If only Bill Gutweiler knew.

He has been able to spend only two nights in their bed since the tragedy, having spent more than a year sleeping under an afghan on the couch.

"I've tried to stay in that bed, but I just can't," he said.

He has not yet touched his wife's clothes. He enters their bedroom only to dust.

"Sometimes I still walk around and realize she's not here and go, 'Oh, God. . . ," he said.

In the beginning, he said, he cried for two months straight.

"I cried until my eyes were sore," he said. "I could not stop, it was like a sickness."

Now, the tears are prompted only by an extraordinary reminder. Sometimes that reminder runs right into his living room.

"Little is number 57," Gutweiler said softly. "I know that now. I'll be watching a sports highlight show and I'll see him come on, and. . . ."

He then quickly changes the channel on his wife's killer, hoping one day the Rams will find it in their hearts to do the same.

POSTSCRIPT: In March 2002, the Rams re-signed Leonard Little to a five-year, $17.5 million contract.

June 21, 2000

The Day After

Stepping around a bonfire along a trash-strewn street near Staples Center late Monday night, I was passed by a laughing kid in a Laker jersey.

"What's he doing out here?" the kid said in my direction while jogging down the road toward another target.

I couldn't tell him then, so I want to tell him now.

I was walking to my car after watching the Lakers win a world championship, moron.

I was soaking in the honking horns, the flapping flags, the little girls sticking their index fingers out the back windows of cars that literally swayed with joy, you fool.

You tried, creep, but you couldn't stop me, couldn't stop the city, couldn't kill the moment.

The big news Monday was that the Lakers won.

The more important news was that you idiots lost.

Desperately trying to steal a show that belonged to the city's basketball team, a relatively small group of vandals did about as well as the Clippers.

Certainly, this is not to minimize the damage of more than half a dozen burned cars and several broken windows.

Obviously, it is not in a city's best interest to have a postgame parade following a route through blazing garbage.

Our hearts and anger are with those who suffered losses in isolated looting.

But the dignified joy expressed by the millions of others in our town was not diminished.

After proving they were more powerful than 28 other NBA teams, the Lakers then showed they were also stronger than a bunch of punks.

In a coat and tie and press badge, rolling my computer along behind me like some lost nerd looking for LAX, I walked 12 blocks to my car Monday night.

I was once turned back by a striding line of policemen. Twice I was detoured by road closures. The bonfires turned up the heat, the low-flying helicopters turned up the volume.

But not once did I feel in any sort of danger.

The idiots' strange chants — they would cry, "Go, Lakers!" before kicking up a pile of fast-food bags — were drowned out by the honking and cheering of the good folks who drove around them.

Their silly little two-fingered waves were overshadowed by passersby flapping the floppy foam finger No. 1.

It was pitiable, perhaps, that the most fat and slow vandals had the nerve to wear Laker jerseys.

But dangerous?

My fears were calmed the moment I saw the punks surrounding and beating the tar out of a . . . newspaper box.

A newspaper box?

How brave. And to think, it wasn't even an L.A. Times box! Guess they would rather pick on some poor weekly.

It was like watching a couple of drunks rolling around on the ground at a picnic, knocking over a couple of chairs, humiliating only themselves.

The news channels did their best to turn them into heroes, but even then, the losers were losers. Especially then.

Judging from the string of monosyllabic and grammatically fractured answers offered during the interviews, this city was apparently being rampaged by a bunch of preschoolers.

They didn't even fool the out-of-town media, which loves our city's troubles the way Kobe Bryant loves Reggie Miller.

Watching the events unfold on television while waiting in the Staples Center press room, the reaction was unusual and refreshing.

They shrugged.

"What is it, a couple of cars?" asked one writer.

"This is a riot?" asked another.

Of course it wasn't. The city was stronger. The Lakers were bigger.

The Staples Center people — thinking they were being good citizens by showing the game on the big screen TV outside — surely will be smarter next time.

I will not remember Monday night for what happened on a couple of downtown blocks, but for what happened in a city's heart.

I will remember it not for bright orange flames, but for multi-colored embraces.

I will remember it not for the smell of burning rubber, but for the aroma of perfume on champagne on cigar smoke.

The face still staring at me today is not some vacant-eyed sheep, but a red-eyed Shaquille O'Neal.

At 2:53 a.m. Tuesday, I received an e-mail. It was from a fan who couldn't wait to wear his O'Neal jersey to places where he had previously been ridiculed.

At 6:07 a.m., I received an e-mail from a fan who wondered what Wilt Chamberlain was thinking.

At 7:22 a.m., I received an e-mail from a fan who was marveling at Monday night's mix of children in Laker clothes and old men in Laker caps.

At 9:30 a.m., I stepped outside and spotted two Laker-shirted maintenance men slapping hands.

Yes, there was violence Monday. The Lakers wiped out the Indiana Pacers.

Yes, there was chaos. Staples Center was hit with a confetti blizzard.

Yes, there was a fire, in the spirit of a city whose dramatically restored bond could not be broken by a relatively few jealous jerks.

Long may it burn.

April 11, 2002

Traditionally, Masters Creates Mixed Emotions

AUGUSTA, GA. — And so, for the 66th time, the sports world gathers today to ponder a question more enduring than an oak, more colorful than an azalea, more compelling than a long amen.

What's with the green jackets, anyway?

Dashing? Or dog ugly?

There are people in this world — 89 this week, in particular — who spend their lives striving to win such a jacket.

There are others, however, who wouldn't dare drape one across the back of anything other than a chair or a thoroughbred.

Welcome to the Masters, a golf tournament that, like sweet tea and sour mash, depends completely on your point of view.

It has been relentlessly billed by its television partner as "A tradition unlike any other."

While absolutely true, that does not mean it is necessarily good.

Throughout the history of organized athletics, there have been other traditions unlike any other.

The Olympics were once contested entirely in the nude. Pasadena once celebrated New Year's Day with a chariot race.

I love the Masters, with its grace and good manners and gumption to resist change.

But there are times I feel awfully guilty about it.

I love it that the world's greatest golf tournament is run by a small club that controls a special course that is open only several months each year.

But this club has no women members and reportedly only four black members and answers to no one.

When asked to explain himself on another topic, chairman Hootie Johnson gave an answer that pretty much covered them all.

"I don't have to give you a reason," Johnson said. "Mr. Roberts wouldn't give you a reason."

He was speaking of Clifford Roberts, a Wall Street sharpie who was one of the Augusta National Golf Club's co-founders with legendary golfer Bobby Jones.

They envisioned this place as a perfect golfing retreat, and, indeed, it is.

Perfectly beautiful.

Perfectly eerie.

I love it that it is the only remaining professional sports event of any magnitude that allows no advertising in its arena, accounting for a golf course that is as dignified as it is quiet.

Yet officials have scolded or blackballed announcers who have criticized the grounds, and until this year they have rarely allowed television to show any part of the front nine.

Oops. They don't call it a "front nine." They call it a "first nine."

They also don't call the area outside the fairway a "rough." They call it a "second cut."

And so will you if you want to talk about it on television.

"I think that Mr. Roberts and Bobby Jones set a pace for excellence and for courtesy and doing the right thing," Johnson said. "We just try to continue that."

As witnessed in the concession offerings — egg salad sandwiches, pink lemonade, headache powder — the right thing is different here than in other places.

Sometimes, certainly, it feels right. Other times, though, it plays as awkwardly as a grainy black-and-white movie with jumbled sound.

The Masters is the only major tournament that has continually invited its former winners to play each year.

It is a lovely practice that came to a sudden halt this winter when officials decided that Doug Ford, Billy Casper and Gay Brewer — the bottom three finishers in last year's tournament and all at least 70 — were just too old.

How did the three men find out?

They were mailed letters.

Brewer was so "devastated," according to Casper, that he boy-cotted this year's Champions Dinner.

When asked whether he should have handled it differently, Johnson said, "I don't look back."

Thus proving that the chairman is as paradoxical as his tourna-ment, a respected banker with a sterling record on diversity who puts on a green jacket and suddenly sounds like an arrogant small-town sheriff.

Everywhere you look here, it seems, it is a tradition that comes with baggage.

I love it that the Masters tickets are incredibly cheap by modern standards — $125 for a four-day pass in a world of $400 Super Bowl tickets.

But the tickets haven't been available for 40 years, passed down from old families, old money, old connections.

While today's average golf crowd is increasingly diverse, the most startling sight here in recent years is that of Tiger Woods walking down a fairway surrounded by cheering throngs that are completely white.

Once inside, the prices get even better, with one able to pur-chase two sandwiches, a soda and chips for $5.

Even the souvenirs, which cannot be purchased anywhere else, or on any other weekend, are the cheapest in sports.

"We think a piece of clothing or souvenir here is kind of special to the people that have been here," Johnson said.

Although located on what appears to be the corner of Waffle House Drive and Bojangles Court in a commercial strip of a cluttered little town, the course itself is a classic souvenir.

The tree-lined entrance area feels like a giant back porch, with green wooden booths and ceiling fans and even an old-fashioned water fountain.

The grounds are so quiet, the most dominating sound for the next four days will be that of the birds.

The air smells as if someone ran down the middle of the fairway spraying pine-scented air freshener.

When the player hits a ball into trouble, that often means he is hitting into something that looks like the showroom of your neighborhood florist.

The grounds are impeccably maintained by kids wearing yellow jumpsuits with caps that read, "Litter."

Even the bathrooms are clean, and permanent, meaning 7,270 yards of course and not one Porta Potti.

The Masters also attempts to be pure in the game itself, and officials have added 285 yards to this year's course in hopes of making it more difficult.

Charles Barkley's silly racist charges aside — hey, this gives Tiger Woods a bigger advantage — most have agreed that the changes will be good.

But . . . and yes, with the Masters, there is always a but. . . .

There are no periscopes allowed. So unless you're in one of the front rows, or camp out on one of the bleachers, you cannot see.

There are, for the first time, no cell phones or beepers allowed.

And the one sin that will get your ticket pulled faster than a Tiger fist pump?

No running.

In other words, don't try to hurry over to watch the new leader, just enjoy the view.

A wonderful assignment, as long as one doesn't look too closely.

February 23, 1999

A High Price
for a Championship

By the time you read this, this town's last family-run sports team
will have a new face.

It has two rings in its nose.

It uses obscenities as if they were prepositions.

It speaks of sexual activities as if talking about housework.

It trashes new teammates even before meeting them.

It insults critics, then weeps when those insults are returned.

All of this occurred during a span of only 20 painfully public
minutes Monday, when self-made bad boy Dennis Rodman
announced he will be signing with the Lakers.

Any guess about the next four months?

In what might have been the most unusual press conference
since Adam disclosed his involvement with an apple, Rodman
broke the news at, appropriately, Planet Hollywood.

The man truly is from a different planet.

And this was as much about Hollywood as basketball.

Reporters entered not through a turnstile but a velvet rope.
There wasn't a ticket taker, but a bouncer.

The room used for the announcement was decorated not in
"Forum blue" and gold, but leopard and zebra.

As at most such occasions, two radio guys sat in the front row.
But these radio guys were wearing dresses.

Nearly 35 minutes late, Rodman emerged from behind a door
marked "Private," accompanied by two bouncers and a woman
who appeared to be uncomfortably trapped in a rapidly shrinking
silver dress.

Only after he later described their bedroom activities could it
be confirmed that this apparently suffocating woman was his wife,
former "Baywatch" actress Carmen Electra.

Even though Rodman said he would be signing with the Lakers
Monday night and would play his first game as a Laker later this

week, there was not one Laker employee in attendance.

There were no basketball officials of any sort.

There were, however, two representatives from the local women's professional team known as the Sparks.

"You never know," one said beforehand. "Maybe he's going to announce he's signing with *us*."

. . .

For all the high-flying exploits of perhaps the most beloved sports team in this town's history, Showtime was always grounded in dignity.

Those Lakers not only flew, but walked. They were stars, but also neighbors. They were not only champions, but friends.

The Lakers who won five world championships during the 1980s were memorable not only for their ability, but for their class.

We loved owner Jerry Buss' commitment to winning, partly because it was a commitment with boundaries.

Eleven years after that last title, those boundaries are suddenly being tested.

Will the Lakers, needing toughness and rebounding to become a championship contender, be a better team with Dennis Rodman? Absolutely.

He has won seven consecutive rebounding titles, and plays the sort of tattoo-rubbing defense that causes opponents to jump out of their skin.

But will Rodman be worth all the trouble he will cause? There was a time when Buss built his team strictly on the advice of his wise and credible lieutenant, Jerry West.

West voted against Rodman. Virtually everyone in the front office who has helped bring this team to the verge of greatness voted against Rodman.

Realizing they were just one more smart acquisition from having a club that could compete for many championships, they voted against taking a shortcut with a 37-year-old guy who once took off his shoes and ignored his coach during a playoff game. . . .

A guy who has left the bench during games, making the coach send a trainer to find him. . . .

A guy who has missed practices to party in Las Vegas. . . .

A guy who has kicked a cameraman in the crotch, head-butted a referee and publicly insulted the entire Mormon church.

With teams that had strong veteran leadership — the Detroit Pistons and Chicago Bulls — Rodman collected five championship rings.

With a team that had young and impressionable leaders — the San Antonio Spurs — Rodman helped cause a meltdown.

Guess which of those teams the growing Lakers most resemble.

Hint: Break out the fireproof suits.

Sure, Disney bought the Angels from sweet old Jackie Autry. But it didn't install Mickey Mouse at shortstop.

Certainly, Fox cashed out the Dodgers from longtime friend Peter O'Malley. But it didn't install David Duchovny as manager.

This is not about how Rodman dresses, which was no different Monday from many people walking outside on the Beverly Hills streets:

Checked pants with a black stripe. Orange shoes with stars. Tattoos and rings over virtually every visible piece of skin. A floppy hat the approximate size of his waiting limousine.

No, the problems Monday were not about how the new face of the Lakers looked, but what happened once he opened his mouth.

He told reporters he didn't want to make a spectacle of himself, but smiled and added, "I must be very important for you guys to be here."

He said he wanted to help the Lakers win a championship, but added, "What I really want to do is give the people what they want. . . . I'm not playing for anybody but the people."

When two reporters questioned his selfish motives in holding his own press conference after waiting two weeks to sign a deal that was not going to change, no matter how long he waited, because of NBA rules, he began weeping.

"I'm never gonna win with you guys," he said, sobbing behind mirrored sunglasses. "No matter what I do in this league, I'm never gonna win."

He then held up a list of charities to which he said he is donating a total of $100,000.

"If this is selfish, we have a problem," he said.

Moments later, he walked off.

Thirty minutes later, in a parking lot below, more than 100 fans surrounded Rodman's empty limousine.

"The antics are the price we're going to pay," said Michael Poret, a stockbroker who works in the building. "But if we get our championship, that will make up for it."

The crowd surged. A security guard screamed at a woman. An excited postal worker with a push-cart spilled her mail. Two photographers exchanged nasty words. Everyone smiled. Anything for a title.

POSTSCRIPT: Rodman was cut 51 days later after showing up late for practice while claiming he forgot his shoes.

January 24, 2001

Without Apology

TAMPA, FLA. — It was scary.

Ray Lewis was Jesus.

"Jesus couldn't please everybody," Lewis said. "He was spit on, slashed at, talked about . . . yet he never said a word. That's my attitude."

It was unsettling.

Ray Lewis was the victim.

"I've got money, I'm black and I'm blessed . . . so it's about me, and that's wrong," he said. "Don't be mad at me because I'm on center stage."

It was sad.

Ray Lewis was everything but sorry.

"People ask me, how do you handle this, how do you handle

that?" he said. "But what do I have to handle? All I have to handle is Tiki Barber, Ron Dayne, and everything else is irrelevant."

For an hour under a bright central Florida sun Tuesday, Ray Lewis chillingly spoke of his involvement with an unsolved double murder as if it had been a missed tackle.

Listening to him, you wanted to run.

Afterward, you wanted to bathe.

Lewis, the centerpiece linebacker in the Baltimore Ravens' celebrated defense, may be the best player at Super Bowl XXXV.

After a smirking, cackling performance on media day, he is also officially the most frightening.

"Yeah, a lot of people are scared of me," he said, laughing. "Come Sunday, those people on the field are going to be scared of me. They're human too."

If only life were as neatly groomed as that field.

The topic was a list of unanswered questions surrounding the deaths of two men in a street fight outside an Atlanta nightclub shortly after last year's Super Bowl

Lewis was initially charged with murder, based on information provided by witnesses who said they saw him throw a punch before speeding away in a limousine. But those witnesses later changed their stories.

Lewis eventually pleaded guilty to a misdemeanor, obstruction of justice, for failing to cooperate with police.

But family members of the deceased say he still hasn't fully cooperated.

And the murders remain unsolved.

On Tuesday, Lewis stepped onto a truly national stage for the first time since that night.

And promptly pronounced the investigation complete.

"That's a chapter that's closed," he said.

(Tell that to the families of the deceased.)

"The people to be mad at are . . . the mayor of Atlanta and the people who never cared at one time to find out who killed those people," he said. "They said, 'We're going to get Ray Lewis,' but Ray Lewis was never the guy."

(Then why wouldn't he help find the guy?)

"You can labor about this, but not me," he said. "We can go someplace else."

(Not in a limousine, I hope.)

He wore a crooked visor and an uneven grin.

Around his sizable neck hung two silver dog tags. One read, "True Soldier Gladiator Warrior." The other, "This Is God's Will For My Life."

The bottom of a panther tattoo sneaked out from underneath the left sleeve of his jersey.

"I've got panthers all over me," he said.

Along with a sense of entitlement that reeked like bad cologne.

It would have been outrageous to expect that Lewis would tell reporters something he didn't tell police.

Certainly, as a football player, he was not compelled to say anything about a crime for which he had already paid his legal price.

But as a human being, he might have shown a little remorse.

Or at least some public feeling for the victims' families?

"Nah," he said. "Uh-uh."

Five minutes into a conversation eventually dominated by football questions because Lewis would give straight answers to nothing else, one dynamic was clear.

It is a feeling that permeates NFL rosters increasingly dominated by players expecting pedestals.

It is about a culture found in the just-completed murder trial of Rae Carruth, and the just-beginning sexual-assault trial of Mark Chmura.

It goes something like this:

Pro football players are special.

The public doesn't understand.

Pro football players, because of the warlike nature of their sport, live by the code of the street.

The public will never break this code.

Pro football players, faced with a natural struggle to leave their aggression on the field, are misunderstood by the Man.

Everybody else is the Man.

Bad enough that Lewis refused to show a shred of sensitivity regarding the murders.

But did he have to seem proud about it?

Asked again about the families of the deceased, he smiled and said, "Football, football, football."

Asked about his reputation, he smiled and said, "Character, character, character."

You wondered, was this how he smiled that night with police? Is this how he answered their questions?

"The most interesting part about this is, I could honestly sit down and give you guys a story," he said. "But some of you would change the whole story."

He was asked if the incident had damaged his chance for endorsements. He laughed.

"The endorsements are crazy right now," he said. "My hand is hurting from all the autographs I've signed."

What about his image?

"If I could go back [to the regular season], I would show you my image," he said. "On Sunday, being introduced to my crowd, the respect those people give me off and on the field . . . that's my image."

He will get that same respect Sunday here when the Ravens play the New York Giants.

He will be the biggest, baddest player in the middle of America's biggest, baddest sporting event.

For four hours, under a colorful shirt and shiny helmet, he will be celebrated as a martyr and a prophet and a gladiator.

And afterward, a certain advertiser might stick a camera in his face while somebody shouts, "So, Ray Lewis, now that you've won the Super Bowl, what are you going to do?"

Heaven help Disney World.

May 16, 2000

Good Knight or Goodbye

The agitated trustee tossed out a statement that clattered like a metal chair across a hardwood floor.

"There are no sacred cows at Indiana University," John Walda said.

No, just silk-suited chickens.

For 29 years, Bob Knight has seemingly brought such great importance to a school with apparently so little self-respect, his immoral and even illegal behavior was a price gladly paid.

Shame on us for thinking judgment day was going to be any different.

The school addressed the Knight issue Monday in a news conference that was far more egregious than any of his stunts.

The university president cowered, its trustees blushed, and integrity flat-out fainted.

A three-game suspension for the sort of choking incident that cost Latrell Sprewell nearly a full season? Of course, Sprewell plays in that moral bastion known as the NBA.

A set of no-tolerance conduct rules that will result in immediate dismissal if they are broken? Um, haven't those rules been in place for 29 years, or has it always been legal at Indiana to throw a vase at a secretary?

A $30,000 fine? That's shoe money.

Presented with a nicely garnished chance to fire a coach who has outlived his methods and overplayed his madness, Indiana officials did what they always do in these situations.

They listened to the coach. They kissed his red sweater. They ran his strange plays.

In doing so, they behaved far worse than Knight has ever dreamed of behaving.

They head-butted morality.

They punched ethics.

They choked dignity.

They did require an individual apology. But that was to the secretary Knight almost beheaded when he smashed a vase against a wall behind her.

What about Neil Reed, the player whose allegations of choking began the investigation, the player university officials tried to smear until videotape proved he was telling the truth?

They are trying to smear him still.

"[Knight] will offer a general apology to all others involved," said university President Myles Brand, sitting amazingly straight for someone with no apparent spine.

And besides, said smirking trustee Walda, "It depends on how you define the word, 'choking.'"

Not only did they not require Knight to face his main accuser, they didn't even require him to face his community.

He might have been sorry, as Walda claimed in a brief message from Knight, but not sorry enough to come to the news conference and tell everyone himself.

"Coach Knight will eventually speak for himself, I'm sure," Brand said.

By the tone of his voice, you could tell that he was not sure at all.

In its finite wisdom, Indiana University has issued a directive to a man who takes orders from no one.

It has drawn up rules for a man who makes his own.

It has penalized a man for whom there is no shame.

It has done nothing to change an environment where bullying continues to be an acceptable form of leadership, as long as that bully wins three national championships and has a chance of becoming college basketball's all-time winningest coach.

Gee, sounds like a great place to send your children.

The message this sends about Indiana and basketball is not just foolish, but frightening.

It's fun to wax poetic about a sport so ingrained in a community, it is like a religion. It's scary when that religion becomes a cult.

The most unsettling thing about Knight's famed chair fling in 1985 was not the actual throw, but the response.

Watch the video. As the chair bounces across the court and nearly hits two cheerleaders, Indiana fans erupt in cheers.

The most uncomfortable thing about all those shoves and head-butts and verbal tirades was never the actual acts, but how everyone else reacted to them.

For nearly 29 years, few people did or said anything.

You can't expect a freshman to fight his coach, but what about the alumni in the stands, or the university officials watching on television? What about a community leader standing up and saying enough is enough?

Are basketball tickets in Bloomington worth that much?

What's most amazing about all the recent allegations toward Knight is not the actual allegations, but that they have been covered up for so long.

Knight is supposedly a tremendous teacher, but are the people of Indiana that desperate for teachers?

Knight is supposedly forever loyal to his players after graduation, but is that a trait so rare that people will let someone punch their neighbors in exchange?

And maybe the most startling thing about Monday's news conference was not the answer, but one of the questions.

A journalist actually asked if this action would have been taken if Knight had not failed to win a national title in the last 13 years.

Good question.

"Our basketball team hasn't been that bad," responded Brand quickly, vehemently, showing far more emotion in defending his coach than in reprimanding him.

A message about Indiana, and a warning for the rest of us.

The sports world is bereft of leaders who stay in one place for long periods of time while demanding consistent overall excellence. We will go to great lengths to place our children in such environments.

But there is always a price. And we have to understand that price before paying it.

Indiana set its price, and it is unconscionably high.

"If Bob Knight persists in this type of conduct, it will not be tolerated," Brand said Monday.

They're giving him 29 more years, tops.

POSTSCRIPT: Four months later, after an altercation with a student, Bob Knight was fired. Six months after that, he was hired to coach Texas Tech.

CHAPTER FOUR

Perfect Games

August 18, 1996

Guardian Angel

ASPEN, COLO. — The 15-year-old girl wins another tennis match, loses another friend. She walks into the locker room and senses them staring, hears them whispering.

It's her body. They are making fun of it. The other top professionals look at the underdeveloped figure and laugh, a teenage girl turned freak of nature.

Andrea Jaeger walks out of the locker room and into a public restroom. For much of the rest of her career, that is where she will dress.

Sixteen years later, an uncertain teenager is lifting her shirt again.

Her name is Pam. She wears a pair of bright boxer shorts on her head to hide her baldness. She reveals a recent cancer surgery scar that winds around her pale abdomen like a zipper.

Andrea Jaeger does not whisper, does not laugh.

She asks Pam about the scar. Asks if it hurts. Asks if it scares her.

Jaeger peers at this girl who has been given no chance of surviving a massive tumor in her chest, and says, "Do you know how incredibly cool you are?"

In the next breath, she adds, "Whadya say we try to market that boxer-shorts look?"

■   ■   ■

Respect and hope. The concepts have replaced serve and volley in the life of America's most charitable former pro athlete.

Andrea Jaeger preaches it daily during her camps for children with life-threatening illnesses, camps that become clubs that become families.

Respect and hope. She talks it at 10 a.m. for a child afraid to take off his wig for a swim . . . at 2 p.m. for the child afraid of skiing with his chest-implanted medication port . . . at midnight for those children who are afraid, period.

Respect and hope are the only currency now for a woman who has traded fame and riches for the full-time company of the young and dying.

Jaeger is asked why she would make such a deal.

It is that 15-year-old who answers.

"I'd be getting dressed before big tennis matches, and fans would find me in the public restrooms and slip autograph slips underneath my stall," she says.

.   .   .

Andrea Jaeger then:

Flying pigtails. Soaring temper. A child prodigy who, in retrospect, makes today's spoiled brats look like so many Shirley Temples.

Smashing rackets against walls. Screaming at linesmen. Publicly calling Chris Evert a "cheat." Once tanking a match when mad. Keeping a computerized list of perceived wrongdoings by her foes. All in the name of a world ranking that crept as high as No. 2 in the mid-1980s.

Andrea Jaeger now:

Owns no car. Makes no money that she keeps. Forgotten about the existence of a hairbrush. Wears nothing but baggy sweat suits, carries around nothing but an old backpack.

Lives in the tiny basement room of a worn mountain chalet. Spends her days bouncing around the street of serene Aspen like somebody half her age, giggling and shrieking and unafraid to scream at anybody who gets in her way.

Doesn't date. Doesn't try to date. Only jewelry is borrowed, only makeup is sweat.

Much too busy chasing kids into the mountains with squirt guns.

"Andrea feels she lost a lot of her childhood on the tour. . . . This is her second chance," said Evert, a part-time Aspen resident. "For the first time she is in her element. She is home."

That home is not the chalet, or the city, but The Silver Lining Ranch, a mythical place that is host to real children.

Five weeks a year, for the last four years, Jaeger and her unlikely team of five have been host to about 20 kids with life-threatening illnesses from around the country.

The kids come to the mountains, all expenses paid, for things like rafting and horseback riding in the summer, skiing and snowball fighting in the winter.

There are kickball games, dance contests, water basketball and a lot of just hanging around.

Kids talking about hair loss. Kids talking about the moment the phone rang with the news that made their parents cry.

Kids talking to some of the only other kids in the world who would understand.

"The people here don't call me Leukemia Master, they don't call me Baldy," said Justin Romano, 12, of Roseville, Mich. "I once pushed a kid's face into his salad because he made fun of me. Here, I can make friends."

Jaeger understands.

"I was different all of my life; I know what that's like," she said. "I never had a peer group. Neither do these kids. Until they get here."

Jaeger takes an extra step that further separates her unconventional camp from dozens of other retreats.

Before the children fly home, they are given a toll-free number, enabling them to phone Jaeger or team members at home at any time.

"Yeah, they all use that number," said team member Heidi Bookout, a former tennis resort manager who lives upstairs from Jaeger. "And yeah, they don't look at the clock before they call. But it rings, and we're there, and it's cool."

Kids are also put on a mailing list for a monthly newsletter edited by a former camper and filled with updates from past campers.

It is as if, a week after taking their first uncertain steps into this high altitude, they are welcomed into a well-grounded family that will remain with them for life.

And in death.

About every three weeks now, that toll-free line rings with the news of the passing of a former camper.

The phone can be heard from Jaeger's basement bedroom. If the voice on the other end is a parent, she knows what comes next.

"We got through that first year in 1993 with nobody dying and we thought, 'This is great!'" Jaeger said. "But now. . . ."

Kevin Smyley, a streetwise former New York City commissioner and team member, explained: "This is like, you're going full speed

down this road, and you're just hoping there's not a wall at the end
. . . because you can't stop."

Smyley, who became involved because he was engaged to another team member, tennis teacher Beene Bookout, flies to Aspen at
least five times a year from his Washington, D.C., home to help out.

He uses vacation time from his employer, Lockheed Martin, for
the days. He uses his own money for the airfare. He uses the top
floor of Jaeger's chalet for sleep.

He recently had these dreams, of two special campers, bright
and alive and laughing, two of his favorites. He awakens, shakes his
head quickly, and reminds himself that they are dead.

"This is not phony stuff," he said.

.   .   .

They are going full speed down this road with a homemade
gearbox and soapbox frame.

The ranch has no permanent housing. No permanent cafeteria. No full-time fund-raising executives. No tear-jerking TV
commercials.

Much of the early money came from Jaeger's now-depleted $1.4-
million career winnings. Her official charity, Kids' Stuff Foundation, is funded through her small income from exhibitions and TV
jobs, and donations she can coax from anybody she can charm.

When she is not arranging or working the weeklong camps, she
is trying to charm with handwritten faxes and homespun speeches
and lengthy notes often signed with a smiley face next to an arrow
that says, "ME."

"I remember doing a one-hour tennis clinic for her kids, and she
sends me this three-page fax thanking me for all that I give," Evert
recalled. "I said to her, 'Andrea, I gave one hour . . . you give a thousand hours! Nobody gives like you. And you're thanking *me?*' "

A hint: Jaeger is not somebody to whom you can leave a message
saying, "Call any time." Because she will call any time. She begins
work at 5 a.m., and wonders why the rest of the world doesn't.

Another hint: If you do not want to donate, you do not want to
sit next to her on an airplane.

"What am I supposed to do?" Jaeger said, giggling. "I start talk-

ing about the ranch, and before the plane lands, the person is giving me his card and sending me a check."

The ranch has only two adult full-time paid workers — Jaeger is
not one of them — and its counseling team is filled by more
unlikely heroes.

Besides the city commissioner, resort manager and tennis
teacher, the team includes another tennis teacher, Katie Anderson,
and Mamta Shah, a registered nurse.

And to think that they spend only about two hours during the
week actually playing tennis.

Even when you include the advisor that each hospital sends
each week with its group of children, the camp isn't exactly run by
the Mayo Clinic.

But it's not supposed to be.

"We're not child-life specialists," Smyley said. "We don't do dying."

Nor funerals. It is their policy not to attend them, partially for
the same reason they never use the word "terminal."

They're too busy living, even at its simplest form.

Jaeger is trying to raise $3 million to build a facility on $5 million worth of donated land, but until then. . . .

Sometimes the team feeds the kids off the grill behind her house.

Sometimes they spend evenings sitting at a downtown Aspen
mall, secretly hoping that juggler drops that torch down his pants.

Sometimes they spend time just bobbing next to each other in
swimming pools.

Jaeger is one of those people who talks in exclamation points.
By the end of each week, even the most subdued campers are
doing the same.

"This is really cool because they just let us hang out with each
other, they give us the freedom to talk, everything is not totally
organized like in other camps," said Pam Thompson of Coos Bay,
Ore., the girl with the scar.

"Everywhere else, everyone treats us different," Thompson
said. "I hate it that people either try to suck up to you, or feel real
sorry for you."

Jaeger and her team do neither. They scream while trying to

whip the campers in ping-pong, they leap to block their shots in water basketball. They scold the selfish ones, give space to the quiet ones, move into their circles without trying.

Shortly after Thompson showed Jaeger her scar, she applied blue dye to Jaeger's blond hair in preparation for the upcoming dance contest.

"Cool," Jaeger said, and she meant it.

In a team meeting before a recent arrival of campers to their middle-class hotel, there arose a typical Silver Lining Ranch debate.

"I think we should limit this week's squirt-gun fighting to below the waist, so nobody gets irritated," Smyley said.

The winner of several national humanitarian awards stood up.

"Are you kidding?" Jaeger said. "What fun is it to squirt somebody below the legs!"

.   .   .

The 15-year-old girl was trying to practice hard, trying to please her father, but she was thinking about things.

Maybe about the kids in the school cafeteria who threw food at her because she was different. After that, she spent her lunch periods grading papers.

Or maybe she was thinking about the older tennis pros who once wondered, aloud, whether her father paid fans to cheer for her.

Whatever it was, she was thinking, and thinking, and soon she wasn't practicing hard. Soon her father was not happy.

Soon she felt his hands on her pigtails, lifting her in the air by her hair. Then she felt those hands smack her body.

She was still not thinking about tennis, but about how somebody's hands could inflict such harm. She would never take that chance, she decided.

And that is why the hardest thing for Andrea Jaeger to give her campers is a hug. It is something she will never give anyone else.

.   .   .

Sixteen years later, another uncertain young adult is scared again.

Her name is Rhea Olsen, she is 20, she lies dying of cancer in her tiny trailer home outside Chicago.

There is a knock at the door, and in walks Andrea Jaeger.

Two years earlier, Olsen attended the first Silver Lining Ranch week. She didn't want to go.

"She thought Andrea was one of those pick-a-disease celebrities, and she didn't want any part of it," recalled her mother, Elsa.

But she went, and felt such a sense of belonging that she began returning regularly as an employee.

"This was not just a neat experience for my daughter, it was a life-altering experience," Elsa said. "At the ranch, everybody was equal, nobody was judging how sick anybody was, and everybody sincerely cared."

None, perhaps, more than Jaeger, who flew to Chicago to share a few of Rhea's final days in February 1995. When Rhea could talk, they talked. When Rhea slept, Andrea laid on the living room couch.

When Jaeger was preparing to leave shortly before Olsen's death — remember, she doesn't do death — she was struck not only with sadness, but irony.

"For the first time in a long time, I really wanted to hug somebody," she said. "But Rhea was in such pain, she couldn't."

Jaeger flew home and her dream grew ever stronger, her hugs of children coming ever easier.

The vision had begun after she moved to Aspen in 1989 to recuperate from an auto accident.

Her tennis career had already ended after nine surgeries. She had no real friends. She had no idea.

"She was, like, socially stunted," said Heidi Bookout.

The Bookout sisters "adopted" Jaeger — took her to dinners, showed her around town — in an attempt to help her grow up.

But Jaeger realized, she didn't want to grow up. She wanted to go back.

"I had worked with kids before while on the tour and I realize, that's who I'm most comfortable with," she said. "That's who I can relate to. That's where I can do some good."

Soon, she had assembled a plan and a team willing to try miracles.

Like the time they were greeted at the airport by a group of campers who were obviously deaf.

"None of us knew sign language so I thought, 'It's going to be a long week,'" Katie Anderson recalled. "But with Andrea, you just do it. So I started making all these exaggerated motions about where to pick up the bags, and how I was going to drive them to the hotel. . . ."

Then everyone sighed when some bald kids stepped off the plane.

"Wait a minute," Jaeger shouted happily. "Those kids are ours."

All sorts of wondrous things happen around Jaeger these days.

She remembers inviting longtime Aspen resident Fabi Benedict to a barbecue, hanging up the phone, and then hearing it ring five minutes later.

It was Fabi.

"You want some land for your project?" she asked.

Turns out, Benedict was staring over her sink at seven empty acres behind her house when Jaeger had called.

"I was asking the Virgin Mary for a sign about my property, and that phone call was a sign," Benedict said.

The land has since been zoned and approved for construction. If Jaeger can raise the money, building can begin as soon as next spring.

Not that she will ever want to invite many more than 20 kids.

"This is about them, and if gets much bigger, it gets away from that," Jaeger said.

Heaven help anyone who crosses those kids. Jaeger is not afraid to shout at passersby for their insensitivity, scold vendors for not delivering exactly as ordered, glare at team members for being five minutes late.

Good thing that phone line into her house is toll-free. She sometimes gabs with former campers for an hour, particularly if there is a good TV show that both are watching.

Friends say since she finally found this safe place, she may never leave.

"She has always played to a different drumbeat," Evert said. "While I always craved to be No. 1, she always craved relationships and friendships. Being accepted was more important to her than Wimbledon."

"I'm sorry," Jaeger said, "but I'm just more comfortable with the kids. It's just me."

Her father and former coach Roland, who Jaeger says both physically and mentally pushed her during difficult teen years, is angered by those who say she is re-creating her childhood.

"Even if she grew up like everybody else, she would be doing something like this, it's her nature," he said. "Everybody in the media talks about this lost childhood. It is the kids who stay home and get in trouble, those are the kids with the lost childhood."

Besides, he said, that childhood was not as bad as she claimed.

"Yes, I laid my hands on my daughter, but it never had anything to do with tennis. . . . I spanked like any other father would spank a child," he said from his Florida home. "And that pigtails thing. . . . I think Andrea likes to say that to add character to the story."

Typical of Jaeger, she giggles about her father and says they are close friends.

"Why would there be a problem?" she asked. "I understood what he was trying to do. I've moved past all that."

She is always full of surprises. Last month, while accepting a Jefferson Award for public service by an individual 35 or younger, Jaeger raised officials' eyebrows in the Supreme Court chambers by recognizing one of her campers in the crowd.

It was Joanna Potter, a college student with cystic fibrosis who had just buried her sister Noelle, who also had cystic fibrosis.

Joanna had made extensive arrangements to crash the party as a thank-you to Jaeger for her support. Jaeger made her stand up, giggling while she did it.

Later, back in her tiny Aspen office in a building where she cannot afford a parking space for the car she does not own, Andrea Jaeger finds Noelle's picture on the wall.

It is a wall filled with pictures, all of smiling kids, some in a Jacuzzi, some at a Christmas party, some playing tennis, Noelle wearing a formal gown and headed for a ball.

More than one-fourth of these children are deceased.

Every three weeks, the toll-free line rings and there is an adult on the other end and that number increases.

"Isn't this like, a wall of . . . death?" she is asked.

"Funny," Andrea Jaeger said. "I was thinking you were going to say life."

POSTSCRIPT: Readers responded to this story with donations that led to the creation of a permanent, 20-room lodge to house campers at the Silver Lining Ranch. Only one room is named for a city. The sign outside the door reads: "City of Angels Gathering Room sponsored by the people of Los Angeles."

November 9, 1995

A Proud Struggle on the Field—and Off

John Aguirre pushes a switch, and day becomes midnight in the gym at James A. Garfield High.

Dark, restless lumps line the floor. The only sound is the heavy breathing of teenagers nervously awaiting their weekly two hours of truth.

Feeling his way through the darkness, carefully stepping over these small men stuffed into big pads, is Aguirre, the head coach of the Garfield football team.

It is a Friday, 4:35 p.m. In less than three hours, the Bulldogs will step outside onto a patch of uneven grass in the middle of a temperamental neighborhood. In front of several hundred people, they will play a game against Bell.

"Gentlemen," Aguirre screams into midnight, "this game is not just for you. This game is bigger than you!"

This is one of nine Garfield games this season. This is one of about 30 games in the average Garfield player's career. That's 30 chances to throw out your chest, 30 chances to have the world scream for you until it is hoarse.

Thirty chances. And no more.

In the last 15 years, not one player from this East Los Angeles school has received a college football scholarship. Scouts rarely even venture inside Garfield's usually locked outer gates. The players are small. Their 40-yard dash times are slow.

All but one of the 48 on this year's team is Latino. The number of Latinos who've ever made it to the NFL is minuscule.

These 48 believe none of it.

They have spent the previous week practicing every day until dark. Juggling jobs and baby-sitting and housework. Dealing with muggings and gang colors.

All for a chance to step on the field and force somebody to notice.

"You are playing not just for yourselves, but for your entire neighborhood!" Aguirre yells. "This is not just for Garfield, it is for all of East L.A.!"

On autumn evenings throughout America, to play high school football is to live a dream.

But for these children of immigrants, single-parent homes and dangerous streets — for these appropriately nicknamed Bulldogs — the dream is awkward, heavy.

The star linebacker sometimes leaves practice early to care for his mother, who is blind. One star running back works as an auto mechanic during the day.

Another starting running back — the team's only black player — missed several practices when Latino gangs tried to force him out of a nearby housing project.

Three of the team's players watched their estranged fathers die from drug- or alcohol-related problems this season.

Tonight, many parents will not be in the stands: Who will pay the bills? Who will watch the children?

Many friends are also absent, having lost a weekly battle to persuade a player to quit. More than 2,200 boys attend this school, these friends say. If only 48 play varsity football — on a team where nobody is cut — how good can it be?

None of this matters to the 48 who, at this moment, feel they have been granted a higher calling. They can sense outsiders looking at them on the street as if they were punks who would be lucky to live past their 18th birthdays. They watch on TV as Latinos are treated like thugs.

Tonight they will be something else. They will be heroes.

As Aguirre pauses to catch his breath, it is so quiet in the Garfield gym that you can hear the whispers of 48 prayers.

"Think about why you are here!" Aguirre shouts. "You just think about it! Just think!"

With the departure of the NFL's Rams and Raiders, critics nationwide have chortled about the fact there is no football in Los Angeles.

Spend a week with the Bulldogs and you realize that, indeed, there is still football here. Football at its sweaty, soul-searching, heart-rending, triumphant best.

MONDAY

Willie Mercado is missing.

The team's first meeting of the week has begun. More than 40 shaved heads and pimply faces gather around a fuzzy TV in a classroom with barred windows.

They will watch films of Bell. They will study a mimeographed game plan. Both teams are 3-1. It is an important contest with playoff ramifications.

But their star defensive back is missing. Where is Willie?

Injury? Hooky?

"Nah," says Victor Ohm, equipment manager and trainer, with a shrug. "Guy got robbed again."

An hour later, as the team takes the field, Mercado shows up. He is wearing a grimace and stone-cold stare. He is 17. He dresses quickly in the cramped locker room. It smells like a subway. The yellow lockers are battered. The wooden benches are reed-thin and chipped. Most of the toilets are clogged. One has a gang symbol carved into its seat.

Yes, Mercado says, his car windows had been smashed during school. His stereo and speakers were stolen. "And my damn books, they got my damn books," he says.

He will practice hard today, smothering smaller players with his long arms, leaping on them with a fury, sometimes kicking them before they get up.

"Kids like Willie, they keep coming here because this is where they are loved," says Ohm. "They don't need gangs, because this is their gang."

And Ohm, 35, is one of their leaders.

An imposing bald man with a stud in one year, Ohm has a constant scowl and a sharp mouth to match. He has been involved in Garfield football for 25 years, lives a few blocks down the road, walks to work every morning at 6.

Every high school team, it seems, has somebody like him.

And no team has anybody like him.

He is not just the equipment manager and trainer, but the players' tormentor and their protector.

He sees their hunger, he buys them lunches. He sees them coming to school with holes in their pants, he buys them blue jeans.

Cleats are not supplied by the school. Many times, they are supplied by Ohm. He gives the sexually active players condoms.

Because of his intuition, most call him "Radar" after the character on "MASH." Some players, however, quietly call him "Dad." Ohm is most beloved for his medical knowledge. As in, he knows where to arrange for free X-rays and treatment.

This is important because the average Bulldog — about 5-foot-8, 180 pounds — is readily injured. Many players are uninsured beyond the school's limited coverage.

Sometimes Ohm relies on doctors who are former students, sometimes he hits up old friends. Other times he relies on his wits.

As practice ends, one of Ohm's children is attempting to hide a slight limp. It is linebacker Douglas Meza, who is recovering from foot surgery. It was performed last summer, after he played on a broken toe for two months during spring workouts because he couldn't afford the medical bills.

Ohm shuffled a few papers, held the boy's hand when doctors were allowed to make the correct diagnosis and arranged for the surgery.

Meza hopes to play in his first game, against Bell. "When I told my mom about the operation, she cried because we had no money," he says. "On Friday, I want her to see this."

TUESDAY

Two hours before the first practice snap, and already there is a problem. A student walks up to Aguirre as he monitors the team during study hall.

"Coach, over there," the boy says. "I think somebody needs you." He is pointing to a player, sitting alone, head buried in his knapsack, softly crying.

Aguirre knows the problem from 10 steps away. It will involve the boy's family. Players have come to him when their father has beaten their mother, or beaten them. Then there are the times their mother has thrown them out of the house for fooling around with football and not getting a job.

Aguirre spends the final 30 minutes of study hall huddled over the player, a stocky defensive lineman with scared eyes. The boy will be sent home from practice. He will not be seen for two days.

But he tells Coach he will be ready for Bell. Aguirre, a product of a nearby project and this high school, wants to believe him. "I grew up in the shadows; I was never anybody," says Aguirre, a small man with a big mustache and soft voice. "Adults would always ask me what I wanted to be, but the choice would always be janitor or machine operator.

"I listened to them, but in my heart, I always wanted to be a coach."

When Aguirre graduated from here 23 years ago, only his mother attended the ceremony. He never knew his father, his sisters were working, and his closest brother was in jail. Aguirre knows about being 17 and feeling alone.

Aguirre is also strict. Again, he says, he has no choice. His team is required to address every adult, in every situation, as "sir." They may miss a block, but they never blow that greeting.

During practice, players on the sidelines stand with their hands behind their backs and do not speak.

Gang members sometimes scream at them from the end zone. Neighborhood women flirt with them from the track.

They do not speak.

Midway through the session, though, bodies begin nervously shifting and eyes glance to the side.

It's Mario Hernandez. He is troubled again.

The star defensive end is pulled out of the scrimmage by two volunteer assistant coaches.

Unlike some schools in Southern California, Garfield has just two paid assistants. Aguirre must rely on seven volunteers, usually former players, who show up after work or between jobs.

Tommy Lopez, who will soon begin training as a prison guard, and medical supplies salesman Lawrence Galindo notice that Hernandez is not playing hard. They surround him.

"Don't b.s. us," Lopez says. "What is wrong with you?"

Hernandez stares down and says nothing. But the coaches know.

Hernandez's father died this season. His mother fears her son has joined a gang, and she wants to send him out of state. After Hernandez missed two recent school days and practices, Lopez and Ohm left the field during drills and drove to the projects to look for him.

They didn't know his address, so they walked through the streets shouting his name. They shouted and shouted until from behind one of the thin doors appeared a woman's face. Behind her was Mario.

Lopez explained to the woman that her son was one of the team's best players and that he was not in a gang. While the assistant coach talked, Hernandez gathered his gear.

He carried it past his mother and into the men's car before she could change her mind.

Today, Hernandez finally admits to his coaches, his mind is on his problems at home. Apparently he is not the only one.

It has been a warm day, the players are tired, but when you have just 30 chances, excuses are few. Aguirre calls the team together, glares and walks to his office.

The final speech of this day will be given, as it always is, by the team's leaders.

"Are you guys scared of something?" shouts receiver and defensive back John Cole, 5-foot-7 but with a 6-5 glare.

The team is kneeling, huddled before him and the other leaders in the end zone.

Linebacker Josh Villalobos is almost hysterical when he shouts, "Remember, every game is our last game. Every play is our last play!"

The day ends with several players walking backward on their hands across the darkened turf. They are being punished by their teammates for messing up, for not remembering.

WEDNESDAY

A typical day in the life of a football team working without a net.

Jose Casagran, the paid defensive coordinator, begins practice by showing more videotape from Bell's last game. But one of the TV wires has corroded. Lopez must stand behind the set and hold it in place to maintain a picture.

They take the field in 90-degree heat and things get worse. Players begin complaining of dizziness. Ohm shakes his head knowingly. It happens about this time every week. Those are the ones who barely have enough to eat.

A couple of children — no more than 8 or 9 years old — gather in the end zone and taunt the offense. "I'm gonna rock you!" shouts one. "I'm gonna screw you up good."

In the other end zone, offensive and defensive linemen practice separately, alone.

Their volunteer leaders have not yet arrived from work and college.

Along the sidelines in this heat walks lineman Eddie Garcia, known as "Flounder," a genuine senior college prospect at 6-3, 245.

That is, if any recruiter could ever find these bleachers. There have been no obvious spectators at practice so far this week. Or for weeks before.

Today they couldn't watch Garcia play anyway. But they could understand a measure of his toughness. He is battling a fever that has reached 102. Yet he won't go home. He won't take off his pads.

He won't even take off his helmet.

For the next two days he will circle the field in full uniform, not playing, not speaking, just circling.

"Sure, I could order him to go home," Aguirre says. "But would you do that to the kid? He would rather be here than anywhere in the world."

Somehow, in the late afternoon, from this madness a football team emerges. The hitting becomes louder, the tackling comes quicker, the players moan longer.

Villalobos has a sprained ankle but won't leave the field. Linebacker Tony Zamorano might have a broken hand, but also won't go.

Ohm shrugs in frustration. Not that he could help. The average Garfield player has other ideas about healing. They are called sabadoras, elderly women who give massages and ointment rubs from homes and storefronts. The coaches liken it to visiting a witch doctor. The players believe it is magic.

Just the other day, a woman rubbed oils and a bit of shrubbery on Mercado's injured back. He hasn't missed a practice since.

"Doctors," Mercado snorted. "Those are for white people."

By the time practice ends, the players are in a good mood. They have seen the injuries, watched Garcia's struggle, felt the strength of their hits. They know they are becoming ready for Bell.

After congratulating themselves for a great practice, the players are screaming at each other about Friday night.

Reminding the players of the race of Bell's star running back, Villalobos yells, "Friday, we're all going to spill n _ _ _ _ _ blood!"

There is silence. The teams look uncomfortably at T.J. Sheppard. He is their star running back. He is the only black on the squad.

A long pause. Then from underneath his helmet, a smile. Relieved cheers.

Sheppard, a junior who leads the team with 350 rushing yards and two touchdowns, understands his teammates' hearts if not their words. He discovered this last season when gangs terrorized him and his mother.

All the windows of his mother's car were broken. The windows of their living room were adorned with "KKK."

His mother, Emma Birden, had seen enough. She made plans to move to another school district.

Then the Bulldogs showed up.

Zamorano and Cole, who both live in the projects, visited the gang members and asked them to back off. For the good of the team, they said. It was the only argument that would work. And it worked.

His mother is happy, and T.J. can't wait for Bell.

"I feel comfortable now," Sheppard says. "My sister and everybody used to say the Mexicans were racist. But not here."

It is dark. Puddles and tape clutter the locker room floor. The last player grabs his knapsack.

It is Zamorano. Senior captain. A SAT score of 1090. One of 20 players with a grade-point averages better than 3.0.

These should be Zamorano's glory days. But these are also his days of drudgery. Back at home in the projects, he must clean his small apartment. He must make dinner. He must shoo away gang-bangers.

It has been this way for several years, since his mother went blind after an illness. He has missed practice to drive her to the hospital. He has rushed home to be her eyes. But she will be here Friday.

That she can't see is the source of his inspiration.

"She sits up where she can hear the public address announcer. She listens for my name," he says. "That is why I make so many tackles. Because that is the only way she will know that I am there."

THURSDAY

The day begins with Ohm leaving the team to investigate reports of taggers on school property. Crime is as common around the Bulldogs as ankle sprains.

Paul Sarni, a junior linebacker, was wearing his blue-and-red jersey before last Friday's game when he visited a doughnut shop with teammates. He was the first to walk outside, where he was accosted by a gang member who demanded his jersey.

"I said, 'No way,'" Sarni recalls.

The gang member threatened to "shank" Sarni.

"I said to myself, 'There is no way I can give him this jersey,'" Sarni said. "How could I go back and face my teammates?"

The punk then threatened to "blast" Sarni. That was enough. He was prepared to undress when his teammates rushed outside. The punk fled to his car.

That night, the team took out its frustrations with an 18-15 victory over South Gate.

Such endings have not always been happy.

Javier Perez, a junior wide receiver, was waiting for a city bus after practice recently when two men approached. One bumped him while the other reached under his knapsack and grabbed his helmet.

He chased the men but could not catch them.

"It was hard coming back to the locker room," Perez says. "I mean, that was my helmet."

Practice ends, as it does every Thursday, on a good, full note. In a small house on campus, Aguirre's wife, Maria, has arranged for a full meal for the team, paid for by Aguirre and donations.

"Tonight, you dream big!" exhorts Aguirre as the carne asada sizzles on the grill. "Then tomorrow, you come out and live it!"

FRIDAY

A day that should be a celebration of life begins with death.

Kickoff between Garfield and Bell is 7 p.m. Just after lunch, three players can be found at Rose Hills Memorial Park in Whittier.

Zamorano, Villalobos and Mercado, decked in their jerseys, are planting flowers, weeping and wondering. They surround the marble gravestone of Carlos "Cooch" Alvarado, a fullback from two seasons ago who was gunned down on this day last year outside the school for no apparent reason.

Mercado sobs.

Six hours to game time.

"I used to think I could never leave East L.A.," Mercado says later. "Now that I look around, I don't see how I could stay."

Three hours to game time. One of the last to arrive at the locker room is Juan Marez, a starting running back. As other players are having their ankles taped, he sits talking with a girlfriend while hurriedly downing a Jumbo Jack.

But he can be excused for rushing. After all, he is a working man.

Marez, who leads the team with five touchdowns, also is the leader in changed transmissions. He is a mechanic for Nungarey Tire Service. He works full time when he does not have a full class load.

"I support myself and help my family," he says. "Sometimes I am tired. But it is my choice."

At 4:30 p.m., the team files into the gym for its weekly hour-long quiet time. After Aguirre's speech, the players will spread out on the floor and sleep like babies.

At 6:30, they are preparing to take the field.

Unlike teams at many schools, during games they do not wear earrings or gloves or tape on their shoes. Some players in this league actually wear gang colors.

"My rules," Aguirre said. "We are not one person. We are one team."

THE GAME

The Bulldogs jog onto the grass amid virtual silence. The band has not started. The bleachers are not half-full.

But when the ball is kicked, the players behave like it's the NFL.

With Sheppard and Marez running through the bigger Bell defense, Garfield moves down to the 16-yard line. Marez runs 15 yards and prepares to score and . . . oops . . . he drops the ball.

Bell recovers.

The Garfield defense takes over. Garcia cannot be blocked. Zamorano has a hand on virtually every tackle. His name is announced so often, his mother can not believe what she is not seeing.

Then, trouble.

Hernandez, who has forgotten his home problems and is playing with a band on, limps to the sideline. It's his ankle.

Ohm runs over. One problem. His tape-cutters are so poor, it takes him five minutes to unwrap Hernandez's ankle. The delay forces Garfield to call a timeout.

Things get worse. Late in the first half, the struggling offense has yet another chance to score. This time, it is Sheppard who fumbles. He stumbles to the sidelines and plops on the bench. Even beneath his helmet, you can see he is crying.

Teammates rush up to hug him. The sobs continue. On this team, the emotion is common.

Once, after a tough loss, Garcia lay down at midfield and refused to go home.

Halftime. 0-0.

The players trudge to the locker room and sprawl in front of the showers. It is the only spot that will hold them all.

The outside doors are carefully closed, and for good reason. Several times each season, gang members wander in at halftime to try to inspire the players or scare them into losing. Each time, Aguirre shoos them away.

"We got 24 minutes, just 24 minutes!" shouts Aguirre tonight.

He says it as if they have but 24 minutes to live.

They begin the second half as if that is true. Moments after Cole recovers a fumble in Bell territory, quarterback Carlos Garcia scores on a 20-yard run.

The defense holds Bell after a long drive, then mounts another long drive. Sheppard runs one direction, Marez runs the other. Bell should stop them but can't.

Then just like that, Sheppard bounces outside with 8:45 left and runs 32 yards for a TD. It's 14-0.

Sheppard's tears are gone. His teammates engulf him.

The defense holds and it is over. Heroes again.

Eddie Garcia falls to the ground in excitement and exhaustion. Meza hops gleefully on his broken foot. Zamorano shuffles and waves his bad hand. Mercado slugs his teammates' shoulder pads, his last bit of anger diminishing for the week.

They run through a tunnel of cheerleaders to the locker room. While the boys dance and sing inside, Aguirre shakes hands and hugs well-wishers outside.

He has not seen any of these people this week. He knows he will not see them until next week. This task of nurturing flowers among the rocks must be handled alone, by him and his coaches.

Right now, it does not matter.

"Our players responded tonight, huh?" he says. "This is what makes it worth it."

He leaves for a steakhouse dinner with his staff. Most of his players are down the street at a loud hamburger stand.

The locker room clears except for one boy, Villalobos. A day that began in a graveyard is ending with a rebirth under a long, long shower. He remains under the water, laughing and singing, when he spots an adult bystander.

The smallest Garfield Bulldog steps out of the stall, covered in soap and a smile.

"Sir! Sir!" he says, as if this were the most wonderful, unbelievable thing in the world. "We beat Bell!"

November 10, 1998

A Long, Tall Glass of—Milk

From the moment he stepped into that loud stretch of land between Slauson and Vernon, David Meriwether just knew people would point.

He just knew there would be stomping.

He just knew there would be chants.

Monday afternoon, amid the dusty haze of history that hangs thick in the legendary Crenshaw High gym, David Meriwether was proven right.

And wrong.

When he was introduced as a junior guard for the Crenshaw High basketball team before the first official practice, more than 1,000 students pointed.

While cheering and whooping and high-fiving.

When he ran to the court to join the state's most celebrated high school basketball program, there was stomping.

As everyone danced on the bleachers.

And yes, by the time he walked into the blue-and-gold embrace of teammates, there were chants:

"Milk! Milk! Milk! Milk!"

Leave it to a bunch of silly teenagers to compose the perfect nickname for this rich, refreshing break from our city's tired sirens of conflict.

Meet David Meriwether, the first white male basketball player in the 30-year history of Crenshaw High.

The students have, and they overwhelmingly accept him.

His teammates have, and they like him.

The coach has, and he thinks Meriwether has a chance to be good.

"This is cool," Meriwether said Monday, bouncing off the shoulders of buddies, posing for giggling girls, looking at home in a place as foreign to most whites as Mars.

Yeah. Cool.

To understand the importance of the enrollment of a single student in a high school of about 2,760, it should be understood who doesn't enroll here.

Whites don't.

You can literally count the number of them at Crenshaw High on one hand.

David Meriwether makes four.

During his first two weeks of school, he was consistently bumped in the halls by gang members and questioned by classmates.

His teammates protected him from the thugs, who would shove him and square to fight before he was ushered away.

He wasn't sure what to do about everybody else.

"Teachers would be taking roll, and somebody would say, 'What are you doing here?'" recalled Meriwether, 17. "People would ask me if I was getting paid to come here."

It was a sense of wonder shared even by his new friends.

"When I was first told he was coming, I thought, 'It's not true,'" said E.J. Harris, Crenshaw's star guard. "There has got to be some pressure on him here. I figured, he has to be pretty strong."

Walking through the campus on a recent afternoon, through its clean grassy courtyard, down its wide and stately halls, the amazement seemed particularly odd.

Crenshaw has a notable program for gifted students, for students who want to become teachers, for those who want to sing in an internationally acclaimed choir.

Crenshaw also gives basketball players a chance to learn under a coach, Willie West, who is considered one of the finest in the country.

Although there is a waiting list for open enrollment permits — for students who want to come here from other areas of town with no special interests — there is room here for those who fit into the magnet programs.

And there is always room for those who live in the neighborhood, which includes whites.

But many eligible kids are steered elsewhere.

"Some people are just afraid," said West, whose teams have won eight state championships and 16 city titles in his 28 years. "It's too bad. It's not fair, but that's the way it is."

For some, it's the poor reputation of the surrounding neighborhood. For others, it's the foreignness of an enrollment that is about 81% African American and 18% Latino.

For West, the scene is always the same.

"The dad and the son will come here and get all excited about it," West said. "Then the mom will show up and say, 'No way.'"

It's happened so often that when Meriwether's father approached West this summer with the idea of his son transferring from Fairfax, West did all but wave him off.

"I told him where to go, who to talk to, what he had to do to try to enroll," West said. "But basically, I was believing it only when I saw him walk through the door on the first day of school."

West obviously didn't know Meriwether's father, also named David.

The Venice man, an Alabama transplant, is a single parent who runs the finances for a garment company and swears by his hometown hero, Paul "Bear" Bryant.

"My son told me he wanted to play basketball and eventually coach," the senior Meriwether said. "When I heard that, I thought, 'He needs to go to a school that helps you become a teacher, and to learn from the Bear Bryant of high school basketball coaches.'"

Meriwether qualified for the teacher training program, so he was able to transfer.

"I didn't even think about the race thing," said the senior Meriwether. "I knew Crenshaw was predominantly black, but I had no idea. To me, it didn't matter."

Even after he impressed West on a summer-league team, the younger Meriwether was required to audition with about 70 other students in West's annual all-comers tryouts. His defense and raw skills were good enough to warrant a uniform, and perhaps a back-up role to Harris.

"Do you know how amazing this is?" asked Kenneth Miller, longtime neighborhood observer and freelance writer. "This is like a black guy starting at quarterback for Brigham Young."

Yvonne Garrison, assistant principal, said, "It's good for him, and others like him, to realize what we have here. And it's good for everyone here to get to know him."

That process continues daily.

The subtle harassment has stopped, and Monday's display of affection should be enough to warm Meriwether through a winter of more questions.

"In class, they will ask me what my life is like, what I talk about at home, what I think about blacks," Meriwether said. "Actually, it's kind of neat, being on the other side of things. I'm learning a lot."

And the chant continues. Everyone who sees him in the halls, in the cafeteria, at local hangouts where he is becoming one of a suddenly expanding group.

"*Yo, Milk! Milk!*"

"That's how we think of him, he's just 'Milk,' no different from most of us," sophomore Monique Newton said. "Most of us are just chocolate milk."

February 11, 1999

Playing Through

Imagine waiting for an earthquake, only the earthquake is inside you.

It sits quietly in the corner of your brain, and sits, and sits, and maybe it strikes tomorrow, and maybe it strikes next week, and maybe it never strikes.

You lie on your back and pray into the empty darkness for that last possibility, but you know how it works. The earthquake probably will strike again, because after sitting quietly for five years, it struck again in December.

All that time sleeping, it woke up angry. It knocked you on the floor of your bathroom, kicked your feet wildly enough to leave marks on the wall, smeared your face back and forth in your blood.

After you regained consciousness and crawled to a phone to call home — "Mom," you sobbed, and she knew — you climbed into bed and looked into that empty darkness again.

And you thought, now what?

Maybe your medicine had stopped working. Maybe your luck had run out.

The earthquake known as epilepsy was back, sitting there again, sitting, sitting, and what do you do?

Do you hide? Do you run? Do you cover your head with your hands and wait just as it waits?

Not Aimee Copp.

She did what she always does.

She flew.

She showed up at practice with her USC women's basketball teammates like always, bruised head, fat lip, lots of stares, and she played.

She ran the floor, leaped to the rim, fought for the ball, and has been doing it ever since.

Basketball is her release. Basketball is her revenge.

"In basketball," Aimee Copp says, "I am free."

She recently suffered a reaction to new medication that caused her to lean trembling against the bleachers while teammates watched in horror.

She bit her lower lip and continued.

Her mind sometimes goes blank for five seconds. The medication sometimes makes her so woozy she must sit down.

She bites her lower lip and continues.

If and when a seizure strikes again, junior forward Aimee Copp has made a decision.

Earthquakes cannot hurt her, because she will be flying.

.   .   .

This was not supposed to be a story about a middle, but an ending. This was supposed to be about how Aimee Copp, after spending most of her high school years on the sidelines dealing with epilepsy, had finally whipped it to become a basketball star.

"I thought it was over," she says quietly.

This was supposed to be about how, while remaining seizure free for nearly five years beginning with senior season at Fullerton High, she had worked eight hours a day to become one of the top junior college players in the country.

She had picked her dream university, USC, over 30 other schools. She was a tough 6-foot-1 junior who could dominate at center or forward. She was scheduled to be eligible at the end of December.

The comeback story was finished.

Then a couple of weeks before her first game, she came home from shopping, put away some groceries, walked into the bathroom, and blacked out.

The next thing she remembers, she was lying on the bathroom floor, hyperventilating, unable to walk for more than 10 minutes because of spasms occurring in seemingly every muscle in her body.

Raising her head, she saw her reflection in a closet mirror. Her face was covered in blood.

The terror was back.

"I crawled into bed and started thinking a million things," she says. "Mostly, it was like, why me? I mean, I thought I had paid my dues."

Two months later, sitting in the spotless living room of her campus apartment earlier this week, she describes how she is still paying them.

Because of the recent seizure, she can no longer legally drive a car — she must remain seizure free for a year to regain her license.

So she moved closer to campus and bought a bike.

Then, last week, somebody stole her bike.

Epilepsy is a chronic neurological disease that causes seizures that can sometimes be prevented with drugs. Her doctor figured that perhaps she had grown immune to her current medication and prescribed new drugs.

But sometimes those drugs leave her feeling drowsy or cause her to briefly lose attention. Sometimes they make everything blurry.

While she is experimenting with the right drug and dosage in an effort to gain control of her life again, anything can happen.

The only thing for certain is, in one way, she is going through it alone.

Despite being surrounded by strong parents and an older brother and close friends and sensitive Coach Chris Gobrecht, there is one part of her life she can not discuss with anyone.

Because she has never met another epileptic.

"What I go through," she says softly, "it's really unexplainable."

Yet she has continued to practice and play and improve, advancing from a raw talent to someone about whom Gobrecht says, "She shows moments of having great things to contribute to this team."

But for how long?

Copp doesn't know. She tries not to think about it.

She just flies, scoring her two points and grabbing her one rebound in her nine minutes every game with the intensity of a double-double.

"If I start believing that my disease is just the way it is, just the way I'll end up, then that's all I'll do in life . . . just end up," she says, her wide eyes growing bright. "I don't want to just end up. I want to do something. I want to have big dreams."

That word, *dream*, is still written in grease pencil on the mirror of the bedroom of her Fullerton home.

It has been there since she used it to inspire her transformation at the start of her senior year.

Before that, since having her first seizure in seventh grade, her high school years were, in her words, "terrible."

Struggling to find the right medicine, she suffered 10-15 seizures a year while losing her hair and suffering incontinence because of the medication.

Once a good student and soccer player, she would sleep 14 hours a day and miss all her classes.

School officials would summon her and demand to know what was wrong. She would break down in tears when they wouldn't understand.

"The biggest thing about epilepsy is the ignorance," says her mother, Phyllis.

Through her parents' persistence, Copp ended up in Loma Linda University Medical Center in the summer after her junior year, subjecting herself to two weeks of observation in hopes of finding the proper medicine.

Confined to her bed with electrodes strapped to her head with gauze, unable to move more than 10 feet for the entire two weeks, she had three monitored seizures that Dr. Carmel Armon — she calls him her savior — used to figure out the right prescription.

"It was like, my life had begun," Copp says.

That fall, she played her first high school basketball, even though she could not dribble with her right hand and her father, John, had to teach her to shoot in the driveway.

The next summer, she spent entire days in gyms, including three hours practicing her dribbling on racquetball courts.

Says Phyllis: "I finally said, 'Honey, what are you doing?'"

Says Aimee: "I told her, 'Let me go, I only have one chance to be young.'"

And so she has grasped that chance, harder in the hard times, so hard now her knuckles are white, absolutely unwilling to let go.

"Sometimes I'm scared, really scared," she says, biting her lip again. "But I am not going to let fear overcome my life."

Unexplainable? Not really.
This is the story of a big, powerful, madly malfunctioning brain.
Being whipped by a heart.

March 8, 2001

A Player With Promise

March Madness carries Michael Schnyder out of the pregame huddle, to a place only he can visit, for a prayer only he can understand.

Before the Glendale College basketball team begins its state tournament quarterfinal game tonight in Stockton, their best player will not gather with his teammates in front of the bench.

He will, as usual, walk to an empty spot near a foul line. Once there, with head bowed, he will speak to the father who left him, on behalf of the mother who will not.

"Daddy," he will pray, "you know what I'm going through. . . ."

Surely his father knows. It was his father who told Michael, in that steady handyman's voice, that his mother should never be put in a nursing home.

Even when her multiple sclerosis became so bad she couldn't hold her gaunt head up, his father told him this.

Even when she moved into a hospital-style bed in their tiny south Los Angeles home, barely able to speak, eating only through a tube, his father told him this.

His father told him this until last June, when Leo Schnyder crawled underneath an ailing car in their backyard and never crawled out.

Died of a heart attack. Left his youngest son to remember his mother and the promise.

"Daddy," he'll pray tonight, nine months later, "I'm doing what you said. . . ."

As he prays, Annie Slaughter will still be in that stucco house, behind those barred windows, still in her bed.

Michael Schnyder, age 20, is her primary caregiver. He is the one who pays the bills, gives the injections, figures the insurance, changes the sheets.

He is also his conference's most valuable player, a high-jumping, tough-shooting guard who is one of the best junior college players in the state and a national Division I prospect.

A prospect who doesn't even open recruiting letters from out of town.

Because he is the one who must come running when his mother calls, and how can he do that from a big city in Texas or a small town in Utah?

In remembering the promise, he has forgotten himself. He has missed practices, nearly left games at halftime, rushed from the court on countless occasions to either drive or phone home.

He has played with no sleep. He has played distracted. He has played in tears.

"I've seen a lot of things here," says his coach, Brian Beauchemin, a 22-year Glendale veteran. "But what this kid is doing, I've never seen anything like it."

This time of year, most college basketball players ask for victory. Michael Schnyder asks only for peace.

"Please, Daddy," he'll pray tonight. "Let my pager stay quiet until we finish this game."

.   .   .

March Madness carries Michael Schnyder hurriedly out of a Glendale gym still filled with his teammates, into a bouncy old Chrysler, down the Harbor Freeway to the promise.

It is three days before the state quarterfinals. Practice is scheduled to last another hour.

"We need him here today," Beauchemin says.

But the nurse who watches his mother during the day has to leave suddenly with a family emergency.

His blue pager beeps. Schnyder runs from the gym without even taking a shower.

Forty-five minutes later, he walks into a yellow two-bedroom house on a cluttered block, into antiseptic-smelling air filled with a familiar cry.

"Michaeeeeel!"

It's his mother. She wants Schnyder to move her head.

He walks into her bedroom. The lights are off, the curtains drawn. A silent television flickers from the opposite wall.

She is propped up against the pillows, a brightly colored blanket pulled up toward vacant eyes.

Her son, whose beard stubble cannot disguise his young face, smiles as if walking into a suite at the Ritz.

"I'm here, Momma, I'm here," he says gently, adjusting her shoulders, kissing her cheek.

"My boy," she groans.

With the exception of school and basketball, her boy is always here.

"I told my father I would never let anyone take Momma," he says. "And I won't."

The state-funded nurse works eight hours a day, six days a week. Schnyder is responsible for everything else.

"I think back to when I had both parents here, and how great it was," he says. "I thought it would always be like that."

Once a pampered child, he now sleeps either on a couch outside his mother's room, or in a recliner next to her bed. He awakens every two hours to move her. He awakens every time the 54-year-old woman cries.

Once a squeamish child, he feeds her every four hours through a tube in her stomach. He dissolves her six bottles of pills into water, and pours them down the same tube. Every other day he mixes medicine in a syringe and injects her hip.

"Used to be, I couldn't even look at a needle," he says.

He also never knew how a washing machine worked. Now, he changes and washes her sheets at least once a day. Because the dryer broke, he sometimes hangs the wet linens on an inside heater.

"She used to change my diaper," he says. "Now, it's only fair that I do it for her."

He had never even seen a bill. Now he pays all of the bills, running to the market to fill out money orders because he has no checking account.

If she has a seizure, which is happening more frequently, he accompanies her to the hospital and stays by her side until she is discharged.

He is always thinking what, perhaps, you are thinking.

"I want everybody at the hospital to know that somebody loves this woman, and cares for this woman," he says. "I want them to know that I am not too young to be that person."

Officials from a social service agency have visited once, and were initially skeptical. He says they checked her medicine, and discovered that she did not have enough to last until the next doctor visit.

"I was one pill short," he says. "I was so scared they were going to put her in a home. I have never been one pill short again."

He says he has nightmares that somebody is going to take her for good.

"I hear ambulances coming, and I see her get taken away, and then they never bring her back," he says.

The day after the nightmares, he says he hugs his mother and reassures her.

"I say, 'Momma, as long as I'm alive and you're alive, we're going to be together,'" he says.

He says she complains when she goes to the hospital and smiles when she comes home.

"I know she is happier here," he says. "This is what my father wanted, this is what she wants. I have to step up and be a man and do this for them."

Beauchemin fits his practices around Schnyder's schedule. On night games, Schnyder either contracts the nurse to work overtime, or relies on friends and extended family members for care.

He has a developmentally challenged older brother, Kenyatta, who recently moved back home. He has four half-brothers — they had a different mother — who are also in town.

All the brothers will be working with the nurse while Schnyder is in Stockton.

"There is so much pressure on him, everything falls on him," says Derek Schnyder, one of his half-brothers. "He's become a real man."

If the Vaqueros have success, they could be in Stockton through the weekend, with the state championship game scheduled for Saturday night. If not, they could be home Friday morning.

As usual, Schnyder is torn.

"I want to win the state championship more than anything," he says. "But, you know, I will be thinking about home."

It is a home that, while once bursting with the richness of a two-parent family, now sits on the edge of chilled poverty.

Schnyder lives on his mother's monthly Social Security check of $721. Because the home belongs to a relative, he pays about $300 a month in rent.

The rest he uses to pay bills and buy supplies, although there's barely enough.

His phone has been turned off. He once recycled bottles for money for bus fare to school. While he is the perfect candidate for a cellular phone, he cannot afford one.

His parents used to cook him a hot breakfast every morning, and had dinner waiting for him when he returned from school. Now he eats out of a refrigerator filled with tinfoil cafeteria leftovers donated by Beauchemin's family.

Schnyder remembers a time when his doting mother would bake him a chocolate cake and pumpkin pie on his birthday.

Last year, he didn't even celebrate his birthday.

He remembers when his parents gave him $150 basketball shoes and electronic equipment for Christmas.

Last Christmas, he says, he received nothing.

He celebrated by lifting his mother into the front seat of that old Chrysler and driving her around the neighborhood. Friends would come to the window and say hello and grab her hand.

"A good Christmas," Schnyder says.

"A 20-year-old kid," Beauchemin says. "Think about it."

. . .

March Madness carries Michael Schnyder through the air, spinning above the rim, into a reverse dunk that turns a passing drill into a highlight reel.

This is his favorite time of day, the time when the squeaking of shoes and echoing of bouncing balls overwhelm a certain beep-beep-beep.

That pager sits on the sideline at practice and on the bench during games.

But sometimes he can get lost in the noise and pretend it doesn't exist.

"I think his personal situation has actually made him a better player," teammate DeJon Lee says. "I think it's given him more focus. In the tougher games, he comes alive."

He didn't begin playing high school basketball until his junior season at Fremont High. Then his mother was diagnosed with MS, and he began missing classes.

He didn't play his senior season because he flunked out of school. He passed his equivalency exam and entered Glendale for a second chance.

The 6-foot-1 leaper was voted the team's top freshman last season, but he was still the pampered child.

There were times he would yell at Beauchemin from the court. Once, after being taken out of a game, he stormed off the bench and into the locker room.

"I don't think I understood what it took," he says.

Then his father died suddenly, and he had no choice but to understand.

"When I first heard about his father dying, I thought, that's it, he's finished here," Beauchemin says. "He would have to get a job and spend all his time taking care of his mother."

That was Schnyder's original idea, until relatives reminded him of something else his father had said.

"My Dad always told me that I was going to be his little NBA player, that I was going to be the one to get them to a better neighborhood," he says. "I knew I couldn't stop playing."

It was hard, then it got harder.

The team played a holiday tournament in San Diego, but Schnyder couldn't stay overnight, so an assistant coach drove him back and forth twice until he was carsick.

At halftime of a game against College of the Canyons, his beeper went off and he phoned home. A friend told him that something must be wrong because his mother was frantically calling for him.

Schnyder got dressed and left the locker room, stopping to phone home one more time. The friend answered and said that his mom was fine, and that he should finish the game.

He undressed again, put back on his uniform, and scored 22 second-half points to lead the Vaqueros to victory.

"One minute he's standing there dressed in his regular clothes and in tears, the next minute he's back on the court scoring," Lee recalls. "It's been a strange season."

But, beginning with that game, an inspired season.

The team was struggling with a 14-9 record before winning nine of its last 10, including an upset of the state's top-ranked team — L.A. City College — in a playoff game last weekend.

Those who voted him MVP of the Western State Conference's Southern Division obviously believed that Schnyder's 18 points, four rebounds, six assists and two steals a game were a big reason.

His appearance at the team's opening playoff game against Cerritos was another reason.

He didn't want to play. He had taken his mother to the hospital the previous night with a seizure and waited five hours until she was checked into a room. Then he stayed by her side until nearly game time, when he arrived at Glendale, exhausted.

"He said he couldn't make it," Beauchemin recalls. "I told him that as badly as we needed him, I understood."

But his teammates didn't. They talked him into playing on no sleep. He scored only 11 points, but the Vaqueros needed all of them in a one-point victory

"You have to remember something about Mike," Beauchemin says. "To him, his mother is the last living thing he has on this earth."

                              ■   ■   ■

March Madness . . . but is it?

Sitting in the middle of his house, Michael Schnyder can pick up his feet and see a grease stain in the middle of a worn blue carpet. It is the mark made by his father's work shirt when they brought him inside after his fatal heart attack.

Facing him is the photo that accompanied his father's casket, plus the silk flowers that surrounded it.

Behind him is his mother's room, the door always open, so he can hear every sound.

He is sitting there on a recent night in basketball shoes, sweat rolling down his face, his teammates still back in Glendale, doing what he should be doing, a promising man crumbling under a promise.

You say, "This is crazy."

He says, "This is family."

POSTSCRIPT: Michael Schnyder is on a full basketball scholarship at Cal State Bakersfield. Donations generated from this story helped him afford care for his mother while he is at school.

August 19, 2001

Her Blue Haven

Bill Plaschke predicted doom for the Dodgers in 2001. . . . Plaschke criticized. . . . Plaschke forgot. . . . Plaschke compared unfairly. . . . The Dodgers need encouragement, not negativity. . . .

• • •

That was part of a 1,200-word screed e-mailed to me last December, a holiday package filled with colorful rips. It was not much different from other nasty letters I receive, with two exceptions.

This note contained more details than the usual "You're an idiot." It included on-base percentages and catchers' defensive statistics. It was written by someone who knew the Dodgers as well as I thought I did.

And this note was signed. The writer's name was Sarah Morris.

She typed it at the bottom.

Most people hide behind tough words out of embarrassment or fear, but Sarah Morris was different. She had not only challenged me to a fight, but had done so with no strings or shadows.

I thought it was cute. I wrote her back. I told her I was impressed and ready for battle.

Little did I know that this would be the start of a most unusual relationship, which eight months later is being recounted from a most unusual place. I am writing this from the floor.

Sarah Morris having knocked me flat with a punch I never saw coming.

May I ask you a question? For two years I have been running my own Web site about the Dodgers. I write game reports and editorials. How did you become a baseball editorialist? That is my deam.

This was Sarah's second e-mail, and it figured. Every time I smile at someone, they ask me for a job.

Her own Web site? That also figured. Everybody has a Web site. The Dodgers guess there are more than two dozen Web sites devoted to kissing the almighty blue.

So my expert wasn't really an expert, but rather a computer nerd looking for work. I didn't need any more pen pals with agendas.

But about that last line. I chewed my lower lip about it. The part about "my deam."

Maybe Sarah Morris was just a lousy typist. But maybe she was truly searching for something, yet was only one letter from finding it. Aren't all of us sometimes like that?

It was worth one more response. I wrote back, asking her to explain.

I am 30 years old. . . . Because I have a physical handicap, it took me five years to complete my AA degree at Pasadena City College. . . . During the season I average 55 hours a week writing five to seven game reports, one or two editorials, researching and listening and/or watching the games.

Physical handicap. I paused again. I was in no mood to discuss a physical handicap, whatever it was.

I have had these discussions before, discussions often becoming long, teary stories about overcoming obstacles.

Courageous people make me jealous. They make me cry. But at some point, they have also made me numb.

Then I read the part about her working 55 hours a week. Goodness. This woman didn't only follow the Dodgers, she covered them like a newspaper reporter.

But for whom? Sarah called her Web site "Dodger Place." I searched for it, and found nothing. I checked all the Dodger search links, and found nothing.

Then I reread her e-mail and discovered an address buried at the bottom: http://members.tripod.com/spunkydodgers.

I clicked there. It wasn't fancy, rather like a chalkboard, with block letters and big type.

There was a section of "News from a Fan." Another section of "Views by a Fan." But she covered the team with the seriousness of a writer.

The stories, while basic, were complete. Sarah's knowledge was evident.

But still, I wondered, how could anybody find it? Is anybody reading?

Nobody ever signs my guest book.

Does anybody correspond?

I get one letter a month.

I read the Web site closer and realized that she does indeed receive about one letter a month — always from the same person.

So here was a physically handicapped woman, covering the Dodgers as extensively as any reporter in the country, yet writing for an obscure Web site with an impossible address, with a readership of about two.

That "deam" was missing a lot more than an r, I thought.

The days passed, winter moved toward spring, and I had more questions.

Sarah Morris always had answers.

I started my own Web site in hopes of finding a job, but I have had no luck yet. I have gone to the Commission of Rehabilitation seeking help, but they say I'm too handicapped to be employed. I disagree.

So what if my maximum typing speed is eight words per minute because I use a head pointer to type? My brain works fine. I have dedication to my work. That is what makes people successful.

I don't know how to look for a job.

A head pointer? I remember seeing one of those on a late-night commercial for a hospital for paralyzed people.

It looked frightening. But her stories didn't look frightening. They looked, well, normal.

Now I find out she typed them with her head?

I asked her how long it took her to compose one of her usual 1,200-word filings.

3-4 hours.

While pondering that the average person can bang out a 1,200-word e-mail in about 30 minutes, I did something I've never before done with an Internet stranger.

I asked Sarah Morris to call me.

I wanted to talk about the Dodgers. I wanted to talk about her stories.

But, well, yeah, I mostly wanted to talk about why someone would cover a team off television, typing with her head for an invisible readership.

I have a speech disability making it impossible to use the phone.

That proved it. My first impression obviously had been correct. This was an elaborate hoax.

She didn't want to talk to me because, of course, she didn't exist.

I thought to myself, "This is why I never answer all my mail. This is why I will never go near a chat room."

The Internet has become more about mythology than technology, people inventing outrageous lives to compensate for ordinary realities.

So, I was an unwitting actor in a strange little play. This woman writer was probably a 45-year-old male plumber.

I decided to end the correspondence.

Then I received another e-mail.

The first sentence read, *"There are some facts you might want to know. . . ."*

In words with an inflection that leaped off the screen, Sarah Morris spoke.

My disability is cerebral palsy. . . . It affects motor control. . . . I have excessive movement, meaning when my brain tells my hands to hit a key, I would move my legs, hit the table, and six other keys in the process.

This was only the beginning.

When my mom explained my handicap, she told me I could accomplish anything that I wanted to if I worked three times as hard as other people.

She wrote that she became a Dodger fan while growing up in Pasadena. In her sophomore year at Blair High, a junior varsity baseball coach, Mike Sellers, asked her to be the team statistician. Her special ed teacher discouraged it, but she did it anyway, sitting next to the bleachers with an electric typewriter and a head pointer.

We had a game on a rainy day. The rain fell in the typewriter, making it unusable, so Mom wrote the stats when I told her. I earned two letters that I am proud of still.

She wrote that her involvement in baseball had kept her in school—despite poor grades and hours of neck-straining homework.

Baseball gave me something to work for. . . . I could do something that other kids couldn't. . . . Baseball saved me from becoming another statistic. That is when I decided I wanted to do something for the sport that has done so much for me.

And about that speech disability?

When I went to nursery school, teachers treated me dumb. This made me mad, but I got over it. I hate the meaning of "dumb" in the phrase "deaf and dumb." My speech disability is the most frustrating.

OK, so I believed her. Sort of. It still sounded odd.

Who could do something like this? I figured she must be privileged. Who, in her supposed condition, could cover a baseball team without the best equipment and help?

I figured she had an elaborate setup somewhere. I was curious about it. I figured she couldn't live too far from Pasadena. I would drive over one day and we would chat.

I live in Anderson, Texas. It's about 75 miles from Houston.

Texas? She didn't explain. I didn't ask. But that seemed like a long flight to see a little rich girl bang on an expensive keyboard.

By now, it was spring training, and she was ranting about Gary Sheffield, and I was hanging out in Vero Beach, and I would have forgotten the whole thing.

Except Sarah Morris began sending me her stories. Every day, another story. Game stories, feature stories, some with missing words, others with typographical errors, but all with obvious effort.

Then, fate. The Lakers were involved in a playoff series in San

Antonio, I had one free day, and she lived about three hours away.

I wrote her, asking if I could drive over to see her. She agreed, but much too quickly for my suspicious tastes, writing me with detailed directions involving farm roads and streets with no name.

I read the directions and again thought, this was weird. This could be dangerous. I wanted to back out.

Turns out, I wasn't the only one.

I'm so nervous about tomorrow. I'm nothing special but a woman with disabilities. I don't know what makes a good journalism story. I don't know if I am it.

I pulled out of my San Antonio hotel on a warm May morning and drove east across the stark Texas landscape. I followed Sarah's directions off the interstate and onto a desolate two-lane highway.

The road stretched through miles of scraggly fields, interrupted only by occasional feed stores, small white churches and blinking red lights.

I rolled into the small intersection that is Anderson, then took a right turn, down a narrow crumbling road, high weeds thwacking against the car's window.

After several miles, I turned down another crumbling road, pulling up in front of a rusted gate, which I had been instructed to open.

Now, on a winding dirt road dotted with potholes the size of small animals, I bounced for nearly a mile past grazing cows. Through the dust, I spotted what looked like an old tool shed.

But it wasn't a shed. It was a house, a decaying shanty covered by a tin roof and surrounded by weeds and junk.

I slowed and stared. Could this be right?

Then I saw, amid a clump of weeds near the front door, a rusted wheelchair.

P.S. We have dogs.

Do they ever. A couple of creatures with matted hair emerged from some bushes and surrounded the car, scratching and howling.

Finally, an older woman in an old T-shirt and skirt emerged from the front door and shooed the dogs away.

"I'm Sarah's mother," said Lois Morris, grabbing my smooth hand with a worn one. "She's waiting for you inside."

I walked out of the sunlight, opened a torn screen door, and moved into the shadows, where an 87-pound figure was curled up in a creaky wheelchair.

Her limbs twisted. Her head rolled. We could not hug. We could not even shake hands. She could only stare at me and smile.

But that smile! It cut through the gloom of the cracked wooden floor, the torn couch, the broken, cobwebbed windows.

A clutter of books and boxes filled the small rooms. There was a rabbit living in a cage next to an old refrigerator. From somewhere outside the house, you could hear the squeaking of rats.

Eventually I could bear to look at nothing else, so I stared at that smile, and it was so clear, so certain, it even cut through most of my doubts.

But still, even then, I wondered.

This is Sarah Morris?

She began shaking in her chair, emitting sounds. I thought she was coughing. She was, instead, speaking.

Her mother interpreted. Every sound was a different word or phrase.

"Huh (I) . . . huh-huh (want to show) . . . huh (you) . . . huh (something)."

Her mother rolled her through a path that cut through the piles of junk, up to an old desk on cinder blocks.

On the desk was a computer. Next to it was a TV. Nearby was a Dodger bobble-head doll of uncertain identity.

Her mother fastened a head pointer around her daughter's temples, its chin-strap stained dark brown from spilled Dr Pepper. Sarah then began carefully leaning over the computer and pecking.

On the monitor appeared the Dodger Place Web site. Sarah used her pointer to call up a story. Peck by peck, she began adding to that story. It was her trademark typeface, her trademark Dodger fan prose, something involving Paul Lo Duca, about whom she later wrote:

" . . . Offensively, Lo Duca has been remarkable. Entering Friday's game, Lo Duca has batted .382 with five home runs and seventeen RBI. Last Tuesday Jim Tracy moved Lo Duca into the lead-off position. Since then, the Dodgers have won six and lost two. Lo Duca has an on-base percentage of .412. On Memorial Day Lo Duca had six hits, becoming the first Dodger to do so since Willie Davis on May 24, 1973. . . ."

She looked up and giggled. I looked down in wonder — and shame.

This was indeed Sarah Morris. The great Sarah Morris.

She began making more sounds, bouncing in her chair. Lois asked me to sit on a dusty chair. There were some things that needed explaining.

Times photographer Anacleto Rapping, who had been there earlier in the day, and I had been Sarah's first visitors since she moved here with her mother and younger sister from Pasadena nearly six years ago.

This shack was an inheritance from Sarah's grandmother. When Sarah's parents divorced, her mother, with no other prospects, settled here.

The adjustment from life in Southern California to the middle of scrubby field more than 30 miles from the nearest supermarket was painful. Sarah was uprooted from a town of relative tolerance and accessibility to a place of many stares.

It was so remote, when her mother once dropped Sarah, helping her out of bed, and called 911, the emergency crew couldn't find the place.

"But the hardest thing for Sarah was leaving her Dodgers," Lois said.

So, she didn't. She used her disability money, and loans, to buy the computer, the television and the satellite dish that allows her to watch or listen to every game.

She doesn't have any nearby friends, and it's exhausting to spend the five hours required for shopping trips to the nearest Wal-

Mart, so the Dodgers fill the void.

They challenge her on bad days, embrace her on good days, stay awake with her while she covers an extra-inning game at 2 a.m.

She covers so much baseball, she maintains the eerie schedule of a player, rarely awaking before 10 a.m., often eating dinner at midnight.

Through the cluttered house, the path for not only her wheelchair, but for the entire direction of her life, leads from her bedroom to the kitchen to the Dodgers.

The air-conditioning sometimes breaks, turning the house into a steam bath. Lois totaled their aging van last year when she hit a black cow on a starless night, then missed so much work that they barely had enough money for food.

Yet, Sarah spends nine hours, carefully constructing an analysis of Gary Sheffield, or two hours writing about a one-run victory in Colorado.

I asked what her Dodger Web page represented to her.

Freedom.

I asked how she feels when working.

Happy. Useful.

I had contacted Sarah Morris months earlier, looking for a fight. I realized now, watching her strain into the thick air of this dark room to type words that perhaps no other soul will read, that I had found that fight.

Only, it wasn't with Sarah. It was with myself. It is the same fight the sports world experiences daily in these times of cynicism and conspiracy theories.

The fight to believe. The fight to trust that athletics can still create heroes without rap sheets, virtue without chemicals, nobility with grace.

It is about the battle to return to the days when sports did not detract from life, but added to it, with its awesome power to enlighten and include.

In a place far from such doubt, with a mind filled with wonder, Sarah Morris brought me back.

I had not wanted to walk into those shadows. But two hours

later, I did not want to leave.

Yet I did, because there was an airplane waiting, and an NBA playoff series to cover, big things, nonsense things.

Sarah asked her mother to wheel her outside. She was rolled to the edge of the weeds. I grasped one of her trembling hands. She grasped back with her smile.

I climbed into the car and rattled down the dirt road. Through the rear-view mirror, through the rising dust, I could see the back of Sarah Morris' bobbing head as she was wheeled back to that cinder-blocked desk.

For she, too, had a game to cover.

If you see Karros, please tell him to watch his knees in 1999. He used to bend them more than now.

Sarah sent me that e-mail recently. It was about the same time she'd sent me an e-mail saying she had finally saved enough money to begin attending a college about 45 minutes down the road in pursuit of her "deam."

I didn't get a chance to pass along her note to the slumping Karros, but it didn't matter.

A day later, he had a game-winning hit. The next game, a home run. The game after that, another homer.

If you watched him closely, you could see that he indeed was bending his knees again.

Eight months ago I wouldn't have believed it, but I could swear each leg formed the shape of an r.

POSTSCRIPT: After this story appeared, nearly 2,000 e-mails and letters of support were sent to Sarah Morris and the L.A. Times, many with monetary donations. She was also hired by Major League Baseball to write a weekly column on the Dodgers' Web site.

CHAPTER FIVE

Halftime

January 29, 2000

He Puts Words
in Their Mouths

It was Cliche Clearance Day at the Super Bowl on Friday, with
two head coaches and a commissioner parading in front of hundreds of reporters for the final time before the big game.

Not to worry. We brought an interpreter.

Paul Tagliabue, NFL commissioner: "It's unfortunate any team
has to move. What [this matchup] does show is that those cities
which made commitments to NFL teams will share in the invest-
ment they made."

*If you agree to have money scraped from your paycheck every
week to buy a stadium for your zillionaire owner, as the dopes in St.
Louis and Tennessee have, you have earned the right to come to a
cold city for a week in January and pay exorbitant prices to cheer
them to a championship.*

Dick Vermeil, St. Louis Ram coach: "John Wooden told me
when I was working at UCLA, he said, 'Players win games, but you
want to strive to be the coach that wins more games with his players than some other coach coaching your players.'"

*If we win Sunday, that means I will have out coached that pret-
ty boy Jeff Fisher, and you can call me the Wizard of Dogwood.*

Jeff Fisher, Tennessee Titan coach: "Our team is not going to
peak today or tomorrow or Sunday morning. They are going to be
ready to play at kickoff."

*Unlike Dick Vermeil's Rams, who have been running their
mouths for the last six days.*

Tagliabue: "The track record of our players [having off-field
problems] is better than society at large."

*You people need to understand that every day in this country,
somebody is evading a murder charge by hiding in the trunk of a
Toyota.*

Vermeil: "The fact that Marshall Faulk caught three passes
and Isaac Bruce caught three passes for a total of 27 yards [in

the NFC championship game], we have got to do a better job, starting with me."

You see what happens when I let my assistants do the play calling?

Fisher: "The thing I take from Buddy [Ryan] most is that he gave me the opportunity to coach. He gave me my first job."

Look, would you stop with the Buddy Ryan-disciple stuff? So the old man once hired me. Big whoop. These aren't his schemes; they are mine, mine, mine.

Tagliabue: "We are concerned at what seems to be some serious deterioration of conduct. We've had conduct that can only be defined as juvenile."

Is it my fault that the average NFL player has the maturity of a 5-year-old?

Vermeil: "My thoughts from time to time were: What the hell am I doing here?"

Three years ago, I took over an absolute sewer of a football program. They should count their lucky stars that I stuck around to save it.

Fisher: "I am sure when the time [for a contract extension] is right for them, they will let me know, but I have got, obviously, more important things on my mind right now."

I'll be quiet now, but if I win this Super Bowl, my cheapskate boss with the pelt on his head better pony up.

Tagliabue: "Eddie DeBartolo will be eligible to rejoin the league after Feb. 1. The issue of who controls [the San Francisco 49ers] is a separate issue."

If you think I'm letting that riverboat rat stick his greasy hands back into this pie, you're dumber than I look.

Vermeil: "I am concerned about my placekicking. . . . My placekicker [Jeff Wilkins] has patella tendonitis in his plant leg. . . . He kicked in the dome yesterday and he feels great."

Doesn't matter what kind of fancy-schmancy name you give his injury, the wimp has no excuses.

Fisher: "If [Yancey Thigpen] convinces me that he can play 35 or 40 plays . . . with the foot condition the way it is right now, then he will play."

Either Yancey Thigpen is a man, or he isn't.

Tagliabue: "I am pleased [with instant replay]. Others are more mixed."

As the boss, I could give a rip what anybody else thinks. Instant replay is not going to be changed, period.

Fisher: "I believe that the [instant replay] system works. I believe the system did exactly what we wanted it to do."

I believe that replay officials will be so happy to read this, this Sunday they will give us a break.

Vermeil: "Leonard Little is a nondrinker. . . . I have had him to my house for dinner, offered him a glass of wine. He does not drink."

The only way we can justify keeping a convicted felon on this team is to believe that friends held him down and poured 14 drinks down his gullet before he killed that woman with his car.

Vermeil: "Some people said, well, you shouldn't bring [Little] back . . . [but] you know, the people in St. Louis are very understanding and very forgiving and, not that we should forgive everybody for every mistake they make, but we have had no problems."

I know a bunch of suckers when I see them. As long as we're winning, Leonard Little will be welcome in St. Louis.

August 19, 2000

You Can't See Much From Tiger's Trenches

LOUISVILLE, KY. — We now take you live to Tiger Woods' gallery alongside the fifth green at Valhalla Golf Club. Listen, won't you, to the sounds of greatness, the sounds of history, the sounds of a champion. . . .

"What's happening?"

"Shhhhh."

"I can't see."

"I can't move."

"What smells?"

"Shhhhh."

"Who's putting?"

"Either Tiger or another guy."

"What are they putting for?"

"Either three or four."

(Loud cheer.)

"What happened?"

"Somebody either made it or missed it."

"For what?

"For either birdie or par."

"This is so special."

"Once in a lifetime."

■   ■   ■

So you want to watch Tiger Woods play golf?

No, you don't.

Watching the sporting universe's most famous resident is like standing in a very small closet. Or a very long subway. Or a very bad dream.

It's dark. It's sweaty. You want your mother.

That way, you can put her on your shoulders and she can tell you what's happening.

Strolling with thousands of others alongside the most exciting athlete of this era is a long walk to nowhere, with occasional stops at nothing.

You can see Tiger. You can occasionally see his swing. You sometimes even can see the flight of his ball.

You can never see all three at the same time.

You might, if you're lucky, watch him putt. Or maybe even watch his putt roll in the hole. But never both.

I know. I tried. I followed him from outside the ropes during the first two days of the PGA Championship this week.

He is leading the tournament with an 11-under-par 133.

But judging from the number of shots I saw from start to finish, he is shooting a 144-under-par zero.

I could have arrived early and camped at one hole and seen everything. Lots of people do that.

But then Woods leaves that hole, and the crowds prevent you from immediately leaving with him, and you're stuck watching Bob Estes and Mathias Gronberg.

For the thousands who insist on following Woods from hole to hole, it's the worst seat in sports.

There are spots behind poles at Fenway Park, but eight profusely sweating people smelling of bourbon won't be leaning on you.

There are places in the stratosphere at the Superdome, but at least you won't spend five hours on your tip-toes.

"This is crazy," said Walter Hill, an Indiana businessman caught in the Woods mob. "So many people, all doing the same thing. You have no idea who is shooting. You have no idea what they shot."

It was worse because Woods was paired with Jack Nicklaus the first two days. But with his six-tournament winning streak and two victories in majors this season, Woods' galleries already had gone from unusual to unbearable.

While crushing other golfers, he inadvertently has crushed his fans.

For them, it's all about noise.

Standing 10-deep around a tee box, they listen for the distinctive sound of his driver.

Standing 20-deep around a green, they listen for the cheers.

A high-pitched shout means that he has just sunk a birdie putt.

A long, low cheer means he has just recorded a par.

A gasp, then silence, then a few stray claps means bogey.

"You learn to listen for the yells," Hill said.

It's also about caps.

When standing on a weed-filled slope on the far side of a green, able to see only Woods' back, one relies on those in front to explain what's happening.

Ask somebody wearing a cap with Dunlop or Mizuno or some resort in Kauai. They always know.

The last time I asked help of somebody wearing a cap with a basketball logo, he told me that he wasn't sure, but he thought

Woods was leading by two points.

For more enterprising fans, it's also about pants.

On several holes Friday, several youngsters waited until everyone was in place around the green before crawling up on their bellies behind them.

Then they watched Woods putt from between people's legs.

"People are like, 'Kid, what are you doing here?'" said Eric Burton, 15. "But how else are we going to see it?"

The only other alternative costs $60, but the crowds were jostling so much, it was nearly impossible to hold one of those nerdy periscopes to your eye.

I watched one tee shot from the middle of a bridge, stuck between two fairways, unable to see or hear or move until Woods already had headed down the fairway and struck his second shot.

I watched one putt while sliding down the back of a green from a spot where, it turns out, I couldn't see anything anyway.

I learned empty fairway viewing spots are empty for a reason.

I ran to one, but it was covered in poison ivy.

I ran to another, and soon was ankle-deep in mud.

But, hey, I was there. I was with Tiger Woods. I breathed his air. I felt his swing. I was in the trenches with him for the beginning of a memorable and dramatic march toward history, a march that will continue today.

What channel is it on again?

September 4, 2001

A State Worth Spinning a Yarn—or a Ball of Twine

Straight up from the storm cellar it comes, rounding the corner, bouncing into our neighborhood. Can you see it? Do you hear it?

Dust on the windshield, wheat stuck to the hood, various other lazy stereotypes belching from the exhaust.

By Saturday it will reach the threshold of our sports conscious-ness, in the form of its two biggest college football teams.

At 9:30 a.m., Kansas University will host UCLA.

At 3:30 p.m. at the Coliseum, Kansas State will invade USC.

An unusual set of pairings, prompting the usual declarations.

Ah, Kansas.

Dorothy, why?

It's difficult to imagine why the innocent young Ms. Gale want-ed so badly to return to the home of the world's most famous Via-gra spokesman.

But it's certainly no coincidence that when she finally did, everything turned black and white.

Ah, Kansas.

Home, home on the range.

That is, of course, the Kansas state song.

It is based on a poem written by an Ohio doctor who reported-ly moved to Kansas only after his fourth wife drove him to drink.

Ah, Kansas.

A great rock band, no?

The good news for Kansans is that the world-renowned group was founded in Topeka.

The bad news is, their biggest hit was about the absolute futility of life.

"Dust in the Wind" is not only a song, it's a Wichita weather report.

Enough, enough.

It is not my mission here to introduce a big-city audience to a small-town opponent by way of tired jokes and arrogant gener-alizations.

Only one person at this newspaper has ever done that properly, and I would never engage in a cheap imitation of Jim Murray.

Besides, I don't want to risk being denied access to the World's Largest Ball of Twine.

Located in Cawker City, it is one of Kansas' top attractions, a 17,000-plus pound ball constructed as an everlasting monument to the dangers of having too much time on one's hands.

Which, really, is the intent of this column.

I wish to warn the locals that, irrespective of speed or strength, these Kansas football players are ominously bored out of their gourds.

There is a point in Kansas, near Lebanon in Smith County that is considered the geographical center of the continental United States.

Which means, then, that the continental United States is a doughnut?

Only through Saturday's appearance of their football teams will some of us realize that Kansas is even there.

It is a state whose most famous town, Kansas City, is mostly in Missouri.

It is a state whose most famous football town, Manhattan, was stolen from New York.

Even the state animal, the buffalo, doesn't belong to them.

It is now the mascot of the University of Colorado, as Kansas State chose another animal common to the state's rolling wheat fields, the . . . wildcat?

Kansas University, meanwhile, decided to attach itself to the name of Civil War guerrillas known as the "Jayhawkers."

There not being many bears roaming Westwood, it is unfair here to criticize nicknames.

Besides, I don't want to be risk being denied access to state's most famous birthplace, the Wichita spot where a couple of guys dreamed up Pizza Hut.

Early American explorers once deemed Kansas, with its endless barren plains, uninhabitable.

That would be news today not only to those farmers who have made this the country's top wheat-producing state, but also to those oddball pioneers who have made this the country's leading purveyor of the eccentric.

Only in Kansas can you find a museum that contains the world's largest prairie dog and two five-legged cows . . . and a town featuring Big Brutus, the giant earth mover.

Equally celebrated are native Amelia Earhart and Grace Bedell

Billings, the little girl for whom there is a monument celebrating the letter she once wrote Abe Lincoln suggesting that he grow a beard.

Fitting perfectly into this genre are the football teams, neither of which, in national polls, has ever finished a season ranked higher than sixth.

Kansas State likes to think it has become a power under Coach Bill Snyder. But USC may be its first non-conference opponent in recent years that actually gives football scholarships.

Kansas, meanwhile, hasn't had a winning season since UCLA wore their offense out in the Jayhawks' 51-30 romp over the Bruins in the 1995 Aloha Bowl.

Most expect Kansas State to defeat USC this weekend, while UCLA is expected to demolish Kansas. But in one way, it has long been a Los Angeles sweep.

You know that movie for which the folks of Kansas are most famous?

It turns out, it was never supposed to involve them.

In the original Wizard of Oz book by Frank Baum, there is no mention of any state.

It was added there by Hollywood, which decided Dorothy should be from Kansas, although somehow resisting having her dance the yellow brick road with a five-legged cow.

January 1, 2001

This Band Has All Others Beat

Hey drum.

Beat it.

I wouldn't dare. I know the rules. Nobody touches you but senior citizens and little kids and celebrities and those six Purdue students who guard you with ax handles.

Those aren't ax handles, they're drumsticks.

Whatever. Some drunk waving a knife once had his arm broken by one of those drumsticks. Among revered and protected Indiana monuments, you rank second only to Gene Keady's hair.

So what are you trying to do, snare me for an interview?

Sort of.

Figures. We brought an entire football team here to play Washington in the Rose Bowl, and you want to talk to the 500-pounder who can't move unless pushed.

No, I don't want to talk to one of your offensive linemen; I want to talk to you.

You're as funny as a Ringo Starr movie.

Well, you are the most famous thing about Purdue. In fact, you're probably the most famous thing about this Rose Bowl. "The World's Largest Drum." A corny, yet compelling symbol of college tradition. Things like you have made the Rose Bowl so special for so many years. The game is not about football, it's about a feeling.

So what do you want to know, other than my exact height?

Why can't you give me your exact height?

My crew is afraid that if they announce my size, then somebody will just build a bigger drum. Let's just say I'm over 10 feet tall when mounted on my carriage.

Doesn't the University of Texas also have a giant bass drum?

Yeah. And back in 1961, we challenged it to a contest to see which drum was the biggest. My handlers drove and pushed me from Indiana to Wichita, Kan., to a band convention for the face-off.

And what happened?

The Texas drum never showed, that little rim shot. It forfeited. I won. So there.

A little feisty, aren't we?

I turn 80 years old today. I've been hearing these questions since I was fitted with my first bullskin head in 1921, back when our band director wanted to build something to help us stand out among the ears of corn.

Will we notice you today?

You'll notice little else. I'll spin. I'll shake. I'll sprint downfield.

*While our band is running around playing the usual patriotic stuff,
I'll be marching to the beat of a different . . . well, you know.*

Just you?

*Well, not only me. My six crew members will push me and pound
me and try not to get squashed. I've given them cuts and sprains and
bruises. They wear cleats, batting gloves, ankle braces. To make the
squad, they have to pass a physical exam, not a musical one.*

But the students get paid well, right?

*They are paid nothing. Purdue doesn't even offer a music major.
The kids work at least 10 hours a week, usually more, for a couple
of hours of band credit.*

That's too bad.

*But you know what they say? They say, "Instead of just attend-
ing Purdue we feel like we are Purdue." Even after 80 years, that
still sounds neat.*

That's sort of the point of this interview. You don't have kids like
this on the sidelines of NFL playoff games. You don't have the
heartbeat of entire sports teams usually based in the whomp-
whomp-whomp of a drum. So, do you have a solo?

*A solo? This is a little embarrassing, but I'm so big, even my own
band can't find room for me in their music. I'm not written into any
songs. My handlers just run me around and pound me whenever.*

What about on the sideline during the game?

*After every Purdue score, they hit me once for every point that
we've scored at the time. I've heard about those Pac-10 defenses. I'm
expecting to take a real beating today.*

Do the players ever hit you?

*After special wins, some of them might come down and take a
swing. But you know the rules. Only special people can touch
me. Harry Truman has hit me. Neil Armstrong has hit me. Rob
Ballard has hit me.*

Rob Ballard?

*He's the captain of this year's B.B.D. Crew. I wanted to get his
name in the newspaper, seeing as he's not paid or anything.*

B.B.D. Crew?

Big Bass Drum Crew. What are you, conga impaired?

So why can't just anybody hit you?

Back in 1940, I was forced into a 14-year retirement because my heads kept cracking and they couldn't find a bullskin replacement. While my heads are made of a synthetic material today, and easy to replace, the school doesn't want to risk me injuring myself again.

So what are the exact rules?

I can be hit by anybody older than 60, or shorter than my crewmembers' waists, or important to the university.

Does all this happen at football games?

Oh, no. I've been in inaugural parades, in hospitals, at festivals, everywhere. I'm a bigger star in Indianapolis than Reggie Miller. The Colts even asked me to appear on a "Monday Night Football" game this year, but once I got there, they wanted to drape a cloth over me that would cover my Purdue logo, so my noble crew drove me home.

Do you have any enemies?

Put it this way: In Columbus, I am pelted with buckeyes. In Ann Arbor, I am hit with snowballs. Last year at the Alamodome, some jokers nailed me with frozen tortillas.

You ever feel like just getting lost?

I have been lost. This prankster — probably an Indiana University, Bob-Knight-loving fool — once lifted me into the rafters of the locked armory where I sleep. Then there was my last trip to the Rose Bowl.

Back in 1967?

On the trip there, I was sitting in the last car on the train. While passing through the Rockies, that car disconnected and rolled back toward Kansas City. Railroad workers eventually caught me and hooked me back up with barbed wire from a nearby fence.

How did you get here this time?

By truck, took five days, spent Christmas on the side of some road in New Mexico. But ask me what part of the turkey I had for dinner.

What part?

The drumstick.

You're as funny as a Ringo Starr financial services commercial.

You can write me the check now.

Check?

For this interview.
You want to be paid for talking to me?
I am a poor boy too, pa-rum-pum-pum-pum.

March 11, 1993

Sticks and Stones May Break My Bones, but Banana Slugs Can Never Hurt Me

Those who still can't believe they are being asked to support a hockey team called the Mighty Ducks can be thankful for one thing.

They could be living in Albany, Ga.

Last year, a Class-A baseball team came to that town without a name. After holding a contest in which fans submitted exciting monikers such as Pine Trees, Pecans and Peaches, a club employee scoured the dictionary for another "P" word.

He stopped at polecat.

The definition: an ill-smelling, long-haired member of the weasel family.

The reality: a skunk.

The owners liked the way it sounded, and the Albany Polecats were born.

"Now we have a giant skunk mascot that the kids love; he doesn't spray or anything," said Scott Skadan, general manager, pausing. "But at first, the name created quite a stink."

A duck is not a skunk, but many local hockey fans pinched their noses when the Walt Disney Co. was awarded a National Hockey League franchise in Anaheim and immediately called the team the Mighty Ducks, named after a successful film that it released last year.

Ira Miller of Irvine wrote: "Can't you hear ESPN showing hockey highlights and saying, 'Let's roll the Duck tape.'"

But do not despair, all of you who will not be able to watch a hockey game in Anaheim without thinking of Emilio Estevez and a bunch of snot-nosed kids. You do not have the worst name in sports.

You are not the UC Santa Cruz Banana Slugs.

Or the Bryn Mawr (Pa.) Mawrters.

Or the Scottsdale (Ariz.) Community College Artichokes.

Or the Presbyterian (S.C.) College Blue Hose.

And chances are, you will never feel compelled to lie about your nickname as Tom Rowland, former football star for the Illinois College Blueboys once did.

Rowland was drafted by the Green Bay Packers in 1968. When he stood on his chair in the training room one night and prepared to make the traditional rookie speech, he panicked.

"I stood up and shouted, 'I am Tom Rowland of the Illinois College Tigers,'" Rowland recalled. "[Hall of Fame player] Ray Nitschke was sitting there looking at me with no teeth. There was no way I was saying Blueboys."

Rowland, the track and wrestling coach at the college, has since tried to change the name to Fighting Blue. But since it came from the days when students fought in the Civil War and were known as Blue Boys, the traditionalists at this oldest school in Illinois (established in 1829) will not bend.

The folks at Concordia College are also not in a hurry to change their name, the Cobbers, even though it originated as an insult from a cross-town rival in Moorhead, Minn.

In the 1940s, the football team played in a cornfield, so they were known as the Corn Cobs. The name was eventually shortened, and accepted.

"It's pretty tough to find a logo," admitted Armin Pipho, athletic director.

In the name business, sometimes the most insignificant bit of history can stick with, and haunt, a school forever.

In 1919, the Arkansas Tech football team upset heavily favored state rival Jonesboro, 14-0, with two 70-yard runs by a 17-year-old quarterback named John Tucker.

A local sportswriter referred to the team as the Wonder Boys, and despite annual protests, the name has remained unchanged.

"The new guys come in here and always want to change the name to some bird or animal," said Sandra Cole, the longtime athletic department secretary. "But then they graduate and decide they want to be Wonder Boys forever."

As those with the Delaware Fightin' Blue Hens will agree, history plays an important role in the acceptance of odd names.

A sports psychologist there, noting that Blue Hens was originally the name of a local militia during the Revolutionary War, says it is this perspective that the Mighty Ducks lack.

"Blue Hens means something to the people here," said Eric Denson, a consultant to the Delaware athletic department. "The problem I see with Mighty Ducks is not so much the name, but how they arrived at the name.

"I mean, to name a team after a Disney movie is a joke."

Jay Coakley, a professor of sociology at the University of Colorado at Colorado Springs, said the naming of the Ducks is part of a recent trend that ignores history.

"Initially, nicknames were descriptive terms referring to a social characteristic of that team, something other than just the team's geographic location, a way of identifying that team," Coakley said. "But more recently, marketing considerations have become much more important in nicknames. And I'm not so sure that was their original intent."

The origin of the Mighty Ducks name, indeed, appears to be a bigger problem than the name itself.

"Ducks, by themselves, are not bad names," said Mike Cunningham, associate curator of birds at the Los Angeles Zoo.

"Ducks fiercely defend their territory," Cunningham explained. "Ducks stick together. And when two ducks fight, well. . . .One duck will grab the other duck with his beak and hold him, then pummel him with his wings.

"That fits the hockey image, I suppose."

Cunningham said, however, that he has never encountered a

"mighty" duck.

"Knowing where that came from, I think that conjures up a whole different image," he said.

Those who named the Mighty Ducks would have done well to follow the example of their fellow quackers in Eugene, Ore. Few make fun of the Oregon Ducks, even though their mascot is actually Donald Duck in disguise.

"We just don't call him Donald," said Jamie Klund, assistant sports information director. "But that's Donald."

Oregon's Ducks evolved from the "Webfoots," a name given to fishermen from Massachusetts in the 1700s. When the fishermen later migrated to Oregon's Willamette Valley, the name came with them.

In the 1950s, it was changed to Ducks to make it easier for fans and headline writers. Leo Harris, then-athletic director, used his friendship with Walt Disney to gain exclusive use of the Donald Duck caricature.

Until last week, Oregon was the only professional or college organization with a Ducks name.

They were also the only organization with a woman's booster club called the Daisy Ducks.

"I tell you what, though," Klund said. "I could think of worse things to be called."

Like the Colby College (Maine) White Mules.

Or the Akron (Ohio) Zips.

Or the New York University Violets.

Or The Evergreen State College (Wash.) Geoducks.

A geoduck (pronounced gooey-duck) clam sometimes is found on the campus of The Evergreen State College. It is also commemorated in a giant clam costume sometimes worn by the school president.

The Anaheim hockey team could also have been called the Mud Hens, a name that is so bad that people often don't believe that the Triple-A baseball team in Toledo is for real.

"Because Jamie Farr wore our hats on the MASH show, quite a few people think we're something just on television," said Joe

Napoli, assistant general manager. "These people will drive through town during the summer and are surprised that we really exist."

And yes, there really is such a thing as a mud hen.

It is the name for a bird that waddled through the marshlands where the original Toledo professional baseball team played in the late 1800s.

Club officials would have adopted the bird's real name, but they didn't want to be known as the Toledo Coots.

The Mighty Ducks at least have the good sense of timing to start up during a sports year in which the world baseball champions were Blue Jays and the national collegiate basketball champions were Blue Devils.

Some in Toronto still believe that the organization wasn't really named after a Blue Jay — "I've never seen one downtown," said Jim Proudfoot, veteran columnist for the Toronto Star — but in deference to the owners' beer operation.

Labatt's, which owned 45% of the club then and owns twice as much now, has a popular beer known as "Blue." Observers say brewery officials would have done anything to make that word prominent. In any case, a public contest was held and Blue Jays was declared the winner.

"No matter what, we can't cast any stones at other nicknames," Proudfoot said. "After all, we have a hockey team that is a grammatical error."

He is speaking, of course, of the Toronto Maple Leafs.

Not to be confused with the Goshen (Ind.) College Maple Leaves.

As the Maple Leafs prove, the Mighty Ducks won't even have the oddest name in the National Hockey League.

After all, what is a Red Wing?

The team in Detroit is actually lucky it is not called the Winged Wheelers, the name of the Montreal-based hockey team for which industrialist James Norris once played.

When Norris founded a team in Detroit, he brought the name with him, then shortened it and added the color of the team's jerseys. A winged wheel is still the team's logo.

OK, you ask, then what about the New York Rangers? How

much sense does that make?

It made plenty of sense to friends of promoter Tex Rickard, who helped bring hockey to Madison Square Garden in 1926. His buddies called the team Tex's Rangers, and it stuck.

Which, of course, does not explain the league's other funky name, belonging to Pittsburgh.

Nobody makes fun of the Penguins' name anymore because, well, after consecutive Stanley Cup championships, people in town would welcome the bird as a pet.

But the truth remains that experts say the penguin can be just as inappropriate mascot material as a duck.

"In fact," said Cunningham of the Los Angeles zoo, "penguins don't necessarily move better on ice than ducks. They can both be pretty clumsy."

So why Penguins? Tom Singer, an Orange County freelance writer, has been thinking about that for the better part of his life.

In the spring of 1967, as a high school senior in Pittsburgh, Singer entered a contest to choose the name of the new hockey franchise.

On a whim, he submitted Penguins.

Shortly thereafter, while he was debating whether to attend the University of Pittsburgh or UCLA on academic scholarship, Penguins was announced as the winner.

His decision was made for him. He flew to California.

"I wanted to get out of town before anybody found out that I had anything to do with that name," he said.

January 31, 1998

He's Just a Tourist at the Track

My first association with drag racing occurred as a cub reporter on the rewrite desk, when a local promoter phoned with information about a race.

The winner, I wrote, "toured the course in 5.1 seconds."

The next day, an editor summoned me with words to live by:

"Son, in drag racing, they do not tour the course."

I thought of that Friday when I drove to a quarter-mile stretch of Pomona concrete and asphalt, attending my first drag race while trying to understand why more than 100,000 will show up this weekend for the NHRA Winternationals.

Once there, interviewing Upland driver Bobby Baldwin in pit row, I was given new words to live by.

"Drag racing is rorrrrrrr, coughcoughcough, sputtersputterputter, and it's good for rrrrrrrr, arggggg, screeeeech and they love it," he said.

Drag racing is loud. It is the loudest thing I have ever attended that didn't take place during a Forum timeout.

It is so loud, the noise literally blows the baseball caps off the guys working the starting line.

It is so loud, the hottest sellers in the souvenir stands are $1 ear plugs.

But I grrrrrrrr howwwwwwwlll digress.

I was hesitant to attend this phenomenon because it violated two personal rules:

1) Never associate with any type of automobile that requires the use of a parachute.

2) Never cover any sports event televised by The Nashville Network.

My fears were initially quelled, though, when it appeared that drag racing is just like the more popular stock car and Indy car racing.

There is a giant inflatable beer can. Cigarettes are cool. The women dress like Johnny Cash.

Along pit row, fans rush to surround any car making unmentionable sounds and spitting out unthinkable poisons. They remain there, holding their ears and sucking in fumes, until the car shuts down, at which point they look as if they just lost their best friend.

It is when those cars leave the pits that drag racing becomes different from other motor sports.

This sport is simple. It's straightforward. Two cars line up side by side, a green light flickers and two drivers respond to the intricate directive of "Floor it!"

In the final race, the first car to cross the finish line wins, and heaven help you if the parachute won't work.

Or, heaven help some poor Pomona citizen. There is a public street at the end of the Pomona Raceway track, beyond a sand pit and a giant net. No car has ever reached that point, but what a SigAlert that would be.

We have a new accident to report. . . . A motorist reportedly traveling in excess of 300 mph hit the back of a truck hauling sofas. . . .

The races this weekend are divided into three, easy-to-understand categories.

There are pro stocks, which means, essentially, your car. Next year I'm thinking about entering my van. Throw some kids in the back, tell me that McDonald's closes in five minutes and I'll win that sucker.

Then there are funny cars, so named because of their unusual design. Not so hilarious are the presence of escape hatches on the hood so, in an accident, drivers can leap out before they become French toast.

Finally, there are top fuels, which look like real race cars and eat fuel like my van. For one five-second race, they use 15 gallons of nitromethane, at about $20 a gallon.

Big Daddy Don Garlits and Shirley Muldowney were once top-fuel drivers, which I mention because, before Friday, they were the only two drag racers I had heard of.

Garlits is retired and runs a museum in Florida. Muldowney — "Heart Like a Wheel," remember? — is still so crusty at age 57, she has trouble getting sponsors for big events and has been reduced to running match races.

Only in drag racing, it seems, could a legitimate legend be forced to continue earning her way.

It is the nature of the sport. Simple rules, no turns and anybody can try it.

Walk through NASCAR pits and bump into corporations like Earnhardt and Gordon and Jarrett.

Walking through the pits of Pomona on Friday, I bumped into a guy who drives heavy machinery during the day, an 18-year-old woman who won a race on prom night, a former NBA star and a Hall of Fame NFL coach.

Not to mention thousands of exhaust-filled fans who take advantage of drag racing's unique rule that allows anyone to hang out with the drivers.

"This is P.T. Barnum out here," said John Force, seven-time national funny car champion from Yorba Linda. "This is the big top."

Force is a former truck driver whose racing has made him a millionaire. He is swarmed by fans at every step here.

Yet if you are saying "John who?" you are not alone.

Drag racing, which officially began in Southern California, is not about showtime. It's about the old times.

"It goes back to the days in California when everybody first realized, to live here, you have to have a car," Force said. "Soon, everybody had cars and people wanted to see how fast those cars would go. . . ."

Today, Cristen Powell, an 18-year-old from Portland, has a car and an NHRA national win.

"You get in there and go 'Whoooh,'" she explained.

Larry Nance, former NBA dunk king, drives a car. Joe Gibbs, former Washington Redskin coach, has two cars.

There is Bobby Baldwin, the heavy equipment operator from Upland, talking about why he left work at noon on Friday to bring a car here for qualifying.

"What I like best is when rrroarrrrrrr you are in that car, going for the finish line, and you can't see grrrrrrr the other car . . . you can only hear it behind you," he said from the pits. "That's the best feeling in the rroarrrrr, grrrrrr, screeeeecch. . . ."

CHAPTER SIX

Fair or Foul?

May 30, 1999

Dodger Victory Is Your Typical Walk in the Park

They were Dodgers, but they weren't. They were part of the club, but not really.

They were like, well, like you and me and anyone else who long ago fell in love with the hometown team and couldn't shake it.

They pitched batting practice. That was their job. Though small and insignificant, that was their link.

It was usually for only home games. It was usually only 15 minutes of pitching, per day, per man, about 125 fastballs down the middle so the Dodger hitters could get loose.

Mike McDermott. Juarez Orman. Tom Aloi.

You've never heard of them. You'd have no reason to hear of them.

In real life, two of them were delivery truck drivers, the other operated heavy equipment. During the summers they were human pitching machines. It's not a big deal.

Until they looked up this season, and it sort of was a big deal. They realized, combined, they had been with the Dodgers for 73 years. Between them they had World Series rings and historic baseballs and memories of every great moment from Koufax to Gibson.

The smallest and most insignificant of link had become, in their minds, a strong one.

"This was not our main job or anything, but it was our family," McDermott said.

Then it wasn't.

Last month, a businesswoman with the new Fox Dodgers summoned them to her office, where an assistant general manager with the new Fox Dodgers fired them on the spot.

Nothing personal, he told them. Your work was fine. It's your salary we can no longer afford.

The three batting practice pitchers each made about $45 a day. Or about $4,000 a year. Or about what Kevin Brown makes for *one pitch*.

They were fired in the middle of the season because they were making too much money in a job that, after a combined 73 years, they would have done for free.

They walked away from the suits in shock. They couldn't sleep. They had trouble facing their friends.

Aloi's wife and children wept. It took McDermott two weeks before he could even tell anybody.

They know they were lucky even to be associated with the team. They know that in the scheme of things, they really didn't matter.

But when you fall in love with something far bigger than yourself, you never realize just how much you don't matter until it's much too late.

It wasn't as if the Fox Dodgers fired three important employees. It was as if they fired three fans.

A metaphor for us all.

■   ■   ■

Mike McDermott remembers the 1977 World Series, standing on the pitching mound at Yankee Stadium, a former neighborhood batboy now throwing batting practice to the National League champions.

"Looking around at all the tradition, thinking that this was really me in the middle of it all. . . ," he said. "It was a feeling I'll never forget."

Juarez Orman remembers the time Bob Welch gave him his first taste of chewing tobacco.

"I'm chewing it on the mound, and I get real dizzy, and Steve Yeager is yelling at me to throw it over the plate," he recalled. "So I yell back, 'I'll throw it over, you just hit the damn ball!' Everybody got real quiet. That tobacco had made me crazy."

They have dusty duffel bags filled with stories like this, of laughter and competition and bonding with what they considered the greatest family on earth.

"When Peter O'Malley owned the team, no matter how small you were, you felt like a part of it," McDermott said. "You were included."

McDermott, 49, known by every Dodger for the last three decades as "Mac," had been here 31 years.

Orman, also 49, had been here 24 years.

Aloi, 43, who also had the thankless job of catching batting practice, had been with them for 18 years.

As the years progressed, their arms grew wearier, their fastballs slowed, but this was only batting practice, and this was a place where loyalty mattered, where Fred Claire once treated them as if they were Orel Hershiser.

And they never took this good fortune for granted.

Even though they wore Dodger jerseys with their names on the back, they never signed an autograph without explaining to the fan that they were "only" batting practice pitchers.

They shagged flies in the late-afternoon heat, played monotonous games of pepper with the likes of Maury Wills and Willie Davis, hustled from the field before the first pitch and dressed in a vacant back room so they could stay out of the way.

"They were great guys, they loved the game, they were fun to be around," Steve Garvey recalled this week, after expressing shock that they had been fired. "Those poor guys' arms have to be hanging after all these years. . . . Did they at least give them a watch?"

Not exactly.

McDermott did receive a 30-year pin during a ceremony this winter. Only four other people — Vin Scully and Tom Lasorda are two of them — had been with the club longer.

"While there had been a lot of changes, I thought, this was so nice, some things have stayed the same," McDermott said.

When he showed up this season, he realized he was wrong.

The new, younger coaching staff was pitching most of the batting practice. A left-hander — an important pregame asset — had been hired to pitch batting practice and work in the video room.

"We were reacting to the needs of the staff," General Manager Kevin Malone said. "While we really appreciate what these three men did for all these years, there was just no longer a need."

Understandable, all of it.

What confused the three men was the reason given to them in that upstairs office after batting practice on April 25.

Said Aloi: "When they told us we were being fired because we made too much money, our mouths dropped open."

Said Malone: "Contrary to popular belief, we do have a budget. We took the money those three guys made and put it into one guy who could also work video and travel."

But do these cost-cutting measures include treating longtime employees like strangers?

None of the coaches said anything to them on the field before they were summoned upstairs.

Since they have been fired, they have not received one call from anyone in the organization.

They were given 10 games' worth of severance pay. They said Gina Galasso from human resources told them they would continue receiving their employee allotment of free tickets whenever they desired.

But McDermott has since learned that his name was taken off the master ticket list. And he says that "seven or eight" phone calls to the human resources office for clarification have gone unreturned.

"You tell them, if they have problems with tickets, anything like that, call my office, we'll take care of them," said Bill Geivett, the assistant general manager who delivered the bad news. "Those guys have put in a lot of years, and they deserve to be taken care of."

That part is probably a moot point. None of the three will be going to games for a while. They never thought losing a part-time job would hurt so bad.

"We all knew our time would come," McDermott said. "But nobody thought it would happen like this. In the middle of the season? Being told like we were told?"

McDermott was so embarrassed, when a longtime friend asked him for some free tickets, instead of telling the friend he had been fired, he quietly arranged for the tickets to be purchased and left at the window like freebies.

When another friend asked McDermott to get a souvenir signed by Raul Mondesi — usually a slam dunk — McDermott said fine.

He still has the souvenir. It is still unsigned. He doesn't know what he will do with it, or when he will tell his friend.

"It's weird, I used to know everybody there, everybody,"

McDermott said. "But now, I feel like an outsider."

Don't we all.

June 27, 1998

All Grown Up

TOMBALL, TEXAS — Twenty-five years later, David Clyde asks if you want to see the scars.

He is shoveling through weeds in a rusty rail yard in southeast Texas. The sun is high, the air is tight, like a wool straitjacket, 100 degrees, an oven-roasted breeze.

Clyde swats at an unseen bug, stares up at a graffiti-covered brown boxcar, hulking and packed with yellow pine. He and his crew have been fighting to move and unload that car for four hours. They will be here four more hours, until 11 p.m., working behind a forklift with lights.

Tomorrow he will get a break, leave the lumberyard, hustle over to watch one of his two boys play baseball. He will crouch behind the home-plate fence for another four hours, working the game as hard as he works the wood.

He lives the furious life of a man making up for lost time, so it's not surprising that he suddenly smiles, puts down the shovel, pulls off his shirt.

There, on his left shoulder, snaking across the white skin, are two red results of operations representing but a cinder in one of the most brilliant burnouts in major league baseball history. So brilliant, sometimes it still hurts to look.

Oh, you say. *Those* scars.

. . .

Twenty-five years later, David Clyde goes to a baseball game. The Texas Rangers play in a new park, but they are still the Texas Rangers, and he still gets free tickets, and he drives up to

Arlington after a long week of work.

He looks around at the fancy new stands and nice seats and con-tending team and can't help but think, if he doesn't take the mound on that June 27 evening in 1973, maybe none of this exists.

He was drafted first in the nation out of high school. Fitted for a major league uniform a couple of days later. Took the mound as an 18-year-old with an entire state hollering in his ear. Breathed life into a franchise on the verge of being shipped out of town.

Now he is a fan. They don't know him. He doesn't care. He takes his seat. The game drags on. It has been a long week. In the eighth inning, his family looks at him with amusement.

At probably his only game this season, David Clyde falls asleep.

"The sport is not what it used to be," says Clyde, and neither is he.

Twenty-five years ago, he was the most famous baseball player in the country, attending his senior prom one day, pitching for the Texas Rangers against the Minnesota Twins the next. No minor leagues, no preparation, all fastball and flash and future.

Today, one 18-win career later, he is the calloused example of why the sports world should never try anything like that again.

Twenty-five years ago, he was a child king, the first of the media age, before Kobe Bryant, before Kerry Wood, before any of those kids incessantly trotted out as the next something-or-other.

Today, with a boxcar full of hardened memories, he is the living lesson that these gifted children should be careful what they wish, and should never do so with eyes closed.

Once he was known as the Houston high school star who struck out three of every four batters and finished his senior year at 18-0 with a 0.18 earned-run average.

Then he was known as the kid who wowed the nation by win-ning a major league game a few days after winning a state high school semifinal game.

Today, the résumé is different:

Only three full major league seasons. An 18-33 lifetime record. More strikeouts in his senior year of high school (328) than in his big league career (228).

Two failed marriages. A bout with alcoholism. A reputation for high and fast and silly living.

A boy who had to fit in among men and, understandably, failed miserably.

Today, around draft time, baseball development people say "David Clyde" the way a mother says, "Measles."

"He was the nicest kid you'd ever want to meet, but he was like Jack Nicholson in 'The Shining,'" said former Ranger teammate Jeff Burroughs. "He did a slow disintegration."

Today, David Clyde has landed in a small country town north of Houston and beyond all that. He has a happy and stable marriage of 16 years, a tough but good job, three children who fill his expansive brick home with laughter.

But the past never quite leaves him, as he hustles about this town of 6,370 as if determined never to be short-changed again.

He runs a successful lumberyard — of which he is the co-owner — like a baseball manager. He gives motivational talks, hands out bonuses, spends eight hours with a boxcar as a manager pitches batting practice.

He works his two teenage boys as if he was their pitching coach. The other day, he was hassling a youth league umpire so much that the ump flashed him an obscene gesture behind his back.

"You can't change what happened yesterday," he says. "But you can sure as hell learn from it."

He wasn't the only one who learned.

Because of Clyde, every professional team sport is careful to offer mentoring and support to the ones who arrive young.

He entered the game as a pioneer. He left it as a sacrifice.

Twenty-five years later, he has grudgingly accepted that one man can be both.

Only sometimes, maybe when the tears flow while reading a scrapbook about a bushy-haired future Hall of Famer that never was, does he wonder why that man had to be him.

"I'm not bitter at all," he says. "Maybe . . . melancholy is more like it."

· · ·

Twenty-five years ago, everyone wanted to be David Clyde.

What mid-1970s high school kid struggling with sports and girls and acne didn't?

We couldn't imagine what it would be like to walk away from the suffocating high school hallway and into the national spotlight, a big league uniform, a big league mound, a nation watching, a beautiful girl waiting.

Some of us would have given the rest of our lives just to be David Clyde on June 27, 1973. Turns out, the only one who did was David Clyde.

The tale is a common one. An owner (Bob Short) moves his struggling team (the Washington Senators) to the Sunbelt (Arlington, Texas, in 1972) in hopes of recouping his fortune.

But the new town's heart is with football, not baseball, and even with Ted Williams as manager, the team loses 100 games and can't draw flies.

In 1973, Whitey Herzog becomes the manager, but the Rangers are still lousy and crowds are still low and Short needs to sell the team, but nobody in Arlington will buy it and here come the moving vans again and. . . .

Along comes a kid from down the road who throws so hard, so fine, that fans stand four deep along outfield fences just to watch him pitch.

Three days before the draft, Herzog calls Gene Clyde, the father of this young pitcher, with some good news and bad news.

"We're going to take your son with the first pick," Herzog told the elder Clyde.

Before Clyde could say anything, Herzog quickly added, "But our owner wants to bring him right to the major leagues. I do not want this to happen. This should not happen. But this is a cruel, harsh world. And it's going to happen."

For what amounted to a $100,000 bonus, the Clydes weren't about to stop it from happening.

"What was I supposed to do, tell them to send me to Pocatello?" Clyde says today. "I still remember that one statement, 'How would you like to go to the big leagues?' That one statement numbed me."

It did the same to 35,698 Ranger fans, who filled Arlington Stadium for the first time in franchise history when Clyde made his
debut against the Twins.

There were cameras at his breakfast table, cameras in the
bullpen when he was warming up, 10,000 fans listening on their
car radios because they could not get in, fans even following on a
scoreboard in the Houston Astrodome.

At the time, it may have been the most publicized regular-sea-
son sporting event in this country's history.

"There were people and cameras and press everywhere — yet I
was more nervous than David was," catcher Ken Suarez remembers.

Clyde walked the first two batters, Jerry Terrell and Rod Carew.
He struck out Bobby Darwin, George Mitterwald and Joe Lis to
end the first inning.

By game's end, he had given up one hit and two earned runs in
five innings with eight strikeouts. And the Rangers had won, 4-3.

"How do you describe living your dream?" Clyde says.

For the rest of the 1973 season, more than a third of the people
who came to watch the Rangers play came on the nights Clyde
would pitch. They saw him win only four of 12 decisions with a
5.03 ERA, but he struck out 74 batters in 93 innings and everyone could see the boyish magic.

What they didn't see were the boyish problems.

His first day with the team, he remembers sitting in a hotel lobby,
wide-eyed, watching the players walk in wearing fancy clothes —
"One of them even carried a purse!" — and fancy attitudes.

The first guy he met was another pitcher who, upon shaking
Clyde's hand, said, "Don't expect me to be your friend, because
you're trying to take my job."

The older guys he met said something equally dangerous,
something about joining them after the game for a drink.

"Some of us bent over backward trying to make him feel at
home," catcher Rich Billings says. "Maybe too far backward."

He began partying after games with a group of thirty-some-
thing players once described as baseball's "Hell's Angels."

At a time when most kids his age were enjoying their last summer at home, he was traveling the country alone, vulnerable and desperate to belong.

"I was honored that they would ask me to go drinking," he says. "So I drank."

A kid who barely drank in high school — and who wasn't even legally allowed to drink in many states — began partying all night after he pitched and showing up at some day games with a hangover.

He once almost didn't show up at all, barely running onto a commercial flight as it was leaving Boston.

His teammates noticed that he was wearing the same clothes from the night before.

"He looked like he had all it took to make it," Burroughs says. "But he was the epitome of a kid who was mentally not ready to make the jump to the big life."

He was never flashy, but soon he was buying expensive jewelry, once being ripped off by a clubhouse salesman with phony rubies.

He walked into a car dealership with $7,500 in bills, hoping to pay cash on the spot for a $6,000 Buick. Where most of the Rangers lived in apartments, he bought a fancy condo.

Then there was his high school sweetheart, who thought his new riches meant they were getting married. She wept when he told her no, so he felt bad and married her anyway.

"He would see all the older players being met by their wives at the airport, and he didn't like being alone," his father says. "It was hard for him to feel like he belonged."

That marriage lasted a year. His second marriage lasted two years. In both cases, it was about a boy trying to hurry his journey into manhood, a boy in a world with no peers or support.

"I never really had anyone," Clyde said.

Although Clyde hated disco music, he would follow the older players to discos. He had never smoked more than a cigarette or two a day, yet soon he was up to two packs a day, even smoking in the dugout runway between innings.

He once phoned his father at 3:30 a.m. and told him that he was firing his agent and wanted his father to represent him.

"I said 'Son, I'll do it, go to bed,'" Gene recalls. "There was a lot of times he should have been in bed."

"But," Billings said, "instead of tucking him in, the older guys were taking him out to get a toddy."

Clyde still managed to stay on his feet until he met Billy Martin.

Martin, who never liked youngsters anyway, replaced Herzog at the end of the 1973 season and made it clear that he hated the very idea of an 18-year-old pitcher.

He told owner Short that Clyde belonged in the minor leagues. Short, needing the money and attention Clyde generated, refused.

In 1974, after Clyde began his second season 3-0, Martin moved him to the bullpen and refused to pitch him for a month.

"It's not polite to speak about someone who can't speak back, but . . . Billy Martin set out to destroy me," Clyde says.

He would ask to throw long relief. Martin said no. He would ask to pitch batting practice. Martin said no.

When he asked to throw in the bullpen during games, Martin agreed, but the minute Clyde bounced a curveball, the phone would ring, and he would be ordered to sit down.

"Billy and I told them all he couldn't pitch here," recalls Art Fowler, Martin's longtime pitching coach. "You couldn't put him in the ballpark, he couldn't throw the ball over the plate."

Records and witnesses indicate otherwise. Several players interviewed for this story said Clyde had an excellent curveball and was improving his control. In 1973, he walked 47 batters in 117 innings, but when he finally was given a chance to pitch, he followed his early win streak with nine consecutive losses.

"I never said anything because I was taught to respect my elders," Clyde says. "But when you hear somebody keep saying you can't do something. . . ."

In 1975, after Martin accused him of quitting on the mound, Clyde was sent to the minor leagues, in Pittsfield, Mass.

Relief? Too late for that. He was as much of an outcast in the minors because of his big league dress and reputation.

Says Clyde: "I'm not going to worry about spilled milk, but looking back, I should have told the Rangers, 'Do not draft me because I will not sign with you. Under any circumstances. For any price.'"

He was eventually traded to Cleveland, where, in 1978, Clyde was 8-11 and Manager Jeff Torborg believed he was finally ready to be a big league pitcher at 23.

But the next spring, his late-night habits persisted, seriously exacerbating an ulcer. Then, within six months of their child being born and home being purchased, his second wife walked out on him.

"All of a sudden, the roof caved in," Torborg said. "It was sad. It was really sad."

Three years and two teams and only three major league wins later, at the ripe old age of 26, Clyde retired.

He was pitching an Instructional League game for the Astros when he looked around the field, noticed that suddenly he had become the old man and realized he was tired of not belonging.

"I thought, 'What am I doing here?'" he said. "I walked off after the game and never came back."

If only he had known that if he had returned to the major leagues for 27 more days, he would have qualified for a pension that today would have paid him as much as $40,000 a year.

If only David Clyde had known a lot of things.

"What they did to him was one of the worst things I've seen in baseball," Herzog once said.

Or, what they didn't do.

And what they will never do again.

"That's one positive," Clyde says. "What happened to me, they won't let happen to anyone else."

•   ■   ■

Twenty-five years later, David Clyde, 43, is feeling sorry for no one.

He has been crouching in his usual position between the backstop and press box at Tomball High, spitting sunflower seeds, wedged in for an inning watching his son Reed, 14, struggle in a youth league game.

This is about the only baseball he sees or talks about these days.

There are a few mementos hanging in a cluttered rec room in his house, including a framed telegram he received before his debut from Sandy Koufax. But nothing at his lumberyard office and store. New employees sometimes work as long as six months before learning of his past life.

He still attends old-timers' games when asked, and the Rangers still treat him like an honored alumnus, but that's no longer his focus.

On this Saturday night, Reed is.

"C'mon, 32, throw the ball," he shouts through the fence. "I mean, 18."

No. 32? That was once David Clyde's number, and is often worn by his sons.

Reed struggles, walking consecutive batters. His father sighs, spits some seeds, shouts, "Relax, 18."

Reed is removed from the game, finds his father afterward, asks for help.

"Can we pitch again on Tuesday?" he says.

"Tomorrow," Clyde says.

February 12, 1998

At Heart of the Cart Issue

Just look at the size of that cart.

It was given by a judge to Casey Martin on Wednesday, and just look at it.

It's more than big enough for a weak-legged golfer who only wanted a chance to make a living playing golf.

It's more than big enough for those disabled citizens asking not for a head start, but equal footing.

It's big enough for all of us, this wondrous cart, deep and wide, with the strength to carry society uphill toward a new level of humanity.

Maybe we moved only an inch Wednesday, maybe not that

much, but we moved, we advanced, the scenery has changed.

So jump on, why don't you?

Maybe you already have.

Maybe you are one of the millions who have never hit a golf ball that wasn't purple, who've dated Big Bertha but would never own one. Maybe by watching this battle between Martin and the PGA Tour, you have realized two very important things.

Golfing is not walking. Walking is not golfing.

You understand that giving Casey Martin a cart, while violating the rules of the PGA Tour, is not like giving a sore-legged baseball player a designated runner.

It is, instead, like giving that player cab fare to the stadium.

You look at the statistics and realize, even when golfers can have carts, as they do on the senior tour, they don't want them.

Golfers lose the rhythm of the course with a cart. Golfers lose time to think with a cart.

You figured out that Casey Martin was not asking for implementation of special treatment, but the end of a silly tradition.

He got it. For the sake of all silly traditions that exclude and isolate, today is glorious indeed, and you celebrate.

But maybe not.

Maybe you are a weekend hacker who still believes that a part of golfing must be walking, because that is the way you were taught, the way it has always been done.

No judge is going to convince you that an entire sport should change its rules for one competitor, because rules are rules, and men are men.

You have to use a cart when you play on Saturday mornings at your country club, but only because it is required, you would never do it on your own, no way, you will walk until you keel.

And if that accident happens to crush the cigar in your shirt pocket and ham sandwich in your side pocket, so be it.

Maybe you think Casey Martin is a coward. A friend who is the parent of a disabled child and sits on the board of a major charity for the disabled thinks that.

He said that Martin dishonors the effort of all disabled by asking for special treatment. He says he is tired after a day of golf, so carts are special treatment.

Or maybe you're just an old golfer who doesn't want to see anything else in your elite sport change. You like the sweaters, the smokers, the walkers.

Maybe you are like Arnold Palmer and Jack Nicklaus, who, during the trial, took time from their unofficial roles as golf ambassadors to hit Martin with chop blocks.

If so, if you lost Wednesday, there is something you should try to see amid the dust surrounding the splendid collapse of another barrier.

Casey Martin cannot hurt you.

Even if Casey Martin could win a PGA Tour tournament — unlikely considering his right leg is deteriorating by the day — he cannot hurt you.

His presence makes the game of golf more inclusive, more personable, more marketable.

He will not only make the sport more popular, he will make you feel better for having played it.

Fine, critics will say. But now what will the tour do? How will it stop everyone with an ingrown toenail from petitioning to ride on a cart?

What will keep the placid, picturesque weekly tournaments from becoming regular traffic jams?

The golfers, that's who.

PGA Tour officials could use this decision to begin tossing cart keys to every golfer, but the officials had better duck.

Because most of those keys will be tossed back.

If surveys are accurate, only three of 10 golfers would ride carts if they were available. And until statistical evidence exists that carts result in lower scores, it will remain that way.

That's not what the tour will do, of course. It isn't tossing keys to anyone.

It will appeal the decision, dragging Martin's mottled leg through the mud a little longer.

Then once it becomes obvious that the tour has no chance at

victory, it will allow only Martin to ride a cart, forcing others with similar circumstances to beg and fight in the same way.

What Wednesday's decision cleansed, the tour will try to make filthy again, which is what elitist organizations always do when imperfections come to their doors.

Only now, it will not work. The cart is moving now, faster every day, steered with courage, navigated by common sense, Casey Martin at the wheel, millions at his side.

A regular joy ride, it is.

October 26, 2001

The Coach Fired Him Up, the Game Took Him Out

A mother's ringless hands rub her delicate face.

A son scratches his neck, checks his watch, scratches his arm, checks his watch, scratches, checks, scratches, checks.

A mother looks across the room with weary love.

A son smiles back from underneath a partially sunken scalp.

"His father wanted him to play high school football," she says.

"My father," he says.

"I thought it was a dangerous sport," she says.

"Dangerous," he says.

"But those things always happened to someone else, so I said OK," she says.

"Someone else," he says.

"I wish I wouldn't have," she says.

"So do I," he says.

■　■　■

Fall Friday night, anywhere, everywhere.

Teenagers thrust gangly arms through giant paper screens and race onto patches of green that have become the center of America's most curiously colored fabric.

It is high school football, a violent game obscured beneath bright swatches of community, status and religion.

Fall Friday night, an endeavor both fulfilling and frightening.

Somebody wins.

Somebody learns discipline and work ethic.

Somebody loses.

Somebody screams in frustration at a coach who wants him to hurl his young body like a man.

Somebody weeps from the pain of being hit by somebody twice his size.

Sometimes, somebody is broken.

Occasionally, somebody is dead.

Then there are the ones who are a little of both.

The ones we forget.

For them, there is not the closure of a funeral, or the healing of an injury.

For them, the two weeks of flowers and prayers are followed by lifetimes of wheelchairs and braces.

Last season, from among the 1.5 million high school football players, one national survey counted 26 catastrophic injuries.

A low percentage, if you didn't know any of those players.

A stunningly high percentage if you did.

If this were boxing, it would be banned.

But it is fall Friday night, so it is embraced.

Parents hold it close, intoxicated by its power, infatuated with its possibilities.

Parents wrap their most precious jewels in this wondrous fabric without completely comprehending its darker shades.

It started, as in all things football, with a pep talk.

Charlene Wedertz can still hear the pep talk.

It was 1990. She was in a room with other parents of potential freshman football players for Santa Margarita High in Orange County. They listened to Coach Jim Hartigan explain his sport's mission.

"They come in here as boys, and leave as men!" Hartigan barked.

She believed him. Anyone would have believed him.

The daughter and wife of former football players, Charlene was ready to run out of that room and tackle someone.

"I was so inflated by those words," she says.

Eleven years later, she is proof that high school football cannot always keep its promises.

She brought Hartigan a boy, her only son, Darren, a 5-foot-7 scrapper who loved to hit. Eleven years later, he is still a boy.

His brain essentially crushed by a tackle, he is 25, going on 10.

"Like he had a lobotomy," she says.

"It stinks," he says.

Then he smiles. He always smiles.

The injury not only robbed him of some mental acuity, it also took away much of his capacity for sadness or depression.

An ironic consolation prize.

He wakes up happy. He walks through the house singing.

In the nearly nine years since the injury, he says he has cried only once.

"I get him out of bed in the morning and he says, 'How's my beautiful mother?'" Charlene says.

"Isn't she great?" Darren says.

He says it in a raspy voice. A new voice. He squeals when he laughs. A new laugh.

"This is not the son I knew," Charlene says.

He can no longer read, because after one sentence, he has forgotten what he started.

He can no longer enjoy TV, because he can't comprehend anything longer than a sound bite.

He remembers names, but by lunch he forgets what he had for breakfast.

He is paralyzed on his left side, deaf in his left ear, and has no peripheral vision.

"He'll never be able to live alone," Charlene says.

There was a time — the sweetest of times — when he would run up the steps and clomp into the house just before his midnight curfew, looking for something to eat.

These days, after attending the renowned High Hopes adult head injury program in Tustin, he is so exhausted he falls asleep by 8.

He constantly itches. He is constantly checking his watch or asking someone else for the time.

He used to think of nothing but football. Now he doesn't have the attention span to even watch a game.

Even if he could, he wouldn't, because the injury took away the aggressiveness that made football such fun.

"This is somebody entirely different," Charlene says.

"No more football," Darren says.

Different, from that moment in 1992 when he made a tackle in a junior varsity game.

There was nobody in the bleachers, because there were no bleachers.

There was neither ambulance nor paramedics nearby.

There was nothing to indicate that this was anything other than an organized sandlot scrum.

Still, it was part of the fabric.

So tangled in it, Charlene Wedertz was initially afraid to leave the sidelines to comfort her collapsed son.

"He told me to never go out there," she says.

"I thought it would make me look like a sissy," he says.

·   ▪   ·

Pop Warner, in his four decades as a college coach, was renowned for his finesse and safety. Yet it was in a Pop Warner League that Darren Wedertz learned to knock the snot out of people.

"He wasn't aggressive enough, and it would infuriate his father," his mother says of her ex-husband, Howard Wedertz. "He would stand on the sideline and shout at Darren to hit somebody like he was protecting his little sister."

Howard, a Southland pilot and former high school football player who was divorced from Charlene before the injury, says football was a teaching tool.

"In the big picture, a lot of people get many positives from football," he says. "They learn discipline, camaraderie, perseverance. Darren was being taught these things."

By the time he was a scrawny high school freshman, Darren had been taught something else.

"I wanted to hurt people," he says. "I wanted to make them cry."

By the end of his first season, he was one of the freshman team's best players.

As a running back in his sophomore season, he was the junior varsity's MVP.

Teammates called him "Squiggs," for the way he eluded tacklers.

He believed he was not only playing football, but answering a higher calling.

After all, he played for a Catholic school that decorated its game program with lines from hymns.

As a member of the school choir, he would walk through the house singing those hymns.

"It was about an entire experience," his mother says. "It was incredible."

Looking back, Hartigan, the Santa Margarita coach, agrees.

"Darren was a tough kid, a hard-nosed running back," he recalls. "He was going to be one of our good ones, and we've had some good ones."

Then, at the beginning of his junior season, things began to change.

Wedertz had inexplicably lost a step. He was slower. He wasn't improving.

He remained on the junior varsity squad and became a target for coaches who were concerned that he wasn't giving his best.

Late in the season, he called his mother from school and asked her to meet him at home.

He told her he wanted to quit. He told her he couldn't take the constant scolding, the exertion of playing in two JV games and a varsity game every week.

"He plopped on the bed and said, 'Mom, I've had it,'" recalls his mother. "He said, 'I'm tired of being yelled at.'"

What happened next is the second pep talk that Charlene Wedertz will remember forever.

"I told him, 'You have a responsibility to the team and other players,'" she recalls. "I said, 'You've got to stick out the year.'"

Good words. Teaching words. The same words spoken every day by responsible parents everywhere.

Two days later, she was at his hospital bedside, thinking about those words.

"When he said he wanted to quit, I wish I had just taken him in my arms and gone on a little vacation," she says.

"Me too, Mom," he says.

. ■ ■

It's rarely the first hit.

Parents who allow their children to play high school football need to understand that brain injuries rarely occur on the first hit.

Matt Colby of Costa Mesa High, the Southland's latest high school football casualty, died last month after collapsing a few plays into a game — but he had been complaining of headaches after two earlier games.

Darren Wedertz's life changed within an hour after he was hit and complained of a headache.

It was Nov. 6, 1992.

In the second quarter of a JV game against Newport Harbor, Wedertz, playing running back, was tackled hard by several players.

He stepped out of the ensuing huddle.

"Boy, that hurt," he said.

In the third quarter, playing defensive back, he made a tackle.

It was such a big hit, he broke the opponent's collarbone.

"I bet that guy's in a lot of pain because my head's hurting right now too," Darren told a teammate.

The last words of his former life.

With everyone gathered around the injured Newport Harbor player, few noticed that Wedertz had collapsed.

There was no doctor there, no certified trainer.

By the time her son went into convulsions, Charlene Wedertz was at his side, screaming. "Somebody do something!" she said.

It was four months before he completely came out of his coma.

It was one year and one day before he left the hospital.

The long stay was not for the head injury, but to battle

leukemia, which was diagnosed six days after he'd entered the hospital. It turns out leukemia was why he had lost his step after his junior season.

At the time, a Santa Margarita official speculated that the leukemia had weakened the blood vessels in Wedertz's head, contributing to the trauma.

Doctors told his mother that was not the case.

Doctors, in fact, told his mother something else entirely.

"The doctor said he looked like he had been playing football without a helmet," she recalls. "What does that say for helmets?"

■   ■   ■

It's an unwritten code woven through the fabric.

A fallen high school football player is instantly a famous player.

But he is eventually only a fallen one.

Nearly nine years ago, there were vigils and prayer services and Santa Margarita kids lining the hospital halls on their knees.

There were benefits and autographs and even a tree planted in Darren's name.

Darren and his mother were embraced by the sorrowing community.

A father bought Charlene a wheelchair-accessible van. Other parents raised money to make her modest Mission Viejo home accessible.

"I can't say enough about the wonderful people here," Charlene says.

But attention wanes. New causes are found. New heroes appear.

This is the first newspaper story on Wedertz in nearly seven years.

Wedertz, who has long since beaten the leukemia, is still visited occasionally by old friends.

"His positive attitude is amazing," says Scott McIntosh, a former teammate and now a Santa Margarita teacher and coach.

Darren spends most of his time with his family — his grandmother, two sisters, a brother-in-law, a niece and a nephew. He will have plastic surgery to level his scalp, but little else in his life is expected to change.

His father's views, however, also have not changed.

Like many, he believes high school football's positives over-whelm its negatives.

"I would not be afraid to let a kid play football," he says. "It does so much for kids. And he could have suffered the same injury if he fell backward off a chair."

His mother, a petite but strong woman, agreed to tell this story for a different reason.

"I just want parents to know, some football helmets do not pro-tect the brain, and they should not get a false sense of security," she says. "I just want parents to open their eyes and check things out before letting their sons play high school football."

He asks my full name. He does not forget it. During two days of interviews, Darren Wedertz repeatedly shakes my hand and some-times asks questions I have answered only moments earlier.

But he always addresses me by my full name.

As I am leaving High Hopes after the last interview, he rests his hand on my shoulder.

"William Paul, you have a son?" he asks.

"Yes," I say.

"William Paul, has he asked you to play football yet?" he says.

"No," I say.

"You know what you tell him, William Paul?" he asks.

"What?" I say.

He tightens his grip, narrows his eyes, concentrates.

"You tell him the story of a 16-year-old boy who made a tackle," he says.

August 3, 2001

The Long Blue Line

While the Dodgers were playing baseball at Dodger Stadium on Sunday, I was engaged in a far more taxing game.

"What's My Line?"

First inning, a line stretching for 20 people, stretching into the second inning, people feeling as beaten as that Paul Lo Duca lead-off home run they just missed.

If you guessed a Dodger Dog booth on the loge level, you win.

"I got here at the start of the game, I've been in the stadium 25 minutes, and I haven't seen a pitch yet," said Jeff Smith of Santa Monica.

Fifth inning, a line stretching for 40 people, lasting three full innings, people numbly trying to imagine the score from the sound of the cheers.

If you guessed the concession stand behind the left-field foul pole on the reserved level, you win.

"I have scouts running in from the seats to give me updates," said Andres Nava of Santa Ana. "It's the only way I can watch."

Used to be, waiting for food was rarely an issue at the Disneyland of diamonds, a place where everyone was served so fast, concession stands never even had — or needed — television sets.

Now, during games with big crowds, long lines in certain sections are as common as baselines, and sometimes stretch even farther.

During a year when an overachieving Dodger team appears ready for a pennant race, its underachieving home park is not.

And it's only going to get worse. The big-drawing Chicago Cubs are in town beginning tonight. The New York Mets, St. Louis Cardinals and Arizona Diamondbacks are here for the Dodgers' other remaining weekend series.

Bring your patience. Better yet, pack it in a knapsack with homemade sandwiches and store-bought sodas.

Happy 40th birthday, Dodger Stadium. Here's hoping you don't have to stand in line for ice cream until you are 41.

"It's definitely worse now than it was 20 years ago," said Sylvia Almaguer, a loge level bartender who has worked in Dodger Stadium food service for 23 years. "Staffing has been a real big issue. They aren't giving us enough people. It's like they want to draw blood."

Almaguer, one of many popular employees customers know by

name, is referring to Aramark Corp., the food service outfit hired by Peter O'Malley in 1994 during the cost-cutting final days of his regime.

Aramark was hired to replace Marriott Corp., whose disastrous three-year reign included the near ruination of the famous Dodger Dogs.

Marriott was hired in 1991 to replace Arthur Foods, a family-type operation that had run the stadium concessions for 29 years.

"After Arthur Foods was gone, everything changed," Almaguer said. "The family feel was gone. Now it's all bottom line, all business, and it affects everything."

Dennis Lamalfa, vice president for Aramark's Pacific region, said the vendors have added staff this season, noting the new food booths on the field level.

"We are constantly monitoring and addressing the situation," he said.

Yet Almaguer, one of the shop stewards for the Local 11 of the Hotel Employees and Restaurant Employees Union, says more respect is needed.

"Certain sections, we have situations where, to do the job right at one stand, we need 13 people," she said. "Yet, they will tell us to do it with 10. That causes extra lines and angry people."

Some days, it's not only the concessions people. On Sunday, it was everybody and everything.

During the sold-out game, the lines were so bad that a fan showing up just before the first inning without bringing enough money could have gone home a couple of hours later without seeing a pitch.

In some places, it required one full inning to pass through the gates because the Dodgers temporarily ran out of Fernando Valenzuela bobblehead dolls.

Then two innings to get money from the ATM.

Then one inning to go to the bathroom.

Then three innings to buy a beer and hot dog.

By that time, it was the eighth inning.

At which point, if you didn't want to get stuck in two innings' worth of elevator traffic, you needed to leave.

"This is the reason I watch it on TV," said Jim Kirksey, who was stuck Sunday in a holding pen where he waited to pick up a Fernando doll. "I drove into the parking lot in the bottom of the first inning. . . ."

And he was still waiting for the doll in the third.

OK, so maybe some of this seems petty.

Some will say, bring your money and quit complaining about lines at ATMs, which host banks are reluctant to place in the stadium because they will sit idle for most of the year.

Still others will say, elevators? Aren't there stairs there? Can't most of you just walk?

And, really, if you want a bobblehead doll, go to the mall.

Fine. But none of that changes the fact that one still should be able to buy a hot dog and a soda without missing one inning for each.

And big crowds are no excuse.

Remember, this was the first baseball stadium to draw 3 million fans in a season. Before this summer, seven of the top 25 crowds in National League history were at Dodger Stadium.

The 54,556 fans on Sunday night were overwhelming? Not quite. It didn't even rank among the top 10 crowds in stadium history.

They've correctly handled big crowds before. They can do it again.

Or can they?

Bob Graziano, Dodger president, said it's sometimes difficult to attract workers to the part-time job that pays about $80 a game for those working in booths.

"When other jobs are paying better, sometimes we've had trouble getting enough employees," he said.

But Almaguer said that some of Aramark's policies have hurt employee morale, making them more likely to seek work elsewhere.

"When you are understaffed and customers are complaining all the time, it's a very difficult situation," she said. "Some employees finally revolt. They said, 'I just can't go back there today.'"

Aramark became infamous in 1997 for firing — then reinstating — peanut vendor Richard Aller after he broke a rule about reselling free peanuts.

Today most agree there are fewer roaming vendors, which means more people leave their seats and get into lines.

"Some of our vendors complain that they don't get enough product to make enough money," said Chito Quijano, a union organizer at Local 11.

The union signed only a one-year contract with Aramark this year — a departure from past multiyear deals — partly because of concerns over staffing.

"We have nothing but respect for Bob Graziano," Quijano said. "We believe he is trying his best to get Aramark to listen to us."

Or maybe, Aramark will listen to the fans.

Any day now, they should be returning to their seats.

February 28, 1999

Little Big Rivalry

PINE RIDGE, S.D. — The mystery sweeps across these desolate grasslands like a cold, haunting wind.

For nearly 70 years, it has been a consistent drumbeat of cluttered life in the biggest village on the Pine Ridge Indian Reservation.

The streets here have no names. The houses have no numbers. Some residents use faded blankets for window panes, splintered outhouses for relief.

The mystery dances through it all, coming to rest in an old aluminum warehouse in the middle of town, in a picture frame that holds a face both beautiful and sad.

Some say this is where the mystery mourns.

Her name was Sue Anne Big Crow.

Seven years ago, she was the best girls' basketball player in the state of South Dakota, scored 39 points a game for Pine Ridge High.

Today, her large senior basketball photograph hangs in a youth center, lovely and radiant.

"And bruised," says her mother, Chick, clenching and unclenching her fists. "Look at the bruises."

Look closely, and you will notice Sue Anne's left cheek and right leg are discolored.

"See what they did?" her mother says.

Shortly before the photo was taken, Sue Anne was in a fistfight with a girl from neighboring Red Cloud High. They rolled around a parking lot of the convenience store hangout, kicking and screaming and punching.

The girls were eventually separated, but so was the town. Again.

Because of that fight, Pine Ridge and Red Cloud stopped scheduling each other in girls' and boys' basketball. Again.

Four months later, Sue Anne Big Crow died in a single-car crash that some Pine Ridge people blamed on Red Cloud's alleged practicing of bad medicine.

The schools have not scheduled each other since, extending one of the strangest, and most bitter, sports rivalries in the United States.

"It's so bad," Robert Yellow Hair, former vice president of the Oglala Sioux Tribe, says as he huddles over a cup of coffee in that convenience store hangout. "It's so unhealthy."

■　■　■

Red Cloud High and Pine Ridge High are only five miles apart, virtual next-door neighbors in this remote, 4,500-person corner of the Lakota Sioux Nation.

The next nearest high school is a 52-mile drive away, along two-lane roads through expanses of nothing.

Yet Red Cloud and Pine Ridge haven't scheduled each other in boys' and girls' basketball for any extended period since they began playing each other in the 1920s.

The teams play only when they are forced to, seeded against each other in preseason tournaments or district championships. This is usually no more than once a year and rarely within 100 miles of their passionate fans' reach.

"We're like Duke and North Carolina," says Mark Prezquez, former Red Cloud player. "Only they play a lot more than we play."

The mystery is, why?

"Why do we have to drive at least 60 miles to play every game when we can drive right down the street?" asks George Bettelyoun, former Pine Ridge star. "The point is, it's ridiculous."

They are of one tribe, these Oglala Sioux, and are known for strong community ties.

They are of one heart, it appears, with seemingly everyone in the village proudly claiming to be related to everyone else.

But they are of two schools that can't stand the sight of each other.

"There's been so much hate," Chick Big Crow says.

Over the years, the games have featured fans brawling in the stands, throwing liquor bottles at one another, chasing others out onto the court.

Before one game, fans from Pine Ridge stoned players from Red Cloud as they were riding through town in the back of a truck.

After another game, a handful of players from each team battled with screwdrivers.

When the teams play in Rapid City, the major town two hours north, there have been fistfights in the lobby of the Civic Center and later in hotel bars.

Winning teams in this rivalry have had the windows of their buses broken. Losing teams have been jeered and taunted on village streets.

"The word 'Lakota' means allies. . . . This shows how far we've degenerated," Yellow Hair says. "We talk about Lakota values, but, in reality, we don't practice them."

The rivalry is so old, so deep, that it has bounced far beyond the simple confines of the reservation's most revered game.

Jobs here are sometimes handed out by tribal officials on the basis of where the prospective employee attended school.

"Red Cloud people won't give jobs to Pine Ridge people that quickly, and vice versa," Yellow Hair says.

Families sometimes spend the winter feuding if high school loyalties are split.

When hospital worker Larry Eagle Bull went against family tradition recently by transferring son Toby from Pine Ridge to Red

Cloud for "academic reasons," he did so at his own peril.

"Everybody looked at me like a traitor. . . . They said my dad would turn over in his grave," Eagle Bull says.

Even in death, the conflict does not diminish.

A woman who had attended Pine Ridge High recently railed against Red Cloud from the pulpit at her husband's funeral.

Then there was the time, several years ago, the Red Cloud girls were leaving town to face the Pine Ridge girls in a district tournament championship game in Rapid City.

Red Cloud's star player was pregnant and had been sent to jail for the duration of the tournament by a Pine Ridge judge after her grandmother had her arrested for truancy.

But a Red Cloud judge intervened, ordering her release. Then a Red Cloud police officer stopped the team bus on the way out of town.

"He told us to take the back roads," says Dusty LeBeau, former Red Cloud coach. "He said on the main roads, a Pine Ridge cop was waiting to stop us and take her back to jail."

So LeBeau drove the bus along the bumpy back roads, reached Rapid City safely and his team took the floor in time for tipoff.

The Pine Ridge folks weren't finished. They pleaded with the referee not to allow the star to play because she was pregnant.

The referees laughed. The teams played. Red Cloud won.

"You draw a line in that town," says LeBeau, who now coaches elsewhere. "You are either on one side, or the other."

LeBeau said he can't explain it. He is not alone.

The only thing that everyone agrees on is that the mystery has become like the wind, strong and self-supporting and seemingly unstoppable.

■   ■   ■

In one corner are the Red Cloud Crusaders, the Catholic school tucked around a dark wooden church behind a hill on the outskirts of town, with an enrollment of about 150.

It is still remembered by some as a place where priests allegedly abused the Indian boarding students and still hold an air of superiority today.

"You know Catholics, they think they're better than everyone else," says Vince Brewer, a tribal elder and part-time judge. "At Red Cloud it's like, 'We're right, you're wrong, there's no in between.'"

In the other corner are the Pine Ridge Thorpes, the colorfully painted government school in the center of town, with an enrollment of about 450.

It is viewed by some as a place that allows students to run wild, perpetuating the myth of the untamed reservation.

"Everybody says kids who want an education come to Red Cloud," senior Rich Patton says. "They say kids who want no life, they go [to Pine Ridge]."

These feelings don't fit easily into basketball, the games summoning a warrior spirit in the descendants of some of this country's greatest warriors.

It was the Sioux who defeated Custer at Little Bighorn. One leader there, Crazy Horse, became a symbol of Indian independence and, after a lifetime battling incursions into the northern plains, was killed during a scuffle with U.S. troops at a government guardhouse.

That legacy lives today. Only the war here is no longer against outsiders.

"How can we talk about reconciliation with the rest of the country," says Brian Brewer, Pine Ridge principal, "when we can't even reconcile with a neighboring school?"

■   ■   ■

As usual, the teams played only once this season, in the first round of the Lakota Nation Invitational tournament at Rapid City in December.

"An interesting draw, wasn't it?" says smiling principal Brewer, who runs the tournament and is trying to bring the schools back together.

Here's how interesting:

Red Cloud takes the floor shaken from the previous week's suicide of a freshman girl and suddenly without star guard Toby Eagle Bull, who disappears at tipoff.

Pine Ridge takes the floor missing three top players, each suspended for one game for breaking team rules.

In the first 30 seconds, Red Cloud's BJ Brave Heart and Pine Ridge's Muilozahe Berg exchange shoves and taunts, and a double technical foul is called.

"This is just a game," Brave Heart shouts.

"No, this is a battle," Berg shouts.

By the end of the first half, there have been five technical fouls and several near fights, and Red Cloud trails, 37-28.

"What in the hell is wrong with you guys!" Will Garnier, Red Cloud coach, yells in the tiny locker room at halftime. "No more technicals! This is just a game."

The sweaty players, mostly small and mostly young, shake their heads. They are old enough not to believe him.

There are no more fights in the second half, but the game stays rough, with players hustling over each other into the stands for loose balls long after Pine Ridge has clinched an eventual 75-60 victory.

"I'm just glad it's over," says Bill Pourier, Pine Ridge coach.

Afterward, there is no fighting among fans, perhaps because there aren't that many fans, this being a weeknight game two hours from home.

The story, instead, is in the Red Cloud locker room, where Toby Eagle Bull's early absence is destined to become another bit of rivalry lore.

He showed up for the game with his hair dyed bright blue in honor of school colors.

"A warrior," he said.

But the referee wouldn't let him play looking like that.

So for most of the first half, the Red Cloud leader was standing in line at a nearby Cost Cutters barber shop waiting for somebody to shave his head.

"Haircut cost me nine bucks, but what was I going to do?" Eagle Bull says. "This is crazy. These games, they're always crazy."

•   •   •

The search for the mystery began with a search for something else.

You heard about a heartwarming little sports program on the

prairie. You called Bob Brave Heart, the Red Cloud principal, to ask him.

He told you about his basketball team, how it is consistently one of the best in the state, despite hours of bus travel in winter conditions to play a simple game.

"Where's the nearest school?" you asked.

"Oh, right up the road, Pine Ridge High School," he said.

"So don't you play them?" you asked.

"Well, no," he said.

"Why not?"

"Long story," he said.

So you flew to Denver, changed to a smaller plane, flew to Rapid City, drove two hours south past Mount Rushmore, nearly hit a buffalo along a deserted, unlit road, then pulled into the hotel closest to Pine Ridge.

Which is 60 miles away.

The next day you drove along a thin strip of deserted highway among miles of swaying hills of grass, into the unannounced border of the second-largest reservation in the United States, past a gleaming gaming facility, past various encampments of hovels and shacks.

The road rose, then dipped into what appeared to be nothing more than a litter-strewn stop along a lost highway. The side streets were filled with roaming dogs, hollowed-out cars, crusted paper plates, dirty diaper bags.

It is Pine Ridge, the center of arguably the poorest county in America, where 70% of those under 18 are living below the poverty level.

You pulled into the gas station-deli in the center of town to make a toll-free call.

Which, here, costs 35 cents.

You climbed back in the car, turned down a dirt road and reached a small aluminum home belonging to tribal elder Joe Blue Horse.

Inside was a story.

Several years ago, Blue Horse was running for tribal councilman.

He did well in the primary and expected to win the regular election.

But he is a longtime Red Cloud supporter. Just before his big day, he sat in the middle of the Crusader cheering section during a district basketball tournament game between Pine Ridge and Red Cloud.

And promptly lost the election.

"There ain't no in-between around here," Blue Horse said. "Once you've gone one way, you've gone that way forever."

You left his home and, and using landmark directions — remember, the streets have no names here — you found Pine Ridge High.

And another story.

It is about 7 p.m., the Pine Ridge boys' basketball team was beginning practice, darkness has settled outside, there seemed to be no one else around for miles.

Yet Pourier, the coach, put strips of paper over the windows of the gym doors so nobody could watch.

Then he hung a paper sign that read, "Players and managers only."

"You never know who is going to be out there," Pourier said.

Like, maybe, Coach Will Garnier of Red Cloud? Like, you guys haven't talked before? Like, every day?

A couple of surprising aspects of the current rivalry are that Red Cloud's Garnier works under Pine Ridge's Pourier at the hospital, and while Garnier attended Pine Ridge, Pourier attended Red Cloud.

Again you ask, why the conflict? Why the deep animosity between people who sometimes are rarely more than five miles apart for their entire lives?

"Can't exactly say," Pourier said.

The next morning, you returned to the reservation, only this time stopping at the edge of town, at the tidy cluster of buildings that is Red Cloud.

You walked into a Native American gift shop, met a frail-looking man with a scraggly beard, the school's unofficial curator and keeper of the records.

If anybody can unlock the mystery, you figure, it is Brother C.M. Simon.

"Records?" he said. "What records?"

It turns out, there are few written records of games between the schools.

Nobody knows how many times they've played, or how many times they haven't, or who has won more.

Because there is no newspaper in town, there are no detailed accounts of fights or vandalism.

The closer you get, the farther away you are.

"It's just always been one of those them-versus-us things," Simon said. "If you know precisely how it started, you tell me. I've been here 35 years and still haven't figured it out."

As with other traditions on the reservation, this one apparently has been passed down orally, through stories swapped at the town's grocery store or the Pizza Hut that looks like a mobile home.

As with other traditions, this one is as old as the wailing chants and drumbeats that float daily from the reservation radio station.

Pine Ridge Boarding School opened its doors in 1879.

Red Cloud, also a boarding school before closing its dorms 20 years ago, opened as Holy Rosary Mission in 1888.

The first recorded basketball meeting between the schools occurred in 1929, when Holy Rosary defeated Pine Ridge in a tournament.

Like most government and church institutions of that era, the schools were trying to strip the Oglala Sioux of their heritage.

They forbade everything from speaking the Lakota language to wearing native dress.

Basketball became one of the few ways youngsters could emulate their forefathers in acts of bravery and skill.

Houses here might have holes underneath the front window and old tires for a porch, but around the back there will be a perfectly good basketball goal.

You found Bettelyoun, 28, the former South Dakota Mr. Basketball, standing near his goal. It is a sturdy backboard and rim nailed to a wilting tree in the front yard of a one-bathroom home he shares with nine people.

Bettelyoun was one of the few who earned a college scholarship, to a small NAIA school in South Dakota. But he has returned because he never felt comfortable on the outside.

"Basketball connects us to the bigger picture," he said. "Many things sacred in our culture are round. The sun. The medicine wheel. Basketball is like that. Sacred."

If it is that important, why can't the two schools be good sports about it?

"Maybe there are other things more important," the Pine Ridge principal, Brewer, said one night while his basketball team practiced down the hall. "Here, I've got somebody you should meet."

Moments later you find yourself in a cozy dorm behind the school, with giggling teenage girls watching a video in a large living room.

There is a heavy-eyed woman watching the girls from behind a desk. Her name is Rita Buckman. She thinks she can solve the mystery.

She said the rivalry was fueled in the mid-1950s when the villagers' children would escape the Red Cloud dormitories and tell their parents about abuse by the religious brothers.

Those children would then transfer to Pine Ridge.

"The priests and nuns, if you had black hair, they treated you like a dog," said Buckman, a dorm assistant who lived at Red Cloud for six years.

She described students being beaten with straps, of having their hair chopped off if they tried to escape.

She said she remembers once being forced to kneel at night in front of an open window during the winter for an hour after misbehaving.

"In their eyes, we were always bad," she said.

Over the next couple of days, her stories are corroborated by several others, including tribal official Everette Tuttle, sitting in a tiny room atop a cramped city hall.

"There's been years of buildup in older people over those problems with Red Cloud," he said. "Lots of angry people who never dealt with it. Back then, there were no counselors, nobody to listen to it."

Tuttle escaped from Holy Rosary in the fifth grade, spent all day hiding in the hills, but was caught and sent back by his parents.

He eventually graduated from Pine Ridge and cheers for that school today.

Back at Red Cloud, Brother Simon acknowledges the former impatience of young Jesuit teachers with the Native Americans.

"When you bring a person from a middle-class white city and plop them into what is essentially an urban ghetto, you have a challenge," he says.

But Father Tom Merkel, school superintendent, adds, "The experience of a boarding school is mixed. . . . Some people are negative, others are positive. It's important to keep balance in that."

You stopped by the Pizza Hut one night before leaving the reservation, and clerk Louis Pulliam told you about balance.

"I had a Red Cloud booster club poster on the wall here," he says. "Then some Pine Ridge people came in and told me I had to put up a Pine Ridge booster club poster."

Pulliam, recently graduated from Pine Ridge, sighed.

"You know, I don't think the kids realize how serious it is until they get out of high school," he says.

You heard this and you remember a group that has been forgotten during the search for this mystery.

You have not asked the children.

This was on your mind later, up in Rapid City, when you were standing in a hallway after Pine Ridge's victory over Red Cloud.

An interesting thing happened to the players when the heated game ended. The bad feelings ended. The aggression ended. They were friends again.

Yamni Jack, Pine Ridge's star of the game, was wearing a funky cap that contained a long, braided wig.

Walking past him is Toby Eagle Bull, the Red Cloud boy who had just shaved his head.

Eagle Bull suddenly grabbed the cap, put it on his shiny dome, and laughed. There was a pause, then Jack began laughing.

Soon, players from both teams formed a nudging, smiling circle of kids from one tribe, one home.

Of course. You have not asked the children.

"It's not about us, it's about the adults," said Red Cloud's Prezquez, back on the reservation. "You walk off the floor talking with your buddies from the other team, then you look up in the stands and see people throwing punches."

Even the adults acknowledge it.

"It's the parents," said John Steele, former tribal president, as he left a Red Cloud girls' volleyball game. "You know how youth are. They listen to their parents. Even when their parents are not talking, they listen."

.   .   .

The search brought you, on the final day of your visit, back to where this story started.

To where the mystery mourns, and where some are convinced a resolution can begin.

It is a drafty old building that used to house a plastic factory.

Now it is the Sue Anne Big Crow Boys and Girls Club, built with the life savings of Chick Big Crow as a memorial to her daughter.

It has a snack bar, game room, study room and one room devoted to Sue Anne's numerous trophies and highlight films.

Most important though, it is filled with students from both schools.

They are hanging out, Pine Ridge with Red Cloud, sharing stories and homework, acting the way the adults only wish they could act.

"Sue Anne was part of the rift," Chick said. "Maybe this place can be part of the healing."

Sue Anne healed many things when she played, a girl capable not only of winning a state championship with a turnaround jumper at the buzzer as a sophomore, but of dunking stereotypes.

During introductions once at an out-of-state school where administrators had balked at hosting Native Americans, Sue Anne put her warm-ups on like a cape and danced around the gym.

She counseled troubled teens in town, urged them to shed the forlorn destiny that was carved for their ancestors, made them realize some things were just plain dumb.

Now they gather nightly under her roof, an inviting place considering the nearest major mall is two hours away and the nearest movie theater is an hour.

They can't help but notice her picture, but this generation does not look at the bruises. This generation sees only the smile.

When somebody in the Red Cloud locker room before the Pine Ridge game told Toby Eagle Bull to be a tough Catholic, he makes an announcement.

"I am not Catholic," he says, wise beyond his sophomore year. "I am Lakota."

It is that statement that maybe turns this into not so much of a mystery after all.

Maybe this conflict is simply about a great nation so overwhelmed by outside forces that have tried to turn it into Thorpes and Crusaders, it occasionally forgets it is simply Lakota.

Maybe this is about a strong, old man who needs his children to remind him how he became so strong, and so old.

"Our ancestors were warriors, fighting for the same thing," Rich Patton of Red Cloud says. "We all want to be the same way. Fighting for the same thing."

The adults have noticed.

Recently, Pine Ridge said it wants to start playing again.

"It is time we sat down," principal Brewer says. "It is just time."

Red Cloud, for the first time, will discuss the issue at its spring school board meeting.

"We should be loyal to one another as a Lakota people before we are loyal to our alma mater," principal Brave Heart says. "We've got to end the hatred."

Shortly after her death, Sue Anne Big Crow's spirit apparently sent a message to her mother.

"She told me to plant flowers at the school, because nothing is beautiful there," Chick Big Crow said, her tired eyes reddening. "Because they fight all the time."

So she did, on the thick lawn across from the plain homes that surround the school, beautiful multicolored flowers.

If you look hard enough, through the swirls of confusion and candy wrappers, you can still see those flowers today. If you look hard enough.

May 12, 1996

Piazza Letter Was Juicy, but Turns Out to Be Thin

The letter arrived in the sports editor's box in the middle of last week, filled with the words that strangle reputations.

Where once there would have been shock, now there were only shrugs.

It had been written about a major league baseball player.

It only made sense.

"My age is 12 and April 28 was my first time to have a front-row seat at Dodger Stadium," Josh Nelson of Northridge wrote in a missive published on these pages.

"I was really excited because I thought I was going to get some autographs."

He continued, "No offense to the other players, but I was mainly trying to get Mike Piazza's autograph. But when I asked him to sign my baseball, he said, 'You got 50 dollars on you, kid?'"

Competent sports journalists and knowledgeable fans love to ask, "Why?"

But this was about a major league baseball player.

So we said, "Why not?"

And we got lazy.

The letter was published with a cursory screening involving a phone call to the boy's mother.

The letter was joined several days later by 10 new letters, letters full of rage toward the once-beloved Dodger catcher who apparently had become just like the rest of them. Another lost soul. Another jerk.

Then it was Mike Piazza's turn. He said the boy was lying. A player asking for money to sign an autograph on a baseball field? How could anybody believe that?

"I wouldn't even joke about something like that," Piazza said the following week. "C'mon, why would I say something like that? I never said anything like that in my life."

Again, we shrugged.

This was about a major league baseball player.

How could anybody not believe that?

The letters ripped, the radio talk shows buzzed, and the dirt was piled higher upon the lifeless form that was once our national pastime.

Which is why everyone should pause today and listen, again, to Josh Nelson.

Who is admitting that part of the letter was fabricated.

"Piazza never exactly asked me for $50," he said when questioned last week.

He said the figure was invented to "juice up the letter a little bit."

He claimed that Piazza had indeed asked him for money, after Josh fought through a crowd, one by one, to approach him by the Dodger dugout during infield practice before a game against the Chicago Cubs.

Exactly what did Piazza say? Nelson wasn't sure, giving three different versions at three different times during the interview.

Which makes you wonder about everything else in the letter.

"We wondered too," said his father, Dr. Michael Nelson, a Northridge internist. "But we've talked to him a lot in the last couple of days, and we believe in the gist of what he said, that Piazza asked him for money."

There is not a parent in the world who would blame the Nelsons. Josh is bright, well-spoken, makes good grades at a private academy, takes piano and guitar lessons, plays three sports, built a backyard tree house.

He also needs to watch where he walks with that imagination. The lessons here are serious ones. Next time, they could be expensive ones.

But this story is not just about Josh Nelson. It is about all of us.

What sort of atmosphere have we created, from the arrogance of the ballplayers to the cynicism of reporters, that would cause a 12-year-old to fantasize about baseball players not as successful professionals, but as arrogant opportunists?

Has our relationship with our former sweetheart become so distant that when a kid writing about baseball pauses to dream, that dream is of extortion?

It's a healthy development that athletes, like Mike Piazza, are no longer automatic heroes. But must they be subhumans?

Why didn't Josh Nelson write a letter fantasizing that Piazza vowed to hit a home run for him?

Twenty years ago, somebody might have done that. Seventy years ago, if you ask Babe Ruth historians, somebody did.

"This is an offshoot of everything that has happened in baseball," Piazza said after being told of the youngster's admission. "After all we have put the fans through, this is what has happened. This is how they think. This is how everyone thinks."

Piazza said he would not have responded if Josh had written simply that he had turned down an autograph request.

Piazza has refused people who have followed him home after games at Dodger Stadium. Followed him into restaurants. Followed him into the men's room.

"The whole autograph thing has gotten totally out of hand," Piazza said. "So if the letter had said that I didn't sign because I was trying to work, that's fine. But to outright lie about my reputation? At some point, this has to stop."

Sure. When the players discover their consciences, and fans lose their bitter memories, and the media regain perspective.

Which isn't happening anytime soon, no matter how you juice it up.

February 27, 1997

He Went Down Swinging

"That S.O.B. won't let me play! It's not fair! He can't do that!"

Bill Spiller fought them to the end, cursing their names in the middle of the night in the small hardwood hallway of his 122nd Street home.

Illness had diluted his mind, but not his indignation, which still covered him like cologne used in quarts instead of drops.

Decades after golf tournaments threw him out because he was black, Spiller would jolt awake, sit up in his bed, shout the names of the long-deceased people who ran those tournaments.

Sometimes he would grab his gun, stalk into the living room, wave the pistol, promise 3 a.m. revenge.

"I'll get them for this, you'll see! I'll get them!"

Bill Spiller fought them night after night, front door to back.

His wife was so worried he might mistake her for a golf official and shoot her, she ordered him moved to a convalescent home.

He died there two years later, in 1988, at 75. His oldest son immediately phoned numerous media outlets — including The Times — with the news.

Gone was the man many feel was most responsible for blacks being admitted to the Professional Golfers' Assn.

Gone was the pioneer who pestered the PGA for nearly 15 years until it finally dropped its "Caucasians-only" clause in 1961.

Contrary to popular belief, Tiger Woods' appearance in this week's Nissan Open is not due to a shoe company, but to Spiller.

The son made the calls because he figured somebody might want to give Spiller's death a headline.

Nobody was willing to give it even a sentence.

"Either they didn't know him, or weren't interested in him or both," said the son.

There was no obituary, so there were no friends at his memorial service. There were no calls from the PGA, no condolences from the organization he fought so intensely.

In the end, even Bill Spiller's demons won.

"Man died with a broken heart," said Maggie Hathaway, a local NAACP activist and former Los Angeles Sentinel columnist who chronicled Spiller. "He should have been the hero. But they made him the scapegoat."

. . .

The history of racial equality in sports is not always as clearly defined as a Jackie Robinson slide or an Arthur Ashe serve.

Sometimes that history is as cluttered as those ordinary neighborhoods from which it springs, as forgotten as those ordinary people who create it.

In the 1940s, South-Central Los Angeles was one of those neighborhoods. Bill Spiller was one of those people.

He was a porter at Union Station, a postal clerk, the owner of a doughnut shop, a resident of 122nd Street in a tidy beige house with a manicured front lawn. He was a father, a neighbor, a fixture.

He was also a golfer, one of many who hung around what is now known as the Chester Washington Golf Course, an unassuming spot of freshness on a blighted block of Western Avenue.

It is there that the only formal tribute to Bill Spiller remains.

It is a simple plaque, leaning back in a glass trophy case overlooking the 10th tee, crowded by haphazardly hung newspaper articles about, ironically, the likes of Tiger Woods.

"To William 'Bill' Spiller," begins the inscription, "In recognition of your achievement as a professional black golfer. . . ."

That's all he ever wanted to do. Make a living playing golf.

He was good enough to shoot a 68 and tie Ben Hogan for second place after the first round of the 1948 L.A. Open, a tournament that consistently ignored the PGA's ban on blacks.

He won many national tournaments held by blacks during that time.

"He was a great golfer, one of the best ever, black or white," said Charlie Sifford, the first African American regular on the PGA Tour.

But Spiller had a problem with patience. While many other black golfers quietly accepted the PGA's assurances that they would soon be allowed to join the tour, Spiller bought nothing.

While others remained quiet for fear of hurting their chances, Spiller howled.

He broke whites-only rules in clubhouses everywhere. He filed a landmark suit against the PGA. And in 1952, he stood in front of a player's swing and stopped an entire tournament in San Diego. That protest helped lead to the rules change that opened the door for the inclusion of blacks on the tour. Many black golfers call it the single most important event in their fight.

Each step brought Spiller closer to his goal, but took him further from the world he so desperately wanted to join.

Typical was that time in Bakersfield in the early 1950s when Spiller and several friends had played well in a tournament, but were denied access to the clubhouse afterward.

"Spiller just walked inside and asked the wife of the club president to dance," said Frank Snow, a former playing partner. "He said that when he came back out, all the other blacks had left him because they were afraid."

Another playing partner, Ed Satchell, remembers having a drink with a PGA official after they had played a round with Spiller and been hassled the entire time about not allowing blacks in tournaments.

"He said, 'Ed, you're a nice guy, you shouldn't be messing around with Spiller,'" Satchell said.

By the time golf became this country's last major sport to officially desegregate, in 1961 after then-California Atty. Gen. Stanley Mosk vowed to fight the PGA to the end of the earth, Spiller was too old to shoot the qualifying scores of his youth and too disliked to be granted any favors.

Sifford became golf's Jackie Robinson while Spiller was frying crullers at the corner of Century and Normandie.

Lee Elder became one of golf's most noted pioneers after becoming the first black to play in the Masters while Spiller was hustling bets as a caddie at Hillcrest Country Club.

The man most responsible for the appearance of blacks on the PGA Tour was never even allowed to become a member of the PGA.

On a recent weekday afternoon, a promotional flier was stuck to the front of the trophy case overlooking the 10th hole, obscuring Spiller's plaque.

Hathaway tore off the paper.

"Everybody still trying to cover poor Bill up," she said.

. . .

Bill Spiller Jr. has a gentle smile, a huge laugh, answers the phone at his Redondo Beach residence by saying, "House of Joy," allows no tears to be shed inside.

"My father was a very angry man, possibly the angriest man I have ever met," he said. "Two chips. Both shoulders. This was his burning cross. He carried it with him to his grave."

Bill Spiller Jr. smiled.

"How angry was my father? He was angry enough to keep this."

In front of the son was his father's scrapbook, brown leather cover, black pages, the usual kind with one exception.

It celebrated as many defeats as victories.

For every faded scorecard with every birdie circled, there was a newspaper story about his protest of some exclusionary tournament.

On one page, there was a yellowed newspaper story about triumph in a black tournament.

On another page, a protest poem he wrote about carrying passengers' bags at Union Station for dime tips.

Spiller carried that basic understanding of life's unfairness with him when he started playing golf, in 1942 at the age of 29.

By then, he knew all about being black in America.

Despite a degree from Wiley College in Marshall, Texas, and a teaching certificate from that state, the best job he could find there was at a rural school for $60 a month.

So he moved to Los Angeles in 1938 to live with his mother. The best job he could find here was as a redcap at newly opened Union Station.

Searching for new ways to gamble with his working pals — besides pool, cards, dice and sports events — he joined a friend for a round of golf on Christmas Eve.

He shot a 114 that day. Four years later, he was winning every black tournament in Southern California.

He bought that house on 122nd Street with $7,000 he won in an all-day golf game with boxer Joe Louis.

Spiller began traveling on the black pro circuit in the mid-1940s, winning tournaments around the country.

In one year, he had one first, four seconds and two thirds while playing in events such as the National Negro Open and Texas Negro Open with equally talented Southern California buddy Ted Rhodes.

Imagine, Bill Spiller thought, how much money he could make if only he could play in the *real* show.

He would imagine, then he would walk into a place such as the Bel-Air Country Club to try to qualify for the U.S. Open. Friends talk of the time Spiller got into an ugly staring match with Fred Astaire there.

"Well, I guess you can stay," Astaire finally told Spiller, according to friends.

Spiller realized he was really supposed to be there in 1948 in the L.A. Open, when he shot a first-round 68, tying him for second.

By the time the weekend ended, though, he had fallen 20 strokes behind eventual winner Hogan. But according to newspaper reports, the unlikely redcap had been followed and cheered by more than 12,000 fans.

He finished well enough to qualify for the next week's PGA tournament in the Northern California town of Richmond.

That is where the trouble started for Bill Spiller.

Rather, that is where he started it.

After playing in two practice rounds, he was confronted by a tournament official who gave Spiller his first look at the PGA constitution, Article 3, Section 1.

It contained the little publicized rule, instituted at the PGA's inception in 1916, that PGA members must be Caucasian.

Spiller had heard about the rule, but to actually see it in print a year after Robinson had integrated major league baseball stunned him.

A couple of days later, according to the golf history book "Get-tin' to the Dance Floor" by Al Barkow, Spiller spent $150 — a first-place purse on the black tour — to wine and dine local newsmen before announcing that he and two others, including Rhodes, were suing the PGA for $250,000.

In Spiller's scrapbook, next to stories about the suit, was pasted a story describing how white E.J. "Dutch" Harrison — "That big fellow from Arkansas" — led the Richmond tournament after three rounds.

On an adjoining page is a photo of a stunned Harrison after he won the tournament, but was given a blank winner's check because Spiller's lawsuit froze all funds.

"Blankety-Blank" read the caption in the San Francisco Examiner.

"Bill Spiller had the original impact," said Jack Burke, former pro and member of the PGA touring committee during Spiller's fight. "He could play, and he deserved a chance. But there was a bunch of people not knowing what they were doing, a bunch of Caucasians not knowing what was going on."

Six weeks after the Richmond tournament, the PGA offered to end its discrimination against blacks if Spiller would drop his suit. He did. It was a huge mistake.

"They tricked him," Sifford said.

The PGA did not change its Caucasians clause, only the name of its tournaments. By calling each tournament an "Invitational" instead of an "Open," it could continue banning blacks with no need for explanation.

Spiller despondently returned to the black tour. He tried to behave like a big-time golfer without the sponsorships or prize money, and his family struggled.

At times, he was reduced to performing a shuffling dance with Rhodes in hopes of persuading wealthy golfers to hire him for lessons. Spiller hated that dance.

"He was sad," Hathaway recalled. "We would go to the bar [at Chester Washington] every day after he played his rounds and he would say, 'Maggie, I've got to play golf.'"

The more he was spurned during the day, the tougher things

became for his family.

He and wife Goldie had two boys and a girl, none of whom play golf. Goldie sold his clubs when he died to rid herself of the memory.

"He was having such a tough time himself, I think he took out a lot of his frustrations on us," said middle son James, an accountant who still lives in his father's home.

The children would often come home to find their father angrily penning a letter of protest, or making a series of frustrated phone calls.

"He would look in the paper, see what somebody on the tour did and say, 'That so-and-so, I can beat him!'" Bill Jr. recalled. "And he would get mad all over again."

While watching Tiger Woods wade through adoring fans at this week's L.A. Open, remember that at the same tournament nearly 50 years ago, Spiller made another memorable scene.

He was angry because the three most prominent blacks in the tournament were grouped together. When the more placid Rhodes told him that it was because some Texans didn't want to play with them, Spiller shouted, "I thought this was the L.A. Open, not the Texas Open. If they don't want to play with us, tell 'em to go the hell back to Texas."

Spiller said he didn't know that the starters' microphone had been turned on during his outburst, blaring his words to the Riviera crowd.

•   ■   •

Fittingly, the most important golf tournament in Bill Spiller's life was one he watched from behind the ropes.

It was the third weekend in January 1952. Spiller had recently played 36 holes in the rain to qualify for a charity event in San Diego that was not an official PGA tournament.

Spiller, Eural Clark, Rhodes, Joe Louis and Leonard Reed were given lockers and assigned caddies.

Just before the tournament began, the PGA disqualified all of them, ostensibly because they didn't have PGA players' cards.

Because Louis was involved, a public outcry ensued. The promoters relented and agreed to allow Louis a spot, but asked the others to keep quiet until the rules were re-examined at a PGA meeting the next winter.

All but Spiller agreed. Spiller was furious and resented Louis being treated as a token. He threatened another lawsuit, barged into meeting from which he had been excluded and charged the PGA with changing its rules to fit its needs.

"Bill was a real fighter there," Clark said. "Fighting to make them change that PGA clause. They held a lot of stuff against him because of that fight."

Spiller stood on the first tee and refused to let the tournament begin. When he was finally talked down by his own colleagues, he confronted PGA officials and warned them that blacks were soon going to be playing in tournaments whether the establishment liked it or not.

Sure enough, the PGA relented and inserted a clause that allowed blacks to play in PGA events if invited by sponsors.

"PGA Clears Path for Negro Golfers" read the headlines.

It was a small change with big ramifications.

"It was the start of the whole thing," Clark said. "San Diego was where everything broke open."

Spiller played in 10 tournaments that year. For younger black golfers, there was finally hope.

"This is when I started playing a lot," Sifford said. "San Diego was important."

The organization also promised to discuss the deletion of the Caucasian clause, and Spiller was going to hold them to it.

"I'll go along with this until the national [PGA] convention in November," Spiller said in a newspaper account of the incident. "Then I want to see something done about that non-Causcasian clause."

It was nearly 10 years before the PGA fulfilled the second part of the deal.

By then, Spiller had been reduced to a caddie.

"How many people do you know became a caddie after they were a pro?" Hathaway asked. "That's the story of Bill Spiller."

Failing eyesight — which family members said was caused by the flour used in his Mrs. Spiller's Old Fashioned Doughnuts store — had forced him to stop playing in big-time tournaments.

In 1960, he was 47 and reduced to making tips and hustling bets.

While carrying bags at Hillcrest he mentioned to member Harry Braverman that he was banned from the tour because of the Caucasian clause.

Braverman promised to speak to Atty. Gen. Mosk, a close friend. At about the same time, Mosk received a letter with a similar complaint from Sifford. Mosk subsequently threatened legal action against the PGA, which had its annual championship scheduled for Brentwood Country Club in 1962.

Mosk lobbied other attorneys general to consider similar action, and by 1961, the Caucasians-only clause was stricken. But before that was done, the PGA had moved the 1962 championship from Brentwood to Philadelphia because of Mosk's challenge.

"I was surprised that the Caucasian restriction was right there in writing. Usually that sort of thing is kept quiet," Mosk said. "I guess just nobody ever thought of challenging it."

So Mosk was given the credit in legal circles, and Sifford is generally given the credit in clubhouses.

While Spiller, forever ignored, retired to Chester Washington, where he played recreational golf until his eyesight got so bad he could no longer make a putt.

He eventually suffered two strokes and Parkinson's disease and found himself in a convalescent home. In his final days he complained to friends that he wanted to return to his house, but his family wouldn't let him because he was so mean.

"This is not my fight," Spiller once said. "It is one of the many phases of the great fight Negroes are waging in all fields of activity to become an actual part of American life."

But it was his fight; and ultimately, his victory.

"I just wish somehow he would know that," said Bill Spiller Jr. "If there is a God, if there is an afterlife, somehow, I think that would make him rest easy."

CHAPTER SEVEN

Safe at Home

November 25, 1999

A Brotherly Bond
That Beat the Odds

He was so small. Expecting to meet a little boy, I had just been introduced to a stick figure.

His jeans hung loosely around dental-floss legs. His T-shirt swallowed the rest.

I reached for his hand, and grabbed him clear up to his elbow. I had just agreed to be Andrew's "Big Brother," yet there was nothing there.

A commitment of three hours a week, each week, for the next year?

What could an active 22-year-old man possibly do with a 7-year-old shadow?

What could we ever share besides an awkward stare?

I had been told that Andrew was suffering from cystic fibrosis, a genetic predator that kills young. But an overeager counselor whispered, "Don't worry, you can't tell."

One look at Andrew's stunted growth and I could tell. One ugly cough and I could hear.

I had just met a boy to whom I was morally bound for the next year, yet I couldn't figure out how to spend the first minute.

"So, um, what do you like?" I finally asked this little thing hugging his mother's legs.

It was then I realized I had missed something: two eyes, flickering under a mop of blond hair, eyes now bigger than all of him.

"Sports," he said, his small voice booming, and I'll remember this as long as I remember anything. "I like sports."

.   ■   .

We like it, hate it, embrace it, denounce it, talk about it for hours, watch it for weekends, rip it for days. We teach with it, blame it, try fruitlessly to play it and hopelessly to understand it.

The one thing we never do, it seems, is pause and be thankful for it.

For me, for sports, this day works as well as any.

This is trying to be a Thanksgiving sports story, but not about sports as names and numbers, winners and losers.

It's about sports as language, as one of this country's most important means of communication, spanning generations, crossing economic classes, giving our diverse people something in common.

It's about how sports connected me with Andrew.

I wasn't trying to save the world. I was trying to save myself.

I had just graduated from college and was working in the swamp bureau for a newspaper in Fort Lauderdale, Fla. I was covering bowling and shuffleboard and hoping for the day when somebody would consider me good enough to cover high school football.

I lived in a one-room apartment with a bed in the wall and roaches on the ceiling. My life lacked any sense of order or importance. I figured the Big Brothers & Sisters program would give that to me.

I met Andrew Fishbein at a Christmas party in 1980.

He said he liked sports.

"What do you know?" I said. "So do I."

On our second visit, I tentatively dumped a pile of baseball cards on the floor. He dropped to his knees and ran them through his hands like money.

"Do you know how to play?" I asked.

He didn't, so I taught him a game I had learned when I was young. Soon we were sprawled out on the carpet, shouting together at little pieces of cardboard, big and little now shoulder to shoulder.

And so the language of our relationship had been established, the currency set.

We played soccer as long as his clogged little lungs could handle it. We pitched baseball until it was time to go home for his medicine.

I was promoted to covering high school basketball, so he attended his first live sports event, Boyd Anderson High versus Dillard High, sitting next to me in the stands, cheering as if it were the Bulls and the Jazz.

Sports was like this for us. A language of laughter and lessons, a bridge between distant lives.

A year passed, my formal commitment to Andrew ended, but our visits continued. Sports had given us a new world — big enough for only two — that neither was willing to leave. There was always another miniature golf course to play, another pretend Super Bowl to enact with a rubber football on the scrubby field behind his townhouse.

Then in the fall of 1983, I landed a job as far from that world as Andrew thought possible. I was going to cover the Seattle Mariners, 3,500 miles away.

I still remember watching Andrew collapse in tears on the floor of his mother's townhouse. To him, I was just another man who had come and gone.

"You'll come see me, I'll stay in touch, I promise," I said quickly. "I'm covering baseball, remember?"

I'm sure he didn't believe it. I don't know if I believed it.

But it was baseball, remember? Within a year, Andrew, by then 10, had worked up the courage to fly cross-country by himself to spend long summer days with me and my wife.

Or, more to the point, to spend an afternoon with the Mariners, running the outfield during batting practice, hanging out in the clubhouse, chaperoned by an unforgettable pitcher named Roy Thomas.

As we grew older, through vastly different situations on different sides of the country, it was sports that gave us both the incentive to keep our relationship strong.

At least three times a year, we would get together, seemingly always to watch a sporting event or to hang out near a sporting event I was covering. Our reunions were, therefore, usually marked by big happy crowds, and our separations usually occurred against the echoes of cheers.

When Andrew was 13, a basketball assignment took me close enough to Florida so I could give the toast at his bar mitzvah, a wonderful celebration of manhood for a child not expected to live long past his 18th birthday.

When Andrew graduated from high school, another milestone for a kid whose lungs and digestive system were weakening by the day, he received a congratulatory phone call from Orel Hershiser.

I've never asked an athlete for anything like that before or since. But Hershiser never held it over my head because he understood the death sentence hanging over Andrew's.

Cystic fibrosis is a genetic, terminal disease affecting about 30,000 children and adults. It causes the body to produce abnormally thick mucus that clogs the lungs and obstructs the pancreas, affecting everything from breathing to digesting.

The language of sports, of course, includes none of those words. It's about life, and I privately rejoiced that the topic of Andrew's prognosis never came up. We were too busy arguing who was better, the Dolphins or Seahawks, the Heat or Lakers.

Many times, for a boy who underwent daily chest-pounding therapies and biannual lengthy hospital stays, sports was also the language of healing.

Despondent over his situation as a freshman at the University of Florida, Andrew once swallowed enough pills to kill himself. Fortunately, a fraternity brother found him in time.

When I was finished being furious, I bought him World Series tickets, and we stayed up all night in Atlanta, talking about comebacks.

It was his first of three World Series games, one baseball All-Star game, one Super Bowl, one national college football championship, one NCAA regional basketball championship.

He has been with me everywhere from Seattle to St. Petersburg, with stops in places like Cincinnati, New Orleans, Charleston, S.C., and even Dodgertown.

He has survived two major surgeries — half of his lungs have been removed — with that same language.

Sitting at his hospital bedside, I would read him the sports pages.

Phoning his room from across the country, I would ask which game he was watching, and turn my TV to the same game, and we would shout at it together, even if he couldn't always shout.

The years passed, and I became a balding middle-ager, and the stick figure became a strong, handsome adult. Yet we stayed together until, at some point, it stopped being all about sports and started being somewhat about us.

That point was reached this fall, when I was scheduled to fly to Boston to cover what became one of the most dramatic Ryder Cup golf tournaments in history.

I flew to Jamaica instead. It was there, on a beach, that his mother and I gave Andrew away at his wedding.

On Wednesday, he flew to join me for this Thanksgiving with his new bride, Sigrid.

Andrew is 26. He is a successful real estate agent. He undergoes countless daily therapies and painstaking hospital stays, but he works out at a gym, and is cut like a body builder. Science has pushed the life expectancy of an individual with CF to 31, and here's betting he doubles it.

Today he will hug my wife as if she is his second mother, which she is. He will roll around the floor with my three children like one of their favorite uncles, which he is.

And with me? What do you think?

Today we'll watch football, eat turkey, watch football, watch more football, then fall asleep in front of the TV while watching everything replayed in 30-second video bites on the highlight show.

Some might call us lazy sports nuts. We just call ourselves brothers.

POSTSCRIPT: Through continued therapy, Andrew has become a thriving 29-year-old man. We still talk constantly, and get together about twice a year. When I was hospitalized in Tampa during an assignment a couple of years ago, it was Andrew who drove up to take care of me.

February 10, 1998

Lesson in Life Wrapped in a Box of Thin Mints

Hi, my name is Tessa, I am buying . . . I mean selling . . . oh, shoot.

Little girl learning to be brave, Take Two.

Hi, my name is Tessa, I have some, can you sell some . . . oh, buy some . . .

Little girl learning to be brave, Take Three.

Hi, my name is Tessa, I'm a Brownie Girl Scout, would you like to buy some Girl Scout cookies?

There. She nails it. The sales pitch that last year caused stammers and sweats, she now belts through our house like a tenor.

I wrap my arms around a fuzzy brown sweater wrapped around a giggling 8-year-old.

"I'm so proud of you, I don't care if you don't sell anything," I whisper.

She sighs, rolls her blue eyes, pushes me away.

"Daddy!" she says. "I'm going to sell a bunch of boxes. I'm going to sell enough to win a T-shirt."

A T-shirt is the prize for selling 100.

Last year, she sold 39.

I hug her again, longer this time, my sweet, brave little girl with freckles on her nose and heartbreak in her future.

She has no chance of selling those 100 boxes.

Because, unlike many other Brownie parents, her Mommy and Daddy aren't going to sell them for her.

This is not about the cookies. They are good cookies. You ask me, one flavor has even replaced apple pie as our nation's dessert.

Mom, hot dogs and Thin Mints.

It's not the cookies, it's the assumptions.

In these competitive times, those who supervise children assume their parents never want them to struggle, stumble, or — heaven forbid — fail.

They assume we will do anything to help our kids avoid life's hardships, even if it means throwing them over our shoulders and sprinting them through the elementary school.

They take advantage of these assumptions by expecting our children to do things they cannot possibly do by themselves.

Used to be, having your parents help you with your homework was cheating. Today, it is curriculum.

The kids are assigned large science projects or book reports, the parents are persuaded to do most of the work, then everyone pats everyone else on the back.

Much is accomplished, yet is anything learned?

The fine line between assistance and plagiarism has been erased such that during a recent visit to Tessa's sophisticated third-grade science fair, it would have taken a scientist to uncover any evidence of third grade.

A couple of days later, I opened my daughter's Girl Scout cookies folder and saw this note:

"Cookie sales begin tomorrow, Jan. 30, at 9 a.m. — so you can let Dad and/or Mom take an order form to work on Friday before girls start going door to door after school."

There it was, in black and yellow. Parents were not only encouraged to help their daughters learn the benefits of salesmanship and hard work . . . but they were actually expected to sell cookies *for* them.

Attached to her main order form was a "mini-order" card that parents are subtly expected to take to the office.

"Huh, Daddy, can you take it to work for me?" asked Tessa. "Please, Daddy?"

This was hard. Tessa struggled last winter, her first in Brownies. She was so shy, she was afraid even to ring neighbors' doorbells, cringing at their sound, even with Daddy standing 5 feet behind her.

She spoke so softly, folks had to step outside to understand her. Make a phone sale? Never, because that would first require an actual phone call.

She wanted it to be easier this year. I couldn't blame her. I despised the Girl Scouts for putting me in this position.

"I can't help you," I said. "And you know why."

"I know," she said. "Re, re-spon-si-bility. I know Daddy. But . . ."

I shook my head. She lowered hers.

The next day she hit the streets while I phoned New York, to the offices of Girl Scouts of the United States of America.

"This activity is for the girls," spokeswoman Marianne Law said. "But you can't tell a parent what to do."

Aren't the mini-order forms telling a parent what to do? Isn't giving awards based strictly on sales — including a 500-box award — telling parents what to do?

My daughter loves hanging out with the other girls at Brownies and, because of money generated from cookie sales, our expenses are virtually nil.

But if it comes at the cost of a lesson in personal responsibility, if the meaning of all this goes no deeper than the co-worker's order form now taped to a wall near our Sports department, then maybe even the Peanut Butter Patties aren't worth it.

So Tessa hit the road. Only this year, it was different. This year, wondrously, she was different.

She marched to front doors, fought with her little sister to ring the bell, looked at her accompanying parents like loiterers.

She worked the phones, calmly apologized for wrong numbers, called boys with no sisters at her school, tracked down our friends, made relatives feel guilty, cut deals.

One parent said she would buy cookies from her if, when her son was selling candy bars for his swim team, Tessa would buy from him. Tessa said she loves candy bars. Done.

At last count, she had sold 75 boxes.

Mommy and Daddy had sold none.

"You know, you're growing up on us," I whispered during a recent hug.

"I know, Dad," she said.

After which, I headed off to buy her the damn T-shirt.

January 18, 1998

This Family Event Is Still Super After XVI Years

The most enduring tradition of our jumbled lives started in the cramped living room of strangers, two toddlers tugging at our feet, trying to watch a stupid football game.

It was January 1982. We were at a party early. We promised one of my wife's co-workers we would visit his family later.

We arrived just as Dan Bunz was tackling Charles Alexander at the one-yard line.

It would be embellishment to suggest we felt anything special as we left their small house after watching the San Francisco 49ers defeat the Cincinnati Bengals in Super Bowl XVI.

"Thanks, that was fun," we said, or something like that. "Let's do it again sometime."

The next year, though still merely acquaintances, we invited the same family to our duplex, on the other side of our Florida town, sitting on saggy couches in front of a dusty TV.

It would be sweet fantasy to think they were sentimental when they left after watching the Washington Redskins defeat the Miami Dolphins in Super Bowl XVII.

"Thanks, that was fun," they said, or something like that. "Let's do it again sometime."

When next January showed up, they were gone, having moved 3,300 miles to Portland.

But, in what we are now certain was not a coincidence, we were also gone, having moved 3,500 miles to Seattle.

We called them shortly after both families had moved in. We didn't want to sound presumptuous, but we did have one thing in common.

"Hey, you guys want to come up for the Super Bowl?"

They surprised us. They did.

Later, lounging around our new apartment after Super Bowl XVIII, we decided the only thing stranger than the Raiders' victory over the Redskins was that our two families had traveled across the country to watch it together.

That tug of tradition we felt that night was real. So, now, is this:

Next weekend the Plaschkes and Kummerers will be celebrating the Super Bowl together for the 17th consecutive year.

This, despite living in the same town for only two of those 17 years.

Eight times they've come to our house. Seven times we've gone to theirs. Twice we've celebrated at neutral sites, including once at the actual game, with tickets for which we are still paying.

We have discovered the only sports bar in the world that was closed on Super Bowl Sunday, a joint in suburban Portland.

We have been so worn out after a weekend with the seven children, my buddy Lou Kummerer fell asleep during Joe Montana's famous drive against the Bengals.

Then, three years ago in Miami, I rushed home from Florida in mid-Super Bowl week for the birth of our third child. Lou gave up his ticket and rushed home with me.

Our worlds are as far apart as the AFC and NFC. The Kummerers have moved to Costa Rica; we live here. Those children who tugged at our feet? One is now a student at Notre Dame, the other a high school senior.

But come January, one family will call the other, and arrangements will be made. When we see each other, we will hug, and we will mean it, another year survived, another return to shore.

We have no idea exactly what we will be doing on the other important days that mark our calendar. Thanksgiving is harried, the holidays are political.

But for 17 years now, we have known what we are doing on Super Bowl weekend, and with whom we are doing it, and in that stability there is a sense of relief that our lives really aren't the madly spinning toys they seem to be.

My hunch is, we aren't the only ones. That is the beauty of next week's game in San Diego, no matter how much the money and hype will try to spoil it.

The Super Bowl is not about the actual game, or it would

have died long ago. It is not about the sport — most members of the Plaschke-Kummerer families don't even follow football the rest of the year.

The Super Bowl is the rarest of occurrences in this age of strike and scandals. It is a day you can count on.

The game might be bad, but the day will be good. From that morning battle of backyard touch . . . to the 60-minute championship that fits as well in rural living rooms as million-dollar luxury boxes . . . to the post-game pizza.

You will probably remember only a couple of players. You won't remember the score. But you will remember the day.

This one should be better than ever. San Diego is a wonderful host for these sorts of things. Next weekend should be a wild mixture of zoo and sea and Old Town.

Me, I'll mostly be home, with the Kummerers, sitting on lawn chairs and playing cards and remembering Dan Bunz.

May 2, 2002

Back in His Old Kentucky Home

LOUISVILLE, KY. — The starting gate was a cracked driveway. The finish line was a crooked crabapple tree.

The course was three-tenths of a mile past the Moirs', past the Browders', past the nasty doctor's wife and the snarling boxer Geronimo and the place where I once pulled a knife on the neighborhood bully.

The horse was a bike.

The jockey was I.

Every first Saturday in May, I would climb aboard my black Schwinn, dip my nose to the metal bar, and race around my neighborhood flapping an imaginary whip, dreaming about a call.

"And down the stretch they come . . . and it's Plaschke aboard the leader . . . it's Plaschke bringing him home. . . ."

Growing up across town from Churchill Downs, I never pretended to make a game-winning basket or hit a game-winning home run.

I pretended to win the Kentucky Derby.

Then I left home, and pretended it didn't exist.

That circular course became a straight line, out of town, through college, to the working world, to the West Coast, far away from a family that cared far too much about two puny minutes.

So what if my great-uncle Ed was a jockey.

So what if my uncle Bill once owned a horse, and has published more than four decades worth of mimeographed derby ratings.

So what if my father claimed to have set a record by drinking 15 mint juleps, after which he retired to watch the event from a backyard tree.

For my family, the Derby is not simply a horse race, it's a tradition that dug and twisted underneath us like the roots of that crooked crabapple tree.

We could bend and crack and still we held firm, in our backstretch work ethic and roses ideals, our life personified in that first Saturday in May.

Some would say we were well planted. I thought we were stuck.

The moment I was old enough to realize the ridiculousness of a 150-pound kid impersonating a jockey, I applied that imaginary whip to my life and away I went, sprinting into a world far from the world of my youth.

"You coming home to cover the Derby this year?" my parents would ask, hopefully.

"I have to cover the Lakers and Dodgers," I would say, somberly, but secretly pleased.

For 25 years, this was my declaration of independence.

Then one day last winter, my father fell down some steps. My mother grew weary caring for him. Their needs were evolving. Their lives were changing.

The only one who was stuck, it seemed, was me.

My parents had long since stopped calling to ask whether I was coming home for the race so, one day, after some gentle prodding from a boss who understands these things, I called them.

"I'm, um, covering the Derby this year," I said.

I anticipated sighs. I prepared for aloofness.

After all these years of covering every major sporting event but the one that mattered most to them, I expected attitude.

Instead, I got questions.

"You want us to pick you up at the airport?" said Dad.

"You want us to fix up a room?" said Mom.

So I'm here, and the name on my press credential is misspelled, and I deserve it.

Bill Plaschge has missed a lot.

The house where mint leaves grew wild around the garage, accounting for my father's record consumption, has long since been sold.

My uncle Bill, who once set a Derby party standard by opening a pari-mutuel window over the patio, has closed shop.

Nobody in our family sneaks through holes in a fence anymore, climbing atop a barn's tar roof and paying for that Derby ticket in second-degree burns.

My people are at the fancy tables now, although not so fancy that I can't hear them, whooping it up in the Eclipse Room, betting the tax refund and eating hot browns and pounding their elbows as if they were at the kitchen table.

Which, now that I think about it, they were.

The reason the Kentucky Derby has lasted 128 years, despite a decline in national horse racing interest, is that it's not about the horses.

It's about that kitchen table, shaped like an oval, covered in dirt, 1-1/4 miles long.

The Derby has been the steady, plain-spoken center of a sports world that has slowly changed around it.

The Masters gets longer. The Indy 500 gets political. The Daytona 500 kills a hero.

Where else but the Derby does the winner simply run faster

than anyone else? Where else do the losers offer no excuse?

There is no trash talking when the competitors can't talk. There is no ugliness when the event lasts only two minutes, and is run for a blanket of flowers.

No other event is so basic, so consistent, so eternal, Aristides becoming Cannonade becoming Monarchos.

The Derby that was here when I left town 25 years ago is the same Derby that was waiting for me this week.

Standing under twin spires that lighted up the predawn darkness like a warm gaze, I saw the spot where I kissed my first girl, drank my first beer, spit out my first nasty-tasting julep.

It was on Derby Day that I first saw my older brother after a yearlong estrangement, hugging him in the infield because that is what you do in church.

It was on Derby Day that I last saw my grandfather, visiting his small apartment, where he lay on his old couch in exhaustion, recounting the race.

Granddaddy Willie died several months later, remembering nothing if not the great ride of Genuine Risk.

It was at the Derby that I first cried at a song, you know which song, and that lump has returned whenever I've heard it since, trying to ignore a race that will not ignore me.

When I walked into my house after flying here Tuesday afternoon, walking past the Derby napkins and Derby cups and framed drawing of a Derby finish, my mother was missing.

She was at the track. Betting the fourth race. On a horse named — and I'm not making this up — Willie Call.

I'm glad I did.

February 26, 2002

In Any Event, Games Did Have Moment of Humility

SALT LAKE CITY — Everyone comes to the Olympics looking for that moment, that one special instant that restores our faith in everything great and important and enduring about the greatest sport spectacle in the world.

On the second night of the 19th Winter Games, I was blessed with that moment.

It was around midnight in downtown Salt Lake City, the streets teeming with celebrating fans, strutting athletes, many languages, one voice.

I was in the middle of a crosswalk, headlights illuminating me from all directions, bathing my body like thousands of shiny medals.

When my snow pants fell to my ankles.

Let me back up here a second.

They weren't my snow pants. I don't do snow pants.

I'm from the South, I live in Southern California, I don't do snow. I don't do slush. I draw the line at Slurpee.

The snow pants belonged to photographer Kirk McKoy. He lent them to me at the opening ceremony, where my knees had started knocking after standing for nearly two hours in a security line in 20-degree temperatures.

McKoy had an extra pair. I tried them on. They fit. I think. I had no idea.

Newly fortified, I walked from the media tent into outdoor Rice-Eccles Stadium dressed as I would be for the next 10 days.

Long johns. Wool socks. Wool pants. Snow pants. Turtleneck. Sweater. Fleece coat. Parka. Inner gloves. Outer gloves. Ski cap.

I waddled to my seat where, just as the Olympic theme was playing and the ceremony was beginning, I dropped my pencil.

I leaned over to pick it up, fell, and couldn't get back up.

It was at this point that a kind volunteer hovered above me and verbalized what became my own personal Olympic theme.

"Um, sir, I think your snow pants are on backward."

So, you see, they weren't my snow pants.

And, having now covered my first Winter Olympics, I can safely say that these aren't my Games.

Not because they were too scandalous, or too maudlin, or too long.

Because they were too cold.

What a great idea, holding outdoor events in the mountains in mid-February. Whoever thought of it should be forced to ride down an icy track on a real skeleton.

The final week here was relatively mild — I wore only one pair of gloves — but that doesn't compensate for the 10 frostbitten days spent standing for hours in 10-degree temperatures watching the final 10 seconds of a ski race.

Haven't these people ever heard of, I don't know, the Fall Olympics?

Every day, it took me at least 30 minutes to get dressed, and 10 minutes to recover from getting dressed.

I wrenched my shoulder trying to put on my coat. I twisted my back trying to put on snow boots. I pulled a calf muscle trying to remove my long johns. I used up all of my complimentary bottles of shampoo trying to wash them.

Once bundled, I would consistently limp outside in all these layers with all these zippers and nearly die.

Not of hypothermia, but of heat exhaustion.

When I desperately shed some of the clothes and threw them on a fence in the skiing corral, then the hypothermia would hit.

During those few moments in the last two weeks when I was not getting dressed or undressed, I examined all the sports here and came to this reasonable conclusion.

There is absolutely no reason the Winter Olympics need to be held during winter.

Snowboarders are skateboarders in thermals. Bobsledders and lugers can do it on wheels. Cross-country skiers can put on cheap running shoes like the rest of us. Ski jumpers can use the pool. And Alpine skiers, well, we stink at that sport anyway.

But back to the crosswalk.

So my snow pants, backward and unbuttoned because I couldn't find the buttons, fell to my ankles. At the same time, the loose waist of my regular pants began dropping.

It was at this point, in the middle of the road, that I was forced to stop walking. Cars started honking. People started laughing.

I could have shimmied away in embarrassment. But no. I hung tough. Still in the crosswalk, I dropped my computer case, leaned down and, in one motion, pulled up the snow pants and found a zipper and fiddled with a button and righted myself before the light changed.

An Olympic moment indeed.

For those keeping score at home, I earned only a 4.9 for technical merit, but a 6.0 for presentation.

June 18, 2000

Look Who's Talking

They have flown over deficits, sprinted past injuries, marched calmly through the most treacherous moments of their professional lives.

But these last two months, the most courageous single act I have seen among the Lakers occurs when one is standing still.

It is Ron Harper.

Every time he opens his mouth.

.   .   .

With the Lakers stuck, stuck, stuck on the verge of a championship today, wondering again when they will win the one game that can make them whole, maybe this is an odd time to write about their aging point guard.

Then again, maybe not.

Ron Harper spends his entire life stuck, stuck, stuck.

Sometimes on a "C." Other times on a "W." Talk about some-body who would open his wallet for a vowel.

Harper stutters.

You may have heard him described as a "recovering stutterer" or "having a speech impediment," but that's simply politically cor-rect blather.

Some words stick to Harper's mouth as though they're glued there. Many that leave, don't do so without a fight.

Harper will take five seconds to start a sentence, and two sec-onds to finish it.

Sometimes he finds a word by rolling his eyes. Other times it sneaks out above a trembling bottom lip.

Ron Harper, plain and simple, is a stutterer.

It takes one to know one.

While growing up, I sounded exactly like Ron Harper.

Today my problem would seem mild, even nonexistent, in com-parison.

This is thanks to years of speech therapy combined with a deci-sion to do something Ron Harper would never do.

I ran.

I avoided words that began with letters — such as "R"— that would get trapped under my tongue.

I changed my everyday vocabulary so I would use only words that were easy to say, and unlikely to embarrass.

Heck, at one point I even considered changing my first name because I kept stumbling on that "B."

Once I began writing, which was another way to avoid talking, I learned other tricks.

I did virtually all of my interviews face to face, not because I was some hard-nosed reporter, but because the silence I anticipat-ed at the other end of the phone would lock my jaws completely.

I would give my interview subjects pet names like "Buddy," not because I was some fun guy, but because I could use those words to start a sentence and build momentum.

But this is not about me, this is about Ron Harper.

Because every time he is interviewed, he puts people like

me to shame.

Harper doesn't run. He stays. He fights. He moves to the next word and fights some more.

He has no tricks, attempts no shortcuts. He says what he wants to say, even if it takes him long, uncomfortable moments of stammering to say it.

"This is me, this is who I am," he says. "I have nothing to be ashamed of."

Harper is undoubtedly the most pained speaker in the NBA, and perhaps one of the most pained in the history of sports, which includes the stuttering likes of Bill Walton, Lester Hayes and Bo Jackson.

Yet no Laker is quoted more.

Think about it.

"What, I'm going to sit home and say nothing because I'm worried that people will laugh at me?" he says. "You can't hide."

Opposing players indeed still mock him — see Portland's classless Rasheed Wallace during the Western Conference finals.

Yet no Laker does more talking during timeouts.

Think about it.

"After all I went through growing up, nothing bothers me anymore," he says. "The special thing about life is that you have to be who you are."

He has always been this way. Growing up in a lower-income environment in Dayton, Ohio, he was never able to get proper treatment for his condition.

He did his therapy on the basketball court.

"Kids would mock me and talk behind my back and I was always like, 'OK, fine, you wanna play me?'" Harper remembers. "That is how I got back at everybody."

He attended Miami of Ohio partially because of the school's speech therapy program. He became more understandable. He decided he could overcome it without challenging every critic to a game of one-on-one.

Today, he has not been to speech therapy in 14 years, and thinks about it no more than he thinks about his fingernails.

"Just look where I've been," he says. "Now I'm like, whatever."

There have been times during these playoffs when, because there was no official practice, the Lakers were required to make only one player available to the media.

That player is almost always Ron Harper.

Think about it.

Walton, who has recovered enough to become an NBC commentator, has thought plenty about it.

"Ron Harper is a testament to a man standing up and being himself," Walton says. "Every day he tells us, 'This is who I am. This is my game.'"

That game is the same with the basketball as with the consonant blocking.

Harper's 35-year-old skills are sometimes as erratic as his speech, yet he doesn't back away.

He struggles, and struggles, and hangs around long enough to beat Portland with a jump shot or Indiana with his defense.

When the team has needed championship focus, he has loudly offered it.

When the team has needed further proof, he has showed his three championship rings.

In Sacramento during a first-round loss, he even slipped one on his finger while sitting on the bench.

He can take one minute to say something everyone else can say in five seconds, but the team is still listening.

"We watch him every day stepping right in front of the cameras," Derek Fisher said. "That's all we need to see to know he's a champion."

This being Harper's first year as a Laker, the team initially didn't know what to make of him. Somebody actually even cracked a stuttering joke.

"Everybody laughed, it went down as one of the funniest jokes of all time," John Salley said. "And nobody has told another one since.

"I tell you what, Ron Harper is a real man."

I agree. I tell Ron Harper this. I break every rule in that little journalist's book and tell him during a group interview session that

I admire him for his courage and his grace.

He stops the interview. He smiles. The eyes are focused, the lips are steady.

"Thank you very much," he says, smooth and clear and perfect.

December 29, 2001

A Sweet Science That Isn't All an Act

So, did you see my movie?

The one about me and this something-or-other boxer?

It's huge. It's everywhere. The biggest Christmas Day opening in history.

People everywhere are falling in love with that mottled face screaming those two probing questions at a vital news conference in the movie's first dramatic moments.

My 15 minutes of fame.

OK, my two minutes of fame.

"Your *10 seconds* of fame," whispered my wife.

"You were good, Daddy, but can we leave now?" whispered my 6-year-old. "The previews gave me a tummy ache."

So, have you seen it?

The movie's original title was "Plaschke."

But the marketing geeks apparently worried that was too many letters.

They fretted about fitting it on T-shirts, mugs, Oscar statuettes, that sort of thing.

So they shortened it, to "Ali."

■   ■   ■

Like many other famous stars, I was discovered in the mailroom. To be more precise, the mailbox.

I was riffling through my junk letters one morning last January when I came upon a much-mimeographed memo saying that the "Ali" folks were looking for people to play reporters.

"That would be a stretch," said a buddy.

I must confess here, I'm not a Hollywood guy. I love a good movie, but only in the manner that I love a good piece of sausage.

I can better appreciate the taste without knowing who made it, or how.

I never drop names, because I don't know any names.

I'm the nerd sitting next to you at the Laker game who's actually watching the game.

Of course, that was before.

Before I discovered that the last scheduled "Ali" tryout coincided with my only day off that week.

Before I realized that my children thought it was a lot cooler to be reading for a movie than writing about a game.

Before the early-evening phone call that changed my life.

"Michael Mann has seen your tape, and he would like you to be part of his movie," a woman said.

"Michael who?" I said.

■   ■   ■

On my first day of stardom on the San Fernando sound stage, the security guard energetically waved at me.

"Only the talent can park in here," he said. "You have to park in a lot down the road."

So my film career officially began while waiting for a shuttle bus, in the freezing rain, at dawn, with dozens of other, um, stars.

These people, I later learned, are called "extras." They are hired by filmmakers to stand or sit or walk around in the background. They are struggling actors and housewives and off-duty security guards.

They are Hollywood's last true believers, it seems, buying into the notion that one big-screen appearance can change a life. They show up each morning with darting eyes, high hopes and paperbacks titled, "Hollywood Here I Come" and "Monologues They Haven't Heard."

They are, I learned, the wonderful soul of the business.

For which they are paid $200 a day and treated like cattle.

"Quiet down and get in line!" an assistant director shouted at us that first day as we exited the bus and stood in another line, in another downpour, preparing to enter the sound stage.

"Makeup over here! Quickly people!" shouted another.

"Move! Move!" shouted a third.

The unheated stage was freezing. The portable toilets outside were leaking. It wasn't yet 7 a.m., and I had already been screamed at five times.

I called my wife, apologized for being a wimp, and told her my movie career was over.

As I prepared for my long, wet walk back to the car, an assistant director named Spoon recognized me from the newspaper.

"Wait a minute," he said. "You're in the wrong place."

Twenty minutes later, I was sitting in a makeup trailer with somebody handing me a razor and telling me to shave my 15-year-old beard.

Now I knew I was really in the wrong place.

"I love my beard," I said.

"You are playing a reporter in Miami in the early 1960s, you have to shave it," they said.

I had seen no script. I apparently had no lines. I was strictly background.

This wasn't worth losing my best friend.

Next thing I knew, I was meeting ringside with Michael Mann.

By then, I had studied enough to know that he was one of the toughest, most exacting directors in the business.

I had no idea he could also be such a good sport.

"I can't shave my beard for a job I know nothing about," I told him.

He stared at me, shrugged and smiled.

"Shave the beard, and I'll give you some lines," he said.

"Hooray for Hollywood," I said.

■   ■   ■

Two lines. Two weeks. Fifteen hours a day.

Actors work harder on one film than many athletes work in an entire season.

Jon Voight, the kind man who played Howard Cosell in the movie, showed up for makeup every day at 3:30 a.m.

Will Smith, who could win an Academy Award for his portrayal of Muhammad Ali, remained in character the entire 15 hours every day, never losing the voice or the bravado.

Mann would shoot each scene about 50 times, it seemed, from every possible angle, with every imaginable kind of lighting.

The scene with my two lines? The shooting lasted 11 hours and required 45 takes, all of them spent standing on a concrete floor with Times co-worker Steve Springer, NBC's Jim Gray and dozens of extras. Everything I now know about movies, I learned from those extras.

"Find out which camera is hot, and go for it," said my extra buddy Walter. "Try to stand next to somebody who has a speaking part, and maybe they'll throw you a line."

Those scenes in "Ali" showing reporters fighting to get close to him? It had nothing to do with acting. The extras were just trying to get into the shot.

The fight scenes with people leaping up and down in the stands? Again, extras hoping somebody notices.

When I said my lines, I had one extra hanging from my back, two others grabbing my coat, and another stepping on my feet.

"Anything to get on the screen," said one.

They are a lovable lot, deserving of much better than the continual public scoldings from the director's low-rung lieutenants.

One extra was fired for trying to be too chummy with Will Smith between takes. Another extra had a bottle of water snatched from his hand because it was reserved for one of the stars.

Of course, with so many extras required for the fight scenes, there was bound to be trouble.

During one scene, an extra sat behind me chanting, "I am not going back to the mental institution." He was later dismissed.

Another extra sat across the ring doing bird imitations before being removed.

My favorite was the fellow who fell asleep at the top of the stands during one fight scene and tumbled down the steps.

But then a ringside cell phone would blare, and it would be Muhammad Ali, himself, asking to speak to Will Smith.

Or, Smith would interrupt the filming on Martin Luther King Jr. Day to read from one of the great man's speeches.

Or, a punch would be delivered by Smith to Michael Bentt that sounded just like something Ali would have thrown at Sonny Liston.

And all this stuff about movie magic, you start to understand, and maybe even feel, and it's a lot like the Lakers, only with more no-look passes.

And then, nearly 12 months later, the theater darkens, the five-story screen brightens, and there it is, bigger than life . . .

A face made for boxing.

"You really should have kept your beard," wrote one of my e-mailing reviewers.

"Hollywood is all about the deal," I smugly replied.

December 13, 2001

No Place Like L.A. for the Holidays

"Do you see him?"

"Where? Where?"

"Out there, right above that tanker."

"That's an airplane. It's buzzing."

"Wait! Wait! Over there!"

"Where? Where?"

"Right above the cliff, way out there, I'm sure that's him."

"Where? Where?"

"Right there underneath those stars. That slow-moving red light."

"Oh, yeah, red."

"You see it glide?"

"'Yeah, like a sleigh."

"Shhhh. Can you hear the bells?"

"Yeah, the reindeer."

"Oh my gosh, it looks like it's turning right toward our neighborhood."

"Daddy?"

"Yes?"

"Can we go home and go to bed now?"

■   ■   ■

Our family knows there is a Santa Claus not because we read about him in tired books or watch him on teary Hallmark movies or visit him in crowded malls.

We know because we see him work. On the busiest night of his year. In the place closest to our Southern California hearts.

Every Christmas Eve, we see Santa in the skies above the beach.

Then we Dasher to the car and Blitzen home, climbing under the covers just before the old guy climbs down our chimney.

So far, so good, although once our young son thought Santa beat us home before we reminded him that, no, it was just the naughty neighbors' ancient, obsolete, stinking eyesore television antenna.

We go to the beach because, well, how else would Santa get here? From the North Pole, south through the Arctic Ocean, over the Bering Sea, then due southeast until turning inland above Zuma, Santa Monica, Carlsbad or somewhere like that.

We don't know where exactly Santa hits land, only that we always see him when he does, a red beacon of promise high above the cold sand and crashing darkness.

The only problem, of course, is that it must be dark. And on Christmas Eve, who can wait for the dark?

For us, this is not an issue, because before Santa, there must be church. That means attending the annual 4 p.m. children's Christmas Eve Mass.

For the uninitiated, a Catholic children's Christmas Eve Mass is like recess with pews. There is screaming, crying, kicking. Occasionally, even the children misbehave. In our dozen years of attending such Masses, I've been able to hear the words of a priest

only once, last year, when our brave padre spoke gently to a parish-
ioner who was running up and down the aisle dressed like the
Grinch.

Exhausted, and occasionally beset with flesh wounds, we
return home for turkey sandwiches and old sweats. Then we climb
in the car and go searching for Santa.

Once on the road, we order the GameBoys turned off, at
which point our three children introduce themselves to one
another. Then we all sing. Nobody seems to know anything other
than the first verse of any carol, and soon our oldest daughter
inevitably begins chortling the schoolyard composition about St.
Nick's body odor.

But by that time, with light traffic, we have reached the beach.
A different sort of holy place on a holy night. Quiet, nearly empty,
whistling air, chilly sand, black water.

For a few moments, standing outside our car, arms wrapped
around one another, we can hear only the thump of the waves. Or
is that our 6-year-old's heart?

Then, together, we all look into the sky. A forever sky. There are
planes with red lights gliding above docked boats with jingling
sails, but that is not where we look.

We look beyond that. We look until all the adult is rubbed from
our eyes. We look until we see.

"Daddy! Daddy! That's him! That's him!"

January 16, 2002

An Experience That Lights Up the Soul

Did you see who was handed a flame?

Amid hundreds of heroes, a lousy storyteller.

A guy who sees Olympic rings and thinks, five iced crullers. A guy who can't ski. A guy afraid to light a match.

Yet Tuesday they gave him an entire flame, in a torch, down on the corner of 14th and Stanford.

Asked him if he could run two blocks with nobody chasing him. Asked him if he could do it while holding a three-pound weight that was not a six pack. Asked him to please not burn the city down.

He said he would try. It was an honor for the torch to pass through his town on the way to Salt Lake City next month for the Winter Olympics, so he would try.

But sitting on the shuttle bus with other Olympic torchbearers early Tuesday afternoon, his legs were cement and his will wavered.

He didn't belong. He knew that now. They picked the wrong guy. How could he do this?

Sitting across from him on the bus was an 80-year-old torchbearer who teaches inner-city children to ski.

Behind him, a torchbearer who gives life to premature infants.

In the middle of the bus, a liver transplant survivor. And in the back row, a kid who beat Hodgkin's disease.

"So why are you here?" someone finally asked the storyteller.

"I'm not sure," the storyteller said.

·   ■   ·

As Olympic moments go, the start of this story carried all the emotion of a slalom preliminary, only without the annoying beeps.

"Hey, you wanna carry the Olympic torch?" asked the storyteller's boss.

"For the United States?" said the storyteller.

"Well, um. . . ." said the boss.

The torch, as the storyteller was quickly reminded, is not about countries.

That is its beauty. That is the one thing that separates it from virtually every other part of the Olympic movement, including those five rings.

The torch does not recognize differences in continents or language. It is the same torch whether it is held by the doctor from

West Covina or west Africa.

The flame is one color, and many colors. The hands that hold it can be old and wrinkled, young and smooth, brown or yellow.

The only requirement, it seems, is that those hands be strong.

The storyteller looked at his hands. They were not particularly strong.

These hands had never cured a child or rescued an animal or bettered the world.

These hands, even while wearing gloves, had no right holding the most endearing symbol of the world's most important sporting event.

The storyteller signed up anyway. He thought it would be fun.

He filled out forms and affidavits. He promised he would not use the torch as a croquet mallet or a birthday candle.

He promised that, for his entire two-tenths of a mile, he would keep his head up and his shoes laced.

One day last week, a package carrying his torchbearer's uniform arrived.

The storyteller's wife unwrapped the box, her eyes darting from the uniform to the storyteller's belly, uniform to belly, uniform to belly.

Then she screamed.

"It's torn?" the storyteller asked.

"It's white!" she shouted.

One crash diet later, the storyteller was rumbling along the streets of Los Angeles with a busload of heroes, a piece of flatware among this city's fine china.

Again, they asked, "So why are you here?"

Again, the storyteller couldn't answer.

So they told him.

Said the doctor: "You're here because everybody touches somebody."

Said the AIDS fighter: "Everything we do affects somebody else."

Alicia Keller, a torch cheerleader who has accompanied it around the country, stood in front of the bus and ended the debate.

"Each of you is here because somebody has seen the flame within you, and your power to spread that flame," she said. "That's what this day is about."

She gently held up an actual torch.

"Read it," she said.

There, in letters that streaked toward the shiny metal base, were the words, "Light the fire within."

As the shuttle pulled up on the corner of 14th and Stanford, the heroes sent him off not with stares, but cheers.

Moments later, the flame arrived, in the hands of a wide-eye high school girl running in memory of friends who had been killed in an auto accident.

The storyteller tipped his torch, and the fire jumped. Now, it was his.

"Remember," Keller had said earlier. "For those few minutes, you will be the only person in the world who has that flame."

The storyteller remembered. As the orange and blue heat flapped wildly in his face, he did the only thing he could think of doing.

On an oily patch in the middle of 14th Street, he dropped to one knee.

It was only for a second. He figured he had to thank somebody.

And then he was off, jogging between rows of aging warehouses that suddenly awakened with faces and hands.

Through the flame, he could see the smiles. Even with the whirring of the security motorcycles, he could hear the cheers.

It didn't feel as though he was carrying the flame. It felt as though he *was* the flame.

The more he stretched out the torch in his left hand, the louder the cheers. He stretched out his right hand, more cheers, as if he were carrying two torches.

Then the storyteller understood what the heroes have seemingly always known, the one thing they were trying to tell him.

Spreading your fire is no more difficult than opening your arms.

Every couple of years, the Olympics embraces the world by simply opening its arms.

The storyteller thought, this is easy. He then turned and opened those arms to the guy running behind him.

His name is Ted Hayes. He is the founder of our Dome Village homeless shelter.

He was not a torchbearer, but a support runner, a person invited to run along with the flame in case the torchbearer falters.

The storyteller thought, why wait? He asked Hayes to grab a piece of the torch, and together they carried it.

"Man," said Hayes, shaking his dreadlocks.

"Man," said the storyteller.

They jogged to the end of the two-block stretch, where the storyteller tipped the flame and passed it to the AIDS fighter.

An official then drove up and turned off the gas, extinguishing his flame.

The caravan of cars and trucks moved ahead, the little street became quiet, then the strangest thing happened.

It was if the torch lit itself again.

A warehouse worker walked up.

"Can I touch it?" he asked.

Another person walked up, and another, each asking only to touch the used torch.

A vagrant walked up, holding a tiny money clip containing what looked like one dollar.

"Here's my wallet as collateral," he said. "Can I touch it just for 10 seconds?"

Sure, said the storyteller, to the warehouse worker and vagrant and anyone else drawn to the flame that briefly filled a tiny corner of our great town.

Touch it. Everyone, please, touch it.

CHAPTER EIGHT

Wild Pitches

August 13, 1996

Rolling in the Aisles

Usher Elliot Berlend leans against a Forum wall, looking pleasant enough for a guy who has been on his feet for most of a sporting event.

"Hey."

"Hey," he says.

"Been busy?"

"You're the first today," he says.

"The first person you've spoken to?"

"The first person I've seen."

.   .   .

Footsteps echoed through concourses. Locked concession stands surrounded spotless bathrooms.

It was so quiet, you could hear the scoreboard.

The final total hummed, Los Angeles Blades 10, San Diego Barracudas 2, but the real story was on the other side of the glass that separates professional roller hockey players from their fans.

Because there were more players than fans.

"I think bizarre would be a very good word for this, don't you?" said Alan Leggett, a Barracuda defenseman.

For the first time in the history of alternative sports in the Southland, bizarre may not even come close.

A professional sporting event was played at the Forum where Los Angeles fans were not invited, parking lots not attended, tickets not taken, hot dogs not sold.

An event was held at the Forum without cheerleaders, celebrities or beer salesmen.

The idea was for the Forum to allow the Barracudas to rent the place for a "home" game against the Blades because the Barracudas say their arena is unsafe.

For it to best resemble a Barracuda "home" game, San Diego owner Dennis Murphy decided only San Diego season-ticket holders would be officially informed. And Murphy decided to start the game at noon on a Monday to scare anybody else away.

The Forum folks, wanting their team to earn a playoff spot without the stain of a forfeit victory, shrugged and let Murphy have his way.

The result?

Estimated paid attendance: 15.

"The only thing I've ever experienced like this was a brawl in junior hockey," said Barracuda forward Stephane St. Amour.

A hockey brawl?

"It was a brawl that happened after all the lights went out," he said. "Guys swinging at each other in the dark. Fans in the stands holding up their lighters so we could see who to punch."

St. Amour shrugged.

"The only thing good about today was, you make a mistake, there's nobody in the stands to yell at you," he said.

The biggest mistake was made by the well-intentioned people who run the Blades and the Forum.

By trying to maintain the integrity of the four-year-old Roller Hockey International League, they undermined that very integrity.

Not to mention, they spilled grease on the reputations of those alternative sports vying for the same respectability among adults that they enjoy among children.

If this can happen in roller hockey, how immune can arena football and indoor soccer be?

Roller hockey's defenders, pretty much everyone in that crowd, angrily accused the media of sensationalizing the game while ignoring a sport that averages 4,671 fans per pro game nationwide.

"It's a shame the news media comes out to a game that's not open to the public," said Amy Fogg, president of the 75-member Blade fan club.

Our point exactly.

How many times has a professional baseball, basketball, football or hockey game not been open to the public?

But back to the grease, which led to the mess.

Murphy alleges that a Gloria Estefan concert recently left grease — from her husband's hair? — on the floor of the Sports

Arena in San Diego. He said it was unsafe for his players and so made arrangements to play his final two home games on the road.

Because one of those games was against the Blades, and because the Blades are fighting for a playoff spot, the Forum folks offered their home for a day.

"What could have been worse than a forfeit? We did not want that to happen," said Tim Harris, Blade general manager.

Murphy admitted he did his best to keep all Blade fans away to appease the fans of teams fighting with the Blades for a playoff spot.

"I wanted to make it as fair as I could for the rest of the league," he said. "We could not give L.A. a home game. We did our best not to."

Instead, he gave us the Ghost Bowl.

A pre-game announcement warning was issued, as it always is, about profanity in the stands.

A similar warning should have been issued to the players, whose every expletive was clear.

Announcements were made about the sale of box lunches in the Forum Club. There are still plenty left.

The crowd grew by one in the first half when San Diego Coach Steve Martinson was thrown out of the game and simply walked up and joined his fans.

OK, so maybe a forfeit wasn't the worst possible thing.

"It's like, no good deed goes unpunished," said Harris.

The Blades, for the record, have been a reasonably successful franchise, averaging 3,639 fans, and can clinch a playoff berth at the Forum tonight at 7:30 against Sacramento.

The Barracudas, for the record, have yet to play their ugliest hand. They will finish their "home" schedule this week with a game against Sacramento at Stuart's Rollerworld in Orange.

"We're playing at a roller rink?" St. Amour said. "I can see it now. Somebody is going to shoot the puck right into the restaurant."

St. Amour sighed into the emptiness.

"I don't know what Stuart's Wallyworld is," he said. "But, right now, I don't want to know."

POSTSCRIPT: The Los Angeles Blades and the Roller Hockey International League folded after the 1997 season.

May 26, 1996

47 Years of Golf Lessons Turn a Guy Tap-Happy

Still looking for a Memorial Day weekend hot spot? We've found one. It's a black Masonite slab in the middle of Ed Coleman's shag-carpeted living room.

First, some background. Throughout the country, Monday's holiday marks the symbolic beginning of The Time When Every Fool Tries Golf.

For the next four months, thousands of innocents will visit quiet, green places in hopes of summer fun, only to endure five consecutive hours of public humiliation.

Then some of them will play the back nine.

For the next four months, with local tournaments and family functions at hand, many are suddenly in need of expert advice on stances, swings, and how to avoid losing those little pencils.

Which, to the man who taught much of this city how to play, means only one thing.

Tap dancing.

After giving as many as 10 golf lessons a day to some of the worst hackers on Byron Nelson's green earth, Ed Coleman unwinds by tap dancing.

He retires to his tiny Westside apartment where he lives alone with the three couches, a card table and no television set since Milton Berle left the screen. He laces up shiny white shoes, turns on Dick Hyman, and bangs across the Masonite for as long as it takes the average person to play three holes.

He does it all with amazing smoothness for a red-faced guy somewhere in his 70s. He just won't say where in his 70s.

"I tap dance because I needed to have something that I could do better as I got older," he said. "It sure wasn't golf."

And Ed Coleman knows golf. For parts of 47 years, and steadily since 1965, he has been a PGA teaching pro at Rancho Park Golf Club in Los Angeles.

It's among the busiest public courses in the country. Catering to players whose first question is usually, "Do we have to count *every* stroke?" he has been one of its busiest instructors.

The way Coleman figures it, this summer he will give his 90,000th lesson.

Which means only one thing.

"There have been times," Coleman said, "when I thought I was a dead man."

Coleman has been hit with drives, which wouldn't be that unusual except he was standing parallel to the driver.

Coleman has had animated discussions with elderly high-school principals, also not unusual, except when considering they are swinging a club at the time and won't shut up.

Then there was the day he walked off a course at the 12th hole. At the time, his foursome had been playing for six hours.

But Ed Coleman said he has also experienced this:

"A very pretty woman, to whom I had given many lessons, once ran to the edge of the fence along the practice tees.

"She shouted to me, 'Hey, I just broke 80! Come over here! I want to kiss you!'

"I said to her, 'What would you want to do if you had broken par?'"

Coleman has broken par on many occasions in his pro career. What he has never done is broken through.

More than 20 times, he has tried to qualify for the U.S. Open. He has never come within a stroke of making it. Nor has he ever come close to qualifying for the regular PGA Tour.

"Sure it's disappointing," Coleman said. "There's about 20,000 club pros out there, and not one of them start out wanting to give 10 lessons a day. All of them wanted to be Ben Hogan. I was no different."

Ed Coleman's biggest wishes were never granted.

Lucky for us.

In working with everyone from Jesse Owens to 100 children in one session, Coleman has been a teacher who has emphasized more than mechanics. In half-hour stints that have added up to a lifetime of influence, he has taught golfers less about the grip and more about the game.

His students don't throw clubs. Or curse. Or improve their lies. Or lie about their improvements. Or they are no longer his students.

"This is still a gentlemen's game," Coleman said. "That much has not changed."

Two things have prepared Coleman for this job, which pays him only a percentage of the $25-a-lesson fee charged by the city.

He was an original student of famed teacher Ernest Jones, considered one of the game's greatest professors. And he was on a tank that landed at Omaha Beach on June 6, 1944.

"After D-day, everything in my life has been a breeze," he said.

He has played under the moonlight, helping a student who shot better at night than during the day.

He has taught students whose clubs are so old and broken, "I get a tetanus shot before the lesson," he said.

Ten reputed Mafia members playing 100 yards behind him once lined up and teed off in unison when they thought his students were playing too slowly.

"If any of them topped the ball, we would have been killed," he said.

But one student once surprised him by filling his date book with a first-class ticket to Europe. Another student showed up 38 years after his lessons just to say thank you.

It has been 47 splendid years, so worth the pain that Ed Coleman, who wants to give his 100,000th lesson before retiring in five years, says, "Teaching golf is wonderful."

Well, almost wonderful.

His favorite sport?

"That would be tennis," he said.

August 8, 1990

This Clown's Not Laughing Inside

ASHEVILLE, N.C.—The summer night air is thick with sweat and Southern accents. Aging McCormick Field creaks under the weight of 4,000 people.

Some have come to take advantage of "Thirsty Thursday," when a 24-ounce beer costs a buck. Others have come to chat with their neighbors while holding their children by their shirttails. Still others have come to watch a baseball game between the Class A Asheville Tourists and the Charleston (W.Va.) Wheelers.

Then there is this 70-year-old man wearing a saggy face and baggy baseball uniform. He has come to entertain.

"Ladies and Gentlemen, introducing the clown. . . ."

The end of the sentence comes out garbled over the scratchy public address system and Max Patkin, the clown prince of baseball, is greeted by only a few cheers and mostly stares as he runs from the third base dugout to his position in the first base coaching box.

He mimics the fielders during an infield drill. He spits on himself. He throws dirt on himself. He lies across first base. He yells out a barely audible joke about chicken cacciatore.

Some people are laughing. Most are still just staring.

Patkin stops.

"Make 'em laugh, damn it," he whispers to himself. "Make 'em laugh."

■   ■   ■

He has been doing this for 45 years, about 80 shows a year, a total of about 3,500 shows. A ton of dirt has been thrown on his face, gallons of water have been spit like a geyser from his mouth, 10,000 bad jokes have been told, and children have laughed a million laughs.

But what makes baseball clown Max Patkin proudest is that he has never failed to show up for work.

He jumped out of a burning plane after it landed in Fayetteville, Ark., to make a date. He once took a cab 300 miles on a flat tire through the middle of Mexico to make a date.

He has performed even when he was so sick others could not bear to stand near him.

"It was in Monterrey, Mexico, 20 years ago, and I had Montezuma's revenge," Patkin remembered of a time he was coaching first base. "All of a sudden, the guy on first base steals second. No big deal, but then the first baseman steals second. And the umpire steals second. I'm standing there all alone when I realize I've had an accident in my pants."

But he finished the show. He always finishes the show.

He has been cursed by minor league managers who won't let him dress in their clubhouses, victimized by players who rub analgesic balm in his athletic supporter, and yet Max Patkin has always been there at the end.

Now, as he nears the end of the time when he is still physically able to perform, Patkin is still here. He is in the midst of doing 60 shows this summer, in minor league ballparks from central Florida to central Canada, from Burlington to Billings.

He still wears a uniform he wore 30 years ago. He still washes his cap by hand so it won't shrink.

And by that part of America he still touches, he has not been forgotten.

"We had an autograph session with him this year, and the line stretched from here to the freeway," said Stan Naccarato, president of the Tacoma (Wash.) Tigers. "The man is an institution within himself."

Added Larry Schmittou, who owns teams in Nashville and Huntsville, Ala.: "The man is like the Globetrotters. He is part of history."

Now, if Max Patkin would only believe that. In becoming part of history, baseball's clown has been disillusioned by it.

His act was never easy, but never has it been as hard as lately. People don't laugh at old men with a handful of teeth anymore, they laugh at chickens. People don't like vaudeville, they like scoreboard videos.

Patkin is wondering these days if their laughter has ever been worth his pain.

"Once I quit, who is going to give a damn?" he said earlier this summer near his Philadelphia area home. "Really now, who gives a damn about a baseball clown? People will think about me and say, 'He used to be funny.' And that's it. That's my story. Used to be funny. Big deal."

■   ■   ■

The crowd at Asheville comes alive. Not because of Max Patkin, but because their team has scored three runs while he is coaching first base in the bottom of the third inning.

As is his custom, he will move to the third base coaching box in the bottom of the fourth inning, then back to first base in the fifth.

But he is not thinking ahead. Struggling with a distracted crowd, he is taking it one joke at a time.

"Hey kids," he shouts to the children while sticking out his neck and scrunching his lips underneath his big nose. "You better be good, or you'll look like this."

He then opens his mouth to show his one prominent bottom tooth. Most of the rest of his mouth is empty, as two years ago he refused to replace a set of bad dentures.

"If you don't brush your teeth, they will look like this!" he shouts to the children.

When he still gets little response, he screams, "What a crowd! I had more people in my bed last night."

The children giggle. Their parents shake their heads.

"I saw him five or six years ago, and just had to come back when I heard he was here," said John Stallings, a football coach who brought two carloads of friends from nearby Burnsville, N.C. "He's still great . . . but it looks like he's aged some."

Max Patkin likes to say that it started during the war, in 1944, when he faced Joe DiMaggio while pitching for a Navy team in Honolulu.

"He hit a home run off me, and I followed him around the bases," Patkin recalled. "I don't know why, I just did. I was just a ham. Soon, admirals were coming out and asking when that goofy guy would be pitching again."

Truthfully, though, he admits it probably started the day he looked in a mirror and realized he looked, um, different.

"I know how I look," he said. "I knew that because of my appearance, I was getting laughed at even when I wasn't trying to be funny. On the field I make myself more grotesque than I am, but I know how it is. I finally figured, the man upstairs makes you a certain way, that's the way it is supposed to be. Maybe the reason I was made this way was, I supposed to make people laugh."

Said Ron McKee, Asheville general manager: "Max is so ugly, people love him."

It was with this understanding that Patkin, a frustrated pitcher who never made it above the middle minor leagues, made his debut as a clown coach for owner Bill Veeck's Cleveland Indians in 1946. In his first game, he set fire to Hank Greenberg's shoes. He has been fooling players and fans ever since.

Fooling most everyone, in fact, except himself. Because from the start, Patkin was uncomfortable with the difference between laughed with and laughed at.

So uncertain of which applied to him in his early years, Patkin grew depressed. One day in 1951, he put his head in an oven and turned on the gas.

"Feeling that I could not make a living in sports except through my funny appearance, I got depressed, nearly had a nervous break-down," he said. "Then one day I could not go on . . . until I smelled the gas — and it smelled terrible. It terrified me. I pulled out. I decided to give my life another try."

Patkin still gets depressed from time to time as he lies in Rama-da Inn or Days Inn or Holiday Inn beds on weekday afternoons in small-town America, waiting to perform at yet another tiny ballpark. He hopes the audience won't notice how he moves slower these days, how he must pause to catch his breath. He hopes the audience will be kind.

"You know, I am really very sensitive about the way I look," he said. "I'll be walking down the street and somebody will call me ugly and I will shoot back with, 'I make a living looking this way. What's your excuse?'

"But it's not funny. I never have gotten the woman I want. I take a lot of abuse. It's not funny."

He thought he had the woman he wanted once, about 30 years ago, and married her. But he said that after he caught her cheating on him, she sneaked up and hit him over the head with a hammer, fracturing his skull. Thirteen years ago, they were divorced.

"You know what the darndest thing about that hammer incident was?" he asked. "A couple of weeks later, I attended this testimonial dinner for Tommy Lasorda. The emcee, Joe Garagiola, looked at me sitting on the dais with my head bandaged. He announced to everybody that my wife had just tried to kill me by hitting me over the head with a hammer.

"And you know what? Everybody laughed. They thought it was a joke."

. . .

Patkin is sweating through his old uniform and Montreal Expo cap, which he wears sideways, as he moves into the third base coaching box for the bottom of the fourth inning in Asheville.

It is a quick inning, but he moves quickly. He blows kisses to the women in the stands. He calls time out and kisses the batter. He spits on himself again. He throws more dirt on his uniform.

Then it is time for his nightly jitterbug dance. With the poor public address system, few can hear the music of "Rock Around the Clock." But the 70-year-old man dances anyway, twisting his feet into the ground and gyrating his double-jointed body as if he didn't care if anyone was watching. Or wasn't watching.

"Because of the bad speakers, that whole part of my act was blown," Patkin said later, shaking his head. "But, hell. Did you see the children who watched me? Did you see their faces?"

Patkin gets $1,500 a game, a pittance compared with the $5,000 per night that many current mascots average. But Patkin has not worked a major league game in 10 years, because his act no longer fits there.

"There is too much at stake for them to worry about me coaching third base during a big inning," Patkin said, slipping into another story. "I remember the time in Toronto, I was working a big game between the Blue Jays and Baltimore. With Jim Palmer pitching against John Mayberry of Toronto in the second inning, I yelled out, 'Fastball! Fastball!' from the third base coaching box. Just a joke.

"But that dumb Palmer, he still throws a fastball! Mayberry hit a homer and Toronto won and I'll never forget how Palmer just stared at me."

Of course, if Patkin had remained a major league act, he might have become as sterile as today's mascots, and thus deprived of adding to his rich and unusual history. He certainly would not have had as many good stories, such as being Lasorda's roommate.

"I was working a Spokane game when Tommy was managing there, and he let me stay in his room that night," Patkin remembered. "But he told me, if his team lost, I could not talk the whole night. And sure enough, they lost. So we go home and he doesn't let me talk for two hours and I'm getting all itchy.

"Finally he says, 'OK, I'll let you say one thing.' I say, 'Tommy, you're a no-good S.O.B.'"

. . .

It is the bottom of the fifth inning, Patkin's final appearance on the Asheville field, and he makes it his best.

Standing in the first-base coaching box, he actually drops his pants. He covers his brightly colored undershorts with dirt. Then, having taken a big swig of water from a soda can, he begins spouting the water in the air. High spouts, and lots of them. It is the feat that, to this day, makes his fans wonder.

"That water thing always amazed me," Dodger catcher Mike Scioscia said. "I don't think any of us ever figured out how he did it."

After the inning, he goes into his grand finale. He runs to home plate, crawls between the catcher's legs, grabs a bat, holds it at the wrong end, swings at a practice pitch, hits a grounder, runs to third base, gets tagged out and then thrown out of the game by a laughing umpire.

By now, the beers have been set aside, the socializing has stopped, and the crowd is roaring. Patkin leaves the field to a standing ovation, the old clown having actually gotten the last laugh.

•   •   •

Max Patkin has had an operation for a herniated disk. He has bone spurs in his feet. He has refused to undergo an operation for torn cartilage in his knee. He carries a blood-pressure card in his wallet, next to the index cards that remind him of his schedule.

This is a clown's life?

He lives with his brother, Edward, in a condominium at King of Prussia, Pa. They have two dogs and a cat. The dogs are so old, they can no longer control their bladders, so one room is completely papered for them.

Neighbors complain about the smell, but Patkin ignores them.

"I know it stinks," he said. "But how can you get rid of something you have had for 13 years?"

Minor league officials often ask him if he is planning to retire.

"I've had him here 11 straight years because he keeps telling me that every year is his last," Asheville's McKee said with a laugh.

Patkin's retirement threat has been just that, but he wonders.

"I'm getting older, my moves aren't what they used to be," he said. "I don't care about the money, I want to be funny. And I worry, are they still liking me?"

A couple of years ago his career was given a second life by an appearance in the move "Bull Durham." Baseball's minor league officials have since crowned him "The King of Baseball," in a corny ceremony annually honoring an individual's contributions.

The pleasures of such achievements, though, have been dimmed by the constant travel and pressures. Just last summer, the manager of the Boise, Idaho, team would not let Patkin dress in the clubhouse, and would not let his players help him. Patkin cursed him throughout his performance.

"When my dance is over, if people are not laughing at me, oh, that would be terrible," Patkin said. "That's why, when I go out there and things are bad, I just keep telling myself, 'Make 'em laugh, damn it! Make 'em laugh!'"

POSTSCRIPT: Max Patkin died Oct. 30, 1999. He was 79.

September 18, 1998

Just a Little Something for Himself

And to think, it was such a perfect catch.

The ball shot off Mark McGwire's bat and, for the first time since he and Sammy Sosa started hitting historic home runs, somebody in the outfield stands actually snared one clean.

"This was my moment, my time," John Grass said from his home south of St. Louis. "I saw it all the way."

Well, maybe not all the way.

. . .

Warning: This is this first story about "the Great Home Run Chase" that doesn't sing.

There are no chills, no flashing lights, no curtain calls.

For the first time, there is a loser.

By now, John Grass has probably figured out he's it.

He's a regular guy. Tends lawns for some St. Louis-area schools. Lives with his wife, three kids, one grandson in a three-bedroom brick home.

He went to a Cardinal doubleheader at Busch Stadium with tickets he bought at a grocery store. Toted an old mitt. Got lucky. Caught a home run ball.

Just so happened, it was McGwire's 63rd, a record at the time.

Officials hustled Grass to an office near the Cardinal clubhouse after the game. In walked McGwire. Grass showed him the ball, a wondrous thing.

McGwire smiled. His previous two landmark home runs were graciously returned to him by the folks who had caught them. He knew the routine.

"So you want a couple of autographed bats and balls?" McGwire asked.

"No," Grass said.

"No?" McGwire repeated.

"No," said Grass, pulling out a piece of paper. "I want this:"

- Seventeen autographed balls for his family and the family of a friend who had bought the tickets with him.
- Seventeen bats.
- Three McGwire jerseys, three caps, three gloves, three photos.
- Four season tickets in the left-field seats.
- Two autographed jerseys from Stan Musial.
- Two autographed balls from J.D. Drew. (Don't ask.)
- An all-expense-paid trip for four to Jupiter, Fla., for Cardinal spring training.
- Arrangements for Grass and his 20-year-old son to throw out the first pitch at a remaining home game this year.

"I don't want to be greedy, I'm not asking for any money," Grass said to the slugger. "I just want a little something to make my family happy."

"See ya," McGwire said.

And today John Grass sits, still holding the ball, still holding the list, wondering how it all became so complicated.

His friends tell him he is doing the right thing. They have since even persuaded him to change his mind and ask for money, in addition to the other stuff.

"Hey, the owners are always asking for money, the players are always asking for money. What's wrong with a fan doing it?" he asked.

Yet he goes on talk-radio shows and is ripped by callers who say he is mercenary.

Strangers find his unlisted number, phone his house, politely ask to speak to him, then scream, "GIVE McGWIRE THE BALL BACK!"'"

Although he returned to the ballpark the next day and was treated fine, his children tried to persuade him to stay home, worried that he would be mobbed by angry fans.

And to think, he was so excited when it happened, he lay awake in bed all night, the ball nestled between him and his wife.

The next morning, so worried that something would happen to his prize, he took the ball and glove with him into the bathroom when he showered.

Now, he sighs.

"I have one heck of a headache," Grass said. "Whatever I do, I am not going to keep this ball."

What would you do?

Judging from the response to the historic homer question posed here last month, as many readers would sell it back as give it back.

Because of what has happened since then, it's clearly time for another question.

What would you do *now*?

The balls McGwire hit to tie and break Roger Maris' 37-year-old record of 61 were returned to him for souvenirs, tickets and some batting practice.

The ball Sosa hit for his record-tying 63rd home run Wednesday night was returned Thursday morning by Fabian Perez Mercado, a bakery worker from Tijuana, for five caps, two jerseys, two balls, two gloves, one bat and 21 Padre playoff tickets.

That was the highest price paid yet by either club, but much of the loot was the Cubs' idea. Mercado wanted to return the ball and wanted only to see some playoff games.

Except for the Cub fan who sold Sosa's 61st homer to a collector for $7,500, the entire thing has been pleasant, civil . . . and it made you wonder.

Could "The Chase," which has stormed through the country breaking down barriers and stereotypes of all sorts, be strong enough to triumph over greed?

Could fans really be willing to serve as role models for the money-minded baseball industry instead of imitating them?

Then a regular guy comes along and gives an answer some of us don't want to hear.

"I am not trying to milk this," Grass, 46, said. "I'm not trying to get everything I can get. This ball is part of the biggest thing in sports history, and what's wrong with me benefiting from it in some small way?"

He loves baseball, played in the backyard with his boy, loves it so much that in May he bought bleacher seats for every home game this month.

He paid $6 apiece for them, and has turned down several hundred dollars each night to give them up.

"I knew back in May that this could be history, and I wanted to be part of it," he said. "Not for the money, but for the history. I love baseball."

He says he even loved his meeting with McGwire, says he was a nice man, even though McGwire took one look at the list, shook his head, and handed it to Walt Jocketty, Cardinal general manager.

Jocketty said it had to be approved by a Cardinal owner who had just left town.

"I want to do it now, I don't want to go home with this ball," Grass told them. "Somebody should do something quick."

The Cardinals never did.

And now the price has gone up by an undisclosed sum that Grass says will supplement his pension.

"I've got somebody out there talking to people for me right now . . . maybe a sheik or somebody will want it," he said. "I wish I could have given it to the Cardinals right then, but I guess they didn't want it."

He said he thought the previous two men who'd caught the historic homers gave up too easily, and at least one person agrees.

Deni Allen, the St. Louis man who caught No. 60, has already publicly expressed regret for being blinded by the lights and not selling the ball for thousands.

Grass said, "Those guys got caught up in the moment. I wasn't going to let it happen to me. The Cardinal people were trying to snow me over . . . telling me that I better hand it over, that the minute he hits number 64, it becomes just another $9 ball."

Grass, however, had already thought this over.

"Hey, the ballclubs charge us $3 for water, and $4 for beer, and Mike Piazza turns down $80 million to play," he said. "You want to call somebody greedy, it's them, not me."

The ball Mark McGwire hit for his 63rd homer now is in a safe-deposit box at John Grass' bank. He passed word from a local TV station to David Letterman that when he takes it out and hands it over, he would gladly do it on national TV.

Letterman's people said they would get back to him.

February 7, 1998

'Toughest S.O.B. You Ever Met'

The breakfast interview ended, the hero stuck out his hand, the reporter gladly shook it.

The hero had something else in mind.

"Help me up, would you?" asked Evel Knievel.

. . .

He was more than a daredevil, more than a crazy man who drank Wild Turkey and rode fast bikes.

For the children of 20 years ago, he was a vision, dressed up like the flag and flying through the air and being a doggone American inspiration when nobody else wanted the job.

Sitting in a restaurant booth Friday morning, black leather jacket on his shoulders, diamond rings gleaming, he is a vision still.

A living testament to how those fearless times did not come free.

Evel Knievel, at 59, doesn't look a day over 70.

"I'm the toughest S.O.B. you ever met in your life," he says.

He has to be, just to get around with that metal walker while recovering from hip replacement and pelvis reconstruction.

He suffers from a staph infection that last year nearly killed him.

He has an esophagus condition that, if he ever dares drink alcohol again, will cause him to vomit blood.

He has liver trouble that he says causes his body to swell up with fluids.

His arms have been so badly broken, he requires help to put on his own belt.

Thirty-five broken bones, more than 3 1/2 years in hospitals, yet he was still able to board a plane at his Florida home and fly here to promote this week's Southern California Boat Show at the Convention Center.

Tough? He's tough as ever, though time has changed the context.

The risks taken by Evel Knievel these days are mostly with his words, leaps over busloads of political correctness, still long and dramatic.

"I will bet Wilt Chamberlain $100,000 that he never slept with that many women, it's impossible; he's a liar, I should know," he said Friday morning.

Sitting alongside him, 26-year-old fiancée Krystal Kennedy glared.

"I once bet buddies that I could sleep with seven women in a 24-hour period, and I ended up with eight, but it's tough," he said. "Even six women in one day is tough."

Kennedy stood up, excused herself.

"I'm going to the bathroom," she said. "I doubt I'll miss anything important."

She walked away, and Knievel laughed.

"This women's liberation stuff, it's B.S., it's sickening," he said. "Women go to work dressed as sexy as they can, then when men don't make passes at them, they sue the men. I know how it works."

Ten minutes later the interview ended, and his fiancée was still missing.

Knievel was last seen shuffling his walker through the hotel lobby, calling her name.

. . .

It's not easy being Evel.

A man recently challenged him to an arm-wrestling match, wanted to brag to his friends that he whipped the greatest daredevil ever, but the great one declined.

"My arm hurts," he said.

He recently taped a series of commercials promoting ESPN's daredevil Winter X Games, then felt like a bad father.

"I watched the tapes, heard myself talking to these children to go for it, and had second thoughts," he said. "I wish I had said something else. I didn't feel comfortable telling them to risk their lives."

Has it really been 30 years since he went tumbling across the concrete while trying to clear those fountains at Caesars Palace?

Twenty-four years since that parachute opened on his rocket over Snake River Canyon?

Eighteen years since his last jump?

"When you were growing up, America was on its butt," he says to the reporter, to anyone who remembers breathlessly watching him clear 13 buses on "ABC's Wide World of Sports." "I came along at the right place, the right time.

"You wanted to see somebody do something for real. You wanted to see somebody do something American."

Or maybe we just wanted to see somebody really die on TV. Whatever, everyone watched, and when he disappeared from the public into a retirement of hard living and high rolling, we knew we would never see anything like it again.

"It's like Elvis Presley or Muhammad Ali," he said, smiling crookedly behind yellow-tinted glasses. "There's something to being first."

And there's something to hanging around. Today, with renewed popularity of disco music and '70s celebrities, Evel is cool again.

There are plans to re-release the popular Evel Knievel doll. There are plans for another movie about his life.

He even has his own crash-filled Web site, consistently voted among the best on the Web.

"W-w-w-dot-Evel-Knievel-dot-com," he says proudly, and you laugh, unable to hide your shock at hearing those words come from that man.

He is also, in his own way, again trying to carry the flag for American values.

He hustles golf.

With a cart, of course.

"I can't believe Arnold Palmer," he said. "If he ever had to use a cart in his life, he wouldn't be saying that Casey Martin shouldn't use one. I can't believe him."

He tells the story of playing a round at Myrtle Beach for $100,000 . . . and getting an eagle on the first hole while whipping another poor sucker.

But he also tells the story of last winter, walking to his ball in the rough, falling down a ditch, then being unable to move for two weeks, prompting him to finally have that hip surgery.

Always these days, there is another story.

He brags about his grandmother living until 103. Yet he despairs about the last time he was affected by the staph infection, resulting in a 104-degree temperature, teeth chattering, an ambulance ride and a prayer.

"I was saying, 'Please God, don't let me die,'" he said.

He brags that once this hip heals and he can walk again, he will feel better than ever.

But when asked about the words he wants chiseled into his tombstone — maybe something about a daredevil leaping to God? — he surprises again.

He says, "Under my name I want it to read, 'See, I told you I was sick.'"

You are thinking about that as you grab his hand and carefully pull him to his feet.

July 10, 2002

The Cold War

SCOTTSDALE, ARIZ. — Here lies baseball's greatest hitter, finally thrown a curve he couldn't reach.

Here lies a summer hero, frozen solid.

Here in this gray cinder-block building, on this scrub brush of a street in an airport industrial park, a marble company on his right, an adjustable-bed factory on his left.

Outside it is 110 degrees. Inside, suspended upside down in a stainless steel tank filled with liquid nitrogen, a legend cools.

Tough, brave, yet not strong enough to avoid being torn apart by his family.

Here lies Ted Williams.

The Splendid Popsicle.

• • •

It is All-Star day, so you have come to this desert neighborhood to pay homage to baseball's ultimate All-Star.

You remember a couple of years ago, when Ted Williams made his final All-Star game appearance, on a golf cart at Fenway Park, in a ceremony that moved modern-day players to tears?

This was a hot-blooded human being who touched people. This was not an ice sculpture.

Yet here he is, at Alcor Life Extension Foundation, a cryonic suspension facility that has parts of about 50 frozen corpses they optimistically call "patients."

Williams arrived here last weekend, shortly after his death at 83.

His son, John Henry Williams, sent him, reportedly hoping to squeeze even more money out of his name, or at least his DNA.

His daughter Bobby-Jo Ferrell, is legally protesting, claiming her father wanted to be cremated, his ashes spread over his beloved Florida Keys.

This messy, spooky affair is as ill-befitting Ted Williams as a ninth-inning strikeout.

Remember how he ended his baseball career with a home run?

Remember how he refused to sit down on the final day of the 1941 season, even though it put his .400 batting average in jeopardy?

This was a man who understood exits.

Is hanging in frozen limbo in the middle of a desert warehouse considered an exit?

. . .

You approach the front door, marked Alcor Marketing and Resource Center, sturdy and gray between two tinted windows.

This could be a cellular-phone store or rug warehouse, until a security guard leaps from his folding chair and blocks your way.

An identification card is passed. The door opens a crack. Another guard reaches outside and takes the card. There is much whispering.

You called ahead, you say. You just need a minute for some quick questions, you promise.

The card is returned. The door slams shut.

They are too busy. They will call you later.

Which, of course, they won't.

"The whole thing is bizarre," says Ron Johnson, owner of a sewing workroom two doors down. "That door is locked all the time. You never see anybody. It's odd. It's not normal. I feel so bad for Ted and what the jerk kid is putting him through."

Neighbors who have toured the facility say that it is essentially a warehouse filled with giant steel containers around what appears to be a surgical unit.

"I think that's for the heads," says Brad Porter, president of the air-conditioning company at the other end of the building.

Porter's outfit knows all about the heads.

Employees at his firm there helped construct racks that hold the severed heads of those who want to freeze only their brains.

They also helped build some of those containers, which are essentially tombs.

"Yeah, it's kind of creepy, I know," says Porter.

The air-conditioning company's phone number is 92-CHILL.

"That should be Alcor's number," employee Sally Kling says.

Neighbors say it's just as creepy outside, where an ambulance drives up at all hours to a back door that warns of hazardous materials.

Out front, a wide-eyed Alcor employee rides around the building on a creaking bicycle.

During calmer times, the windows are not tinted, and neighbors are treated to a window display of one of the giant tombs.

"Every time somebody new works here, they are taken past that window to get their reaction," Kling says. "When they took me, I was like, 'Oh my God.'"

Ted Williams, one of our most honored athletes, has been consigned to a sideshow.

"He's in there with all the other stiffs, and I mean stiffs," Kling says.

Ted Williams, the guy who used to tell the jokes, is in the middle of a bad one.

"We tell people, 'Why go over there and get frozen, when you can come here and get turned into beautiful stone?'" says Beverly Durigon of Travertine International, the marble company next door.

Ted Williams has gone from the baseball family to . . . "The Addams Family," says another business neighbor, and on a steamy All-Star afternoon, the whole room howls.

January 1, 2002

His Spirit's Unflagging

"Old Glory."

May she always fly high and free

∎   ∎   ∎

So reads the inscription at the base of the 132-foot pole in the front yard of the Southland's star spangled manor.

Thomas "Ski" Demski lives here. He does flags.

Painted on his car, painted on the side of this converted Long Beach duplex, flying so largely atop that pole that he had to fight city fathers to keep it there.

"Something about the flapping being in violation of the noise ordinance," he says. "But you can't silence Old Glory."

Nor its owner, a 72-year-old rascal best described as Old Glorious.

In the cackling home he shares with two dozen birds, Demski has flags on his walls, and over his floors, his light switches and his heart. Literally.

There are flags covering his entire torso, tattooed forever on the chest of the free and the back of the brave.

Right next to the tattooed phone numbers of his doctors.

One of them solemnly met Demski in an examining room last summer.

"Ski, I've got bad news for you."

"What is it, doc?"

"You've got my wrong number."

When it comes to flags, Demski wears them, bares them, dares them.

But mostly, he shares them.

With folks like us, in places we can understand.

Demski is the guy who rents the giant flags to the giant sports events.

The compelling flag that nearly covered the Dodger Stadium field in their first home game after the Sept. 11 tragedy? That odd-looking fellow marching alongside it was Demski.

In exchange for the use of Old Glory, he wanted to appear Half Monty, topless, with his flag tattoos in full view. The Dodgers said no. He brought the flag anyway.

"These are the sacrifices you make," he said.

That flapping, emotion-building flag that sprawled across the Rose Bowl field in UCLA's first football game after the tragedy? Demski again.

He has supplied the flags for everything from Army-Navy football games to the Super Bowl. Since the World Trade Center tragedies, he has been working since the dawn's early light, filling flag orders from a nation that finally shares his national pride.

His latest triumph will appear today, during the pregame show at the Fiesta Bowl, when 300 band members will unfurl a flag the size of the Sun Devil Stadium football field.

If recent flag ceremonies are any indication, some will have tears, others will have goose bumps.

Ski Demski will have a little of both.

Because he is dying.

Talk about your star-spangled ironies.

Just as the rest of the country is catching up to the fervor of one of its leading 72-year-old patriots, the flag man is out of breath.

It's his heart. He's already had one multiple bypass operation and the arteries are clogged again and nothing more can be done.

Last summer he passed out twice at home and nearly died.

This winter, for the first time in several years, Demski couldn't play Santa Claus for the local kids.

For the first time in 15 years, he did not accompany his flag to the Fiesta Bowl.

"All I do is lay around and sleep," he said.

"I'm fighting to keep him from giving up," said best friend Jim Alexander.

Demski hopes they broadcast his Fiesta pregame event on television, hopes there are enough people there to spread his flag across the field and give it the respect it deserves.

At the end of a life that Sept. 11 has transformed from eccentric to compelling, Demski fittingly said it's not about him.

It's about the flags.

"I'm just waiting to roll over and die," he said quietly in an interview in his cluttered home. "But my flags, I have made sure that they will always fly."

Like any man whose collection includes the world's largest flag — it cost $80,000, weighs 3,000 pounds, and covers nearly three football fields — Ski Demski can dazzle you with numbers.

But none are more compelling than this:

In 21 years owning and displaying flags in all parts of the country, none have been vandalized.

Nothing stolen, nothing burned, nothing clipped, nothing tagged.

On a street filled with barred windows, his giant flagpole stands unmarked, while a painted flag and surrounding eagle remain untouched.

"The flag, I guess, is one thing everyone understands," Demski said.

Driving up the freeway 21 years ago, disabled from his construction job because of a back injury, Demski understood.

He saw a giant flag flapping from a pole in front of a car dealership.

"I thought, that really looks good," he recalled. "I thought, why not try that?"

Unmarried, with no children and no job, perhaps Demski saw the flag as one part of the American dream that he could own.

Seeing as he was never in the military — he worked in the Pennsylvania coal mines, he said — maybe he felt he had some catching up to do.

Whatever the reason, and Demski isn't exactly sure himself, he drove home and erected the flagpole. And began buying flags. And soon he became one of the few people in the country to buy and rent the big ones.

He made his money printing bumper stickers. But he made his impact with stars and stripes.

"Someone like me was really drawn to him," said Alexander, a retired Coast Guard commander who helps run the Super Flags company. "He really loves his country."

Demski's company draped flags on the Washington Monument, Hoover Dam, in county fairs and veterans events everywhere.

After 15 years and one heart operation, he had become so associated with flags, he didn't blink at a tattoo artist's idea during a talk show.

"The guy saw my bypass scar and said, 'You know, that would make a great natural flag pole,'" Demski said. "So I got my first tattoo."

Five years later, he is covered with them, highlighted by a flag outline of the United States on his back.

Some find him weird. President Bush's people found him charming. Last winter, Demski and Alexander and their flag became the only sole-California entries in the inaugural parade.

None of which prepared him for the outpouring of emotion — and business — after Sept. 11.

"Somebody told me it was like everyone was just realizing what I've always known," Demski said. "It was really something."

It was also really expensive. Their http://superflag.com Web site was overloaded, so it cost them to expand it. While they never made any money on the flag rentals, the increase in travel costs caused them to lose money.

The bills have mounted about the same time Demski's ability to travel has stopped.

"He stuck his neck out as far as he could," said Alexander.

"I've been quite depressed," said Demski.

His last big trip was to New York, where he managed to reach Ground Zero and fly one of his flags from a crane.

He cradled his WTC identification card in his hand like a jewel. He sighed.

"This is so hard," he said.

It's gotten so bad, he's even put the world's largest flag up for sale, $100,000, because Demski is worried that it's not being shown enough.

"These flags deserve more than I've been able to give them," he said, shaking his head.

He misses the eyes of those holding the giant flag for the first time . . . and the squeals of those who get briefly caught underneath it.

He already missed one trademark moment, at Phoenix's Bank One Ballpark during the recent Insight.Com Bowl.

Shortly before the game, Alexander had rounded up only 36 firemen for an unfurling job that required 150 people. He asked the fireman to go into the stands for help.

By the time the flag had been carried from the mobile home to the end zone, there were 200 people waiting to grab and flap.

"The best thing about all this is, it brings people together," Demski said.

And ultimately leaves them alone.

Demski spent Thanksgiving by himself, in bed. Same for Christmas.

"There's nothing I can do right now," he said, looking at bottles of unopened pills on his aging desk. "Everything is coming down at once."

Old Glorious has already planned his wake and funeral. A couple of years ago, he even held a dress rehearsal with friends.

A hypnotist calmed him enough so he could lie for an hour in a Plexiglass, mirrored casket in his garage while his friends ate corned beef sandwiches.

The casket is Plexiglass and mirrored, of course, so everyone could see the tattoos on both sides of his torso.

The plan is for a cremation, with the casket to be brought out on the anniversary of his death and donated as a coffee table for the homeless.

His ashes? Where else?

He has ordered them placed into the golden eagle at the top of his flagpole, above the ashes of a friend whose remains are already stashed inside the pole.

"A good place, don't you think?" he said.

May he always fly high and free.

POSTSCRIPT: 18 days after this story ran, Thomas "Ski" Demski died at his Long Beach home. His death was ruled a suicide.

May 3, 2002

Ain't Life Grand at 50-1?

LOUISVILLE, KY. — His room is on the backside of the backside, a stall facing the street, miles from the cameras, days from the finish line.

His name tag is a homemade wreath tacked to a wall above a pitchfork and a rake.

His protection is a homemade blanket one size too small.

He arrived at Churchill Downs not because of victory, but because of a recent late-night phone call from owner Darwin Olson to trainer Wilson Brown.

"Let's run him in the Derby," Olson said.

"What Derby?" Brown said.

His name is It'sallinthechase.

But it should be changed to Ain't Never Been.

"I ain't never been to a Kentucky Derby," said Brown, the trainer from Cement, Okla.

"I ain't never been neither," said Rusty Paul, the red-headed groom who lives wherever her trailer is parked.

The owner ain't never had a horse in the Derby.

The jockey ain't never ridden in a Derby.

The jockey, in fact, ain't never even officially ridden this horse.

It'sallinthechase, a 50-1 longshot to be ridden by Eddie Martin Jr. Saturday, is a plodding example of the excesses that are supposedly ruining this race.

And a wonderful example of how they only make it better.

Although It'sallinthechase was one of the bottom three horses that fattened this field to 20, this is not about an excess of bodies.

It's about an excess of hope.

"Everybody writes that we have no chance," Brown said. "But, you know, the horse can't read."

It's about an excess of innocence.

"I got here and they gave me a car to use all week for free," Brown said. "I thought that was the most amazing thing until I realized they also put gas in it."

It's about an excess of humor.

"I saw three ladies watching him work the other day, reading their form," Paul said. "I bet that under his name, it read, 'Ha, ha, ha.'"

What such an assessment lacks in details, it makes up for in accuracy.

In his last race, the Arkansas Derby three weeks ago, It'sallinthe-chase finished ninth.

He hasn't finished higher than third in any race this year.

He has, in fact, never won a race that wasn't held at minor-league Remington Park in Oklahoma.

"After the Arkansas Derby, I cried all the way home, because I didn't think we had a chance at Kentucky," Paul said.

But she was forgetting what Bob Baffert says is the best thing about this big event.

"It's a race that allows owners to dream in Technicolor," he says.

And so, back home in Rochester, Minn., where he owns an insurance agency, Darwin Olson dreamed.

"I thought about how my heart pumps so fast when my horse is running, it's like I'm having a child, and you can't put a price on that," Olson said.

He thought about how his family — and Brown's family — might never have a chance at a Kentucky experience again.

"We're first-timers, and maybe only-timers," he said.

He then rechecked his balance sheet and saw that, with $117,000 in graded stakes earnings, It'sallinthechase was 18th on the top 20 money list and would qualify for the race.

Some say that system, because it allows for so many horses, is dangerous.

I say, because it allows for so many of those Technicolor dreams, it's splendid.

It's like the NBA, at the end of every season allowing every team with 39 wins to take one shot at the Lakers.

It's like It'sallinthechase is the Clippers.

"Say what you want, it isn't like we didn't earn our way here," Olson said.

Thus it happened that Olson paid more to enter the Derby ($30,100) than he paid for the horse that he entered ($27,000).

It is a horse that must now compete against horses purchased for as much as $2.3 million.

Trainer Brown heard the news, and phoned his brother.

"He has the truck that we needed to haul the horse here from Oklahoma," he said. "I guess some people actually fly their horses here, huh?"

Then, when he realized that regular jockey Gerald Melancon couldn't ride at Churchill Downs because of a past infraction here, Brown had to make another phone call.

"I needed to find me a boy to put on the horse," he said. "Somebody told me that Eddie Martin really liked our horse, so I called him."

While Brown is a respected trainer at smaller tracks, his most famous winning trip involved not a race, but a fight.

A losing trainer once insulted him after a race, so Brown decked him in the winner's circle.

And while Olson is considered a good owner, his most famous victory occurred in the *Indiana* Derby.

Did you even know there was an Indiana Derby?

Regardless, the horse is here, and his handlers are taking no chances.

It'sallinthechase was walking toward the track for a workout the other morning when a black cat crossed his path.

"I said, 'No way, we're getting out of here,'" recalled groom Paul, who immediately turned the horse around and entered the track from the other side.

Then, while getting accustomed to the race-day paddock, Brown summoned the horse into stall No. 13.

"I told him, 'I'm not bringing him in there, so you better move,'" Paul said. "So he moved."

She told the story and howled, her laughter carrying through the backside of the backside. It is the music of a horse that, on this most serious of weeks, is also a message.

It'sallinthechase, indeed.

POSTSCRIPT: It'sallinthechase finished 16th in the 2002
Kentucky Derby, approximately two days behind winner War
Emblem.

February 12, 2002

A New Marquee Event
That Is Worlds Apart

SALT LAKE CITY—The future of Olympic sports McTwisted
and Stalefished across America's front porch on Monday.

Its jeans hanging halfway off its rear end.

Its hair hanging tangled off its head.

Its dreams not exactly the dreams of heroes past.

"I would never want to be on a Wheaties box, I never eat the
stuff," said Danny Kass, smiling. "Put me on Count Chocula."

Draped in heavy metal and big air, the future of Olympic sports
landed square in the middle of America's fears that its children will
go too fast, risk too much, hang too loose . . . and get away with it.

Does a medal sweep by three of our kids in something called
halfpipe snowboarding qualify as getting away with it?

It sure sounded as if it did at raucous Park City, where Ross
Powers, Kass and J.J. Thomas won the gold, silver and bronze
medals, respectively, in only the second U.S. winter sweep ever.

After which, Powers and Thomas autographed the bare breasts
of an excited female fan.

Then Kass acknowledged a male blowup doll he jokingly called
his team manager.

Yeah, this is not going to be easy.

That's four U.S. snowboarding medals in two events that look
like skateboarders doing tricks in overcoats.

The question is not whether America is the new dominant

power in what could be the Winter Olympics' new dominant game.

The question is, does it want to be?

Snowboards, after all, are more than two skis tied together.

They are a culture apart.

The sport is more than the traversing of a hill, it is the empowering of a generation, with a sometimes reckless, sometimes rebellious attitude that sometimes irritates instead of inspires.

What adult skier has not looked either angrily or jealously at the young tattooed soul flying past him on a snowboard?

Snowboarders are often viewed not as young people lawfully flexing their voice, but as transplanted bums from the mini-mart parking lot.

Loiterers, only faster.

The average American sports fan understands the athlete who listens to music on headphones before the competition.

But those who wear rockin' headphones *during* the competition?

"Why not? It's cool," Kass said.

And doesn't the average American sports fan want athletes to, like, lift weights?

"I haven't been to a gym in, I don't know, two years," Kass said.

Certainly, America wants its athletes to at least act like athletes.

"I try not to think of myself as a jock," Kass said.

Regardless, snowboarders were shoved into the Olympics four years ago by officials who viewed them not necessarily as studs, but marketers.

As figure skating attracts women, and downhill skiing attracts men, snow boarding could speak — and sell — to young adults.

"If you understand kids," said Kass, 19, "then you understand us."

But many still didn't understand.

And when that 1998 winner of the first Olympic snowboarding event, Canada's Ross Rebagliati, tested positive for marijuana and temporarily lost his medal, the news was greeted with rolled eyes and tongue-clucking.

You see? Thought so.

Many figured that snowboarders would eventually just go away, much like skateboarders are eventually kicked out of grocery-store parking lots.

"Yeah, I've been kicked out of a few parking lots," Kass said.

Yet suddenly, in the middle of last week, they showed up again.

I know because I was there, at the news conference for the half-pipe folks, the longest hour in the history of the hired interpreters.

"A lot of those words they used, there's no translation for them," said frustrated Renate Dallmann, a German expert. "I had to reach way back to high school for some of the other words."

By the end of the session, everyone was staring at Kass because, with shaggy hair and distant eyes, he looked just like the infamous "Fast Times at Ridgemont High" burnout Jeff Spicoli.

Sounded like him too.

When asked how he liked being a first-time Olympian, he squinted.

"The uniforms are pretty mommy," he said.

When asked how he deals with the pressure of being a first-time Olympian, he squinted.

"Maybe lots of video games?" he said.

When asked about his sport's reputation, though, he frowned.

"You can't do this sport if you're high, you can't do it if you're drunk," he said. "That's just crazy."

Crazy, perhaps, but Monday morning, the Salt Lake Tribune carried a story written by Kirsten Stewart with this first paragraph:

"University of Utah fraternity bashes are like Tupperware parties compared with the drunken, late night revelry of snowboarders renting the Beta Theta Pi house during the Olympics, says an angry Greek Row neighbor."

Turns out, those snowboarders aren't Olympians, but workers at a nearby extreme-sports expo. But to the public, a snowboarder is a snowboarder is a . . .

Then later Monday, America's Olympic snowboarders brought the party where it belonged, to the snow, and above the snow, with acrobatic moves and tricks that would have won a gold medal for any gymnast or diver.

They are different. But they are athletes. And they aren't going to leave the room while you wait for them to grow up.

"It's like in high school, the cool kids were on the football team . . . but the skateboarders were stealing all their cheerleaders," Kass said, grinning. "I know some kids from my high school are really surprised when they see me on TV. They're probably like, uh-oh. . . ."

Probably. Right up until they see the silver medal draped around his neck, and hear our national anthem played for another dude just like him.

April 1, 2000

Cornucopia

MITCHELL, S.D. — It is a story as old as basketball shorts are long.

While a country boy leads his college basketball team toward a national championship in a big city far away, the hometown locals flock to the gym where it all began.

Only, the tale of Florida's Mike Miller is a little different.

These locals are pigeons.

In a cluttered little corner of a wind-swept prairie, they will flock to the gym in an attempt to eat it.

.   .   .

You want a corn-pone Final Four?

You want corny reminders this is still a sport of playgrounds and driveways and barns?

You want corn-fed college athletes?

Mike Miller can give you more than that.

He can give you an entire palace.

The Corn Palace.

"The World's Only Corn Palace," reads the advertisement, and no man worth his salt (and butter) would argue.

Before Miller led the Gators into the national semifinals, against North Carolina tonight in Indianapolis, before he made enough big shots to become the biggest player in this tournament, he ruled the Corn Palace.

"If you haven't seen it, you'll never believe it," Miller said.

Once you have seen it, you will believe in all of it, especially the part about small-town roots enabling the Final Four to withstand storms and remain this country's most popular collegiate event.

Located on the corner of Seventh Avenue and Main Street in the farm town of Mitchell (pop. 14,191), the Corn Palace is where Miller played his high school basketball.

For the Mitchell Kernels.

In front of a mascot that resembles a winking ear of corn.

In games broadcast by, among others, radio station KORN.

Ready for a real earful?

On the front and side of the gym, as well as on three walls around the actual court, townspeople annually staple hundreds of thousands of ears of corn of various colors.

Those ears, combined with various types of grain, create various murals.

This year's theme being the millennium, one can plow along the sidewalk in front of yellow-and-black depictions of Martin Luther King and Elvis.

Inside, players shoot free throws while staring into a corn-cobbed version of Mount Rushmore.

Townspeople put together the murals based on a local artist's drawing.

"It's like, corn by numbers," said Dale Odegaard, the Corn Palace's director of marketing and merchandising.

The corn-tage is reworked every year out of necessity because of, well, those pecking pigeons.

New York has "The House That Ruth Built."

Mitchell has "The World's Largest Bird Feeder."

Have we mentioned the roof? It is adorned with decidedly un-Dakota-like minarets, turrets and domes.

Sitting across the street from Casey's General Store and Uncle Zeke's Black Hills Gold Jewelry, the joint looks like something straight from the set of "Ernest Goes to Moscow."

The birthplace of corn-unism.

Tourists stalk it every summer with one question:

"They all ask, 'Why?'" Odegaard said.

Well, OK, not all of them.

"They come up and say, 'What the heck is that?'" said Robin Ackman, co-owner of the nearby Scoreboard tavern.

The answer to both queries is the same. It is an answer that can be found at the wick of the flame that drove Miller, a 6-foot-8 sophomore, from these desolate rolling fields to this weekend's national stage.

Built to bolster town pride, the Corn Palace now breathes it.

"You learn, if you want somebody to notice you from South Dakota, you have to bring something different," Miller said.

Like his driving shot that beat Butler in the final second of overtime in the tournament opener. Like how he doesn't want to be like Michael Jordan, but Larry Bird.

And like, well, the Corn Palace, which was appropriately built to honor the historical equivalent of a blocked shot.

Explorers Lewis and Clark once said they thought this area would be good for nothing. Some frost-resistant pioneers threw it back in their faces by growing long fields of corn and soybean.

In 1892, the Corn Palace was established to celebrate that highlight reel. It was redone in 1921, the roof was detailed in 1937 and the rest is agri-sports history.

"Yeah, we've all heard of the Corn Palace," said Udonis Haslem, one of Miller's Florida teammates from inner-city Miami. "I told him, if my high school team ever played up there, we would put so much heat on them, it would become the 'Popcorn Palace.'"

Surrounded by fields dotted with red barns that look like Monopoly hotels on Marvin Gardens, the Corn Palace has become as reliable as Free Parking.

On nights when cattle die and cars stall and the wind chill hits 50 below, it becomes a community's hearth.

"It's like our own little Boston Garden," Odegaard said.

This is where 3,500 fill the seats for nearly every home game during basketball season to cheer the state's most prolific program, which won five state titles in the 1990s.

Many of those same fans also attended the road games, no small feat considering the nearest one is 50 miles away.

This was where Miller, whose family still lives in a modest wood-frame home across from a field filled with farm equipment, learned that basketball was more than just basketball.

And that his calling was higher than any leaping dunk.

"It doesn't seem like you get a lot of credit, being from South Dakota," he said. "It's important I can show everyone about what people from there can do."

Those people have already shown Miller.

Early in his high school career, during morning shoot-arounds on game days, he would be curious about all the coats draped over the Corn Palace's front-row seats.

Turns out, those were people saving their seats for the game. Nine hours later.

Ernie Kuyper, Miller's cousin and best friend, remembers once when the team turned its game cameras to the Corn Palace's front doors when they opened in mid-afternoon.

"Everybody would come through the door and run to their seats," he said. "It was amazing."

When people here aren't watching basketball players, they are searching for them.

Miller was discovered in fourth grade, not by legendary Kernel Coach Gary Munsen, but by Munsen's wife, Sheryl.

"She was his teacher, and she would watch him during recess, and one day she told me that this boy was something special," Munsen recalled.

The high school coach visited the class to put on a basketball exhibition, dribbling around his back and through his legs and sinking a right-handed hook.

He then gave the ball to Miller, who did the same thing, only he made the shot left-handed.

"Son, are you left-handed?" Munsen asked.

"Nope," the boy said.

Munsen knew.

Sheryl died of breast cancer a few years later. "I'm sure, looking down from where she's at, she knows too," Munsen said.

Miller's only problem was his weight. When he showed up in eighth grade at about 6 feet, 125 pounds, everyone called him "Skinny."

To this day, nobody in town but his parents calls him anything else.

Only those in his new life call him Mike.

Skinny grew, and grew, and eventually became a high school All-American and perhaps the best basketball player to ever come from South Dakota.

Not to mention, king of the Corn Palace.

Recalled cousin Kuyper: "He was signing autographs for a half-hour before the games when he was a junior."

Said Miller, surrounded by cameras and note pads in Indianapolis on Friday: "My status today has actually *decreased* from when I was in South Dakota."

While many college players decorate the tape above their ankles with the names of a parent or brother or girlfriend, Miller simply writes, "Family."

His father, Tom, a former player, is principal at a local elementary school.

In other words, he always had keys to the elementary school gym.

"People ask me a lot about parenting and I always say, 'Spend time with your children,'" said Tom, sitting in his easy chair during a last moment of calm before leaving for Indianapolis. "Basketball enabled me to spend that time. We would just go over to the gym and shoot all night."

Skinny still does. This summer, Miller and Kuyper would unlock the school doors about 11 p.m. and play until 2, pulling garbage cans in the middle of the court and avoiding them as if they were defenders.

The two friends came together again last weekend. Miller was the outstanding player of the East Regional in Syracuse; Kuyper and friends drove 22 hours to watch him.

Miller, whose parents couldn't make the trip, passed a Final

Four T-shirt to Kuyper in the stands. Then later, by the bus, he handed him his snippet of the net.

"Ern, will you drive this home to my dad?" Miller asked. "I owe him."

"Will do, Skinny," said Kuyper.

Twenty-two hours later, the snippet was in the living room of that modest wood-frame home across the street from the farm equipment and down the road from a gym covered with a vegetable. A mother cried. A father beamed.

How corny. How cool.

CHAPTER NINE

Time Out

September 12, 2001

Play Is Stopped

I won't miss the games. Suddenly, I don't care about the games. It will be a while before any of us truly cares about the games.

Baseball is closed, Pac-10 football is closed, maybe the NFL will soon be closed, and you know something? The only thing I miss about the games is that ritual that precedes them.

Lord, what I wouldn't give right now to hear a national anthem.

A nice, long national anthem. Doesn't matter if some of the lyrics are wrong, or the key is off, or the musician is one of those long-haired saxophone players who keeps Laker fans standing for five jittery minutes.

A national anthem, just one, echoing through a stadium of people feeling strong again, accompanying a game that will make us feel real again.

■   ■   ■

You may not be sure why you're reading this section today. I'm not exactly sure why I'm writing for it.

There's no news here. Set against a horrible big picture few of us ever thought we would live to see, the names here suddenly mean virtually nothing. The numbers here don't count.

After spending two hours watching the news of the terrorist plane crashes in New York and Arlington, Va., early Tuesday morning, I unfolded this section, tried to read it, and couldn't.

The names were odd, jumbled, lacked all perspective. A baseball team so dear to me yesterday was now a collection of strangers. A home run record was simply another statistic. A star running back was just some kid.

Reading about sports while your country is under attack is like reading a phone book. I scanned parts of two stories, folded the section back up, and returned to the TV.

During times like these, this is why the sports world is the first to turn the lights out.

We don't want anyone confusing ball and bat with life and

death. We don't want our endless trivialities taking up space better used for things that actually matter.

This is where you turn for escape. But during times of national tragedy, there can be no escape. We can offer little insight. We can be of no help.

You know this, and so do I.

Yet we are both here today anyway.

Perhaps this is because we know that the sports world is also the first to turn those lights back on, a bright blaze under which a weary community gathers, a first stop in a long journey back to normalcy.

It was Babe Ruth who swung us out of World War I. It was Joe DiMaggio who helped us endure World War II.

And who can forget Super Bowl XXV, smack in the middle of the Gulf War, 73,000 people showing up in Tampa, to remind themselves and the world that America was still beautiful.

Remember Whitney Houston that night? Now *that* was a national anthem.

Friday night football helps high school communities heal. On the night President Ronald Reagan was shot in 1981, a college basketball game between Indiana and North Carolina helped the nation endure.

That is perhaps why you are here today, wondering when such a healing will happen again. That is certainly why I am here, believing that it will.

Just not yet. It's far too soon. The damage to our nation has been far too great. The lights here are still out.

Pete Rozelle regretted his decision to hold NFL games on that 1963 weekend after John F. Kennedy's assassination. The NFL cannot be criticized if it chooses to step slowly this time.

Out of respect for the incredible suffering of our families and cities and psyches, nobody in the sports world should be criticized for whatever decisions are made to honor the loss.

But don't give up hope. Keep checking with us. When the country is ready to resume living, you will feel it here first. It will sound like Whitney Houston. I strain to hear her now.

INDEX

G

H

I

J

K

OTHER BOOKS FROM
THE LOS ANGELES TIMES

DRAWING THE LINE
by Paul Conrad
Two hundred drawings, spanning the period from the late 1960s to President Clinton's impeachment trial, from America's premier political cartoonist. $25.45

ETERNALLY YOURS
by Jack Smith
Who can forget Jack Smith, the *Los Angeles Times*' columnist for nearly 40 years? When he died in 1996, we all lost a treasure. But at least his words survived. Here, Jack's widow, Denise, and his sons, Curt and Doug, have collected some of their favorite columns. $16.95

CURBSIDE L.A.
An Offbeat Guide to the City of Angels
by Cecilia Rasmussen
Enjoy a truly eclectic tour of Los Angeles. Explore the L.A. you've not seen with enticing excursions into the city's peerless history and diversity. $19.45

DAY HIKERS' GUIDE
TO SOUTHERN CALIFORNIA
by John McKinney
Walks in Southern California, from the simply scenic to the challenging, as described by *Los Angeles Times* hiking columnist and author John McKinney. $16.45

52 WEEKS IN THE
CALIFORNIA GARDEN
by Robert Smaus
How to make the most of your garden by the foremost authority on gardening in Southern California. $17.45

ANSWERS TO YOUR CALIFORNIA
GARDENING QUESTIONS
by Robert Smaus
For decades, gardeners in Southern California turned to Robert Smaus, the *Los Angeles Times*' gardening editor, for practical, expert advice. This book is full of those questions and Smaus' authoritative answers. An excellent companion to *52 Weeks in the California Garden*. $21.45

IMAGING LOS ANGELES
Photographs of a 20th Century City
Foreword by Ray Bradbury
Collected here are some 175 photos from more than a dozen Southern California archives that tell the tale of men and women from all over the world who hoped and dared on a grand scale and who turned Los Angeles into the quintessential 20th century city. $28.95

L.A. UNCONVENTIONAL
by Cecilia Rasmussen
Where some people see roadblocks, others, such as the men and women in this volume, see possibility, opportunity and excitement. $30.95

THE SAN FERNANDO VALLEY
America's Suburb
by Kevin Roderick
Valley native Kevin Roderick recounts the area's vibrant past, from its Native American residents through the Spanish, Mexican and American settlers, spinning along the way the tales that give the Valley its unique history and culture. $26.45

LAST OF THE BEST
90 Columns from the 1990s
by Jim Murray
The best of Jim's columns from the last decade of his life are included in this paperback volume compiled by *Los Angeles Times* Sports Editor Bill Dwyre and featuring a foreword by Dodger legend Tommy Lasorda. $19.45

THE GREAT ONES
by Jim Murray
The top men and women of the sports world written about as only this late, great sports columnist could. Foreword by Arnold Palmer. $24.45

LOW-FAT KITCHEN
by Donna Deane
From the pages of the *Los Angeles Times* Food section come more than 110 recipes that use fresh food avor, not fat, to satisfy your taste buds. $20.45

THE LOS ANGELES TIMES' MODERN CALIFORNIA COOKING
Staff of The Times' *Food section*
A sequel to the 1981 best seller, *California Cookbook, Modern California Cooking* offers more than 300 recipes that reflect the cutting edge, international cuisine for which Southern California has become so famous in recent years. An ideal companion to the 1981 volume. $22.45

SOS RECIPES
30 Years of Requests
by Rose Dosti
This best-selling hard-cover book offers hundreds of tried-and-true recipes for all-time favorite dishes that literally range from soup to nuts. $19.45

DEAR SOS
Favorite Restaurant Recipes
by Rose Dosti
Rose Dosti has culled her perennially popular column in the *Los Angeles Times* Food section to hand pick 225 of your all-time favorite recipes from restaurants throughout the country. $22.45

ANSWERS FOR CALIFORNIA GARDENERS
by Robert Smaus
Expert advice in an easy-to-read Q&A format from the foremost authority on Southern California gardening. An excellent companion to Smaus' *52 Weeks in the California Garden*. $21.45

SUNSET BOULEVARD
Cruising the Heart of Los Angeles
by Amy Dawes
A guide to the sights, experiences and lost legends of Los Angeles' most famous boulevard. Loaded with photos, maps and tips on where to dine, party and shop. $28.45

ICONIC L.A.
Stories of L.A.'s Most Memorable Buildings
by Gloria Koenig
The architecture and drama behind 13 of Los Angeles' most recognizable landmarks, including the Bradbury Building, the Getty Museum, Disney Concert Hall and the LAX Theme Building. With an introduction by Frank O. Gehry. $29.95

To order, call (800) 246-4042 or visit our Web site at http://www.latimes.com/bookstore